D0673124

Who Is Jesus?
An Introduction to Christology

Thomas P. Rausch, S.J.

A Michael Glazier Book

LITURGICAL PRESS
Collegeville, Minnesota

www.litpress.org

A Michael Glazier Book published by the Liturgical Press.

Cover design by David Manahan, o.s.b. Illustration: *Christ Pantocrator,* Encaustic ikon of the 6th cent. Monastery of Saint Catherine, Sinai.

Scriptures selections are taken from the **New American Bible** Copyright © 1991, 1986, 1970 by the Confraternity of Christian Doctrine, 3211 Fourth Street, NE, Washington, DC 20017-1194 and are used by license of copyright owner. All rights reserved. No part of the **New American Bible** may be reproduced in any form or by any means without permission in writing from the copyright owner.

© 2003 by The Order of Saint Benedict, Collegeville, Minnesota. All rights reserved. No part of this book may be reproduced in any form or by any means, electronic or mechanical, including photocopying, recording, taping, or any retrieval system, without the written permission of the Liturgical Press, Collegeville, Minnesota 56321. Printed in the United States of America.

4	5	6	7	8

Library of Congress Cataloging-in-Publication Data

Rausch, Thomas P.
  Who is Jesus? : an introduction to christology / Thomas J. Rausch.
    p. cm.
  Includes bibliographical references and indexes.
  ISBN 0-8146-5078-3 (alk. paper)
    1. Jesus Christ—Person and offices. I. Title.

BT203.R38 2003
232—dc21   2003044616

For my students,
past and present

Contents

Acknowledgments

This book is not intended to be a general survey of recent works on Christology. My position is that of a teacher who has tried to survey the best of contemporary Christology, in order to develop a competent introduction to the discipline. I have drawn on more critical mainstream scholars as well as Evangelical authors, acknowledging with Ben Witherington that too many mainstream scholars ignore the work of Evangelicals who use historical critical methodology.[1] I would like to acknowledge some of those scholars whose works I have found particularly helpful.

Edward Schillebeeckx and John P. Meier both have contributed very careful works on the historical Jesus. Schillebeeckx's *Jesus: An Experiment in Christology*,[2] drawing on an incredible range of European scholarship, is a good source for ascertaining the "critical minimum," even if he tends to be something of a hyper-critic. Meier's much more recent work, *A Marginal Jew*, now in three volumes, is not only extremely helpful; it always makes for excellent reading.[3]

N. T. Wright, an Evangelical scholar long at Oxford, is now Dean of Lichfield Cathedral in England. Though he attributes far more to the self-consciousness of Jesus than many other scholars would do, his work is extremely helpful.[4] He is skeptical of the modern tendency of form critics to reduce the Gospel tradition to disconnected fragments. His work has the

[1] Ben Witherington III, *The Jesus Quest: The Third Search for the Jew of Nazareth* (Downers Grove, Ill.: InterVarsity, 1997) 257.

[2] Edward Schillebeeckx, *Jesus: An Experiment in Christology* (New York: Seabury, 1979); see also his work on soteriology, *Christ: The Experience of Jesus as Lord* (New York: Seabury, 1980).

[3] John P. Meier, *A Marginal Jew: Rethinking the Historical Jesus*, Vol. One; *The Roots of the Problem and the Person* (New York: Doubleday, 1991); Vol. Two, *Mentor, Message, and Miracles* (New York: Doubleday, 1994); Vol. Three, *Companions and Competitors* (New York: Doubleday, 2001).

[4] N. T. Wright, Vol. One: *The New Testament and the People of God* (Minneapolis: Fortress, 1992); Vol. Two: *Jesus and the Victory of God* (Minneapolis: Fortress, 1996).

enormous merit of taking the Jewishness of Jesus seriously and of reading his story against that tradition of Torah and Temple as it was in his day. He also has contributed a fine introduction to the history of Christology.

Roger Haight's *Jesus: Symbol of God* is a massive achievement, one that all future works will have to deal with.[5] While I have difficulties with some of his interpretations, Haight provides a very helpful overview of the tradition and has the gift of being able to say things clearly. More importantly, his efforts to rethink the way we talk about salvation in Christ is a very important aspect of his work.

Brian O. McDermott's *Word Become Flesh* represents a fine effort to situate Christology against both the doctrinal history of the church and more contemporary approaches.[6]

While I am appreciative of contemporary approaches to Christology from the perspectives of liberation theology, feminist theology, and religious pluralism, that has not been my principle concern here as it is beyond the scope of this book. However, I have tried to take note of scholars working in these areas and have drawn on their insights. I refer the reader to the works of Haight and McDermott as well as to Witherington's book on the Third Quest for a survey of contemporary approaches.[7]

I am grateful to my graduate assistant, Ryan Ignatius Pratt, for his careful work in reviewing the manuscript; to Barbara Murphy for her help with the index; and to Aaron Raverty, O.S.B., for his copyediting. I also want to express my gratitude to my students over the years who have helped me to see more deeply into the mystery of Jesus and his continuing relevance to our lives. It is to my students that I would like to dedicate this book.

Thomas P. Rausch, S.J.

---

[5] Roger Haight, *Jesus: Symbol of God* (New York: Orbis, 1999).

[6] Brian O. McDermott, *Word Become Flesh: Dimensions of Christology* (Collegeville: The Liturgical Press, 1993).

[7] Witherington, *The Jesus Quest.*

Abbreviations

DS   Denzinger-Schönmetzer, *Enchiridion Symbolorum* 33rd ed. (Freiburg: Herder, 1965)

DV   *Dei verbum*: Vatican II, Dogmatic Constitution on Divine Revelation

JVG   N. T. Wright, *Jesus and the Victory of God* (Minneapolis: Fortress Press, 1996)

LG   *Lumen gentium*: Vatican II, Dogmatic Constitution on the Church

LW   Martin Luther. *Luther's Works*, ed. Jaroslav Pelikan and Helmut T. Lehmann (St. Louis: Concordia Publishing House)

NJBC   *New Jerome Biblical Commentary*, ed. Raymond E. Brown, Joseph A. Fitzmyer, and Roland E. Murphy (Englewood Cliffs, N.J.: Prentice Hall, 1990)

PBC   Pontifical Biblical Commission

Introduction

Who is Jesus? This is the fundamental question for Christology. From the first days of the Christian community there have been various answers to this question. The earliest Christians used various titles, most of them drawn from the Old Testament or Hebrew Scriptures, to express their faith in Jesus. They called him prophet, teacher, Messiah, Son of David, Son of Man, Lord, Son of God, Word of God, and occasionally even God. The New Testament offers a rich variety of Christologies, as we will see below.

Images of Jesus

The Christian tradition has been no less rich than the New Testament in reflecting on the mystery of Jesus. The earliest representations of Jesus in Christian art, found in the catacombs, portrayed him as a shepherd. The Church Fathers saw the pierced side of Christ as the source of the Church and the sacraments. Medieval Christians often saw Jesus as the coming judge who would separate the saved from the damned, a scene frequently represented over the lintels of their churches. But medieval art was also fascinated with the humanity of Jesus. Monastics and mystics meditated on the wounds of Jesus and there was a growing devotion to his heart, precursor to the Catholic devotion to the Sacred Heart of Jesus. During the Renaissance many works of art focused on the genitalia of the Christ.[1] Behind this emphasis on Jesus' sexuality lies the importance of the Incarnation in Renaissance thought; humanity in all its concreteness was the bearer of the divine. In the last three centuries rationalists, writers, and theologians recreated Jesus largely in their own image; he became an ethical teacher, a noble

---

[1] Leo Steinberg, *The Sexuality of Christ in Renaissance Art and in Modern Oblivion* (Chicago: University of Chicago Press, 1996).

but human religious ideal (Thomas Jefferson), a loving, misunderstood figure (Renan), or a messianic schemer.[2]

The image of Jesus is infinitely adaptable. In an article based on his 1986 presidential address to the Catholic Biblical Society, Daniel Harrington presents seven different images of Jesus proposed in recent years by scholars, all based on different Jewish backgrounds. They include Jesus as a political revolutionary, magician, Galilean charismatic, rabbi, proto-Pharisee, Essene, or eschatological prophet.[3] Under the influence of liberation theology, Jesus has been portrayed as a social revolutionary, even as a guerrilla clad in military fatigues. Some gay writers have described Jesus as a gay man on the basis of his relationship with the "beloved disciple" of John's Gospel. Feminists have changed his gender, using a cross with a crucified figure of a woman, "Chresta." Elisabeth Schüssler Fiorenza offers a Jesus who saw God, not as "Abba," despite numerous attestations of this in the tradition, but as Divine Sophia, a female Wisdom figure, and himself as Sophia's prophet.[4] John Dominic Crossan, a member of Robert Funk's Jesus Seminar, presents Jesus as a Jewish magician and wandering peasant philosopher in the Cynic tradition whose sayings advocated a radical egalitarianism that challenged established structures and hierarchies.[5] To celebrate the beginning of the Third Millennium, the *National Catholic Reporter* sponsored a contest called "Jesus 2000," seeking an artistic representation of Jesus for the new millennium. The winning portrait, chosen by Sister Wendy Beckett, shows a dark skinned, androgynous Jesus, obviously someone from the Third World. The artist explains that though her Jesus was portrayed as a man, the actual model was a woman.[6]

Popular Christianity today tends to focus on the divinity of Jesus, often at the cost of his humanity. Catholics refer to Jesus as Our Lord or simply as Christ. Many honor him as Christ the King. Those with an Eastern European background often have a devotion to the Infant of Prague, which portrays the child Jesus in the robes and crown of a king. Orthodox Christians honor Jesus as the eternal Logos, and as the Pantocrator, the ruler of the universe who often appears in their iconography. Protestants call on

---

[2] See Earl Richard, *Jesus: One and Many: The Christological Concepts of the New Testament Authors* (Wilmington, Del.: Michael Glazier, 1988) 26.

[3] Daniel J. Harrington, "The Jewishness of Jesus," *Bible Review* 3:1 (1987) 33–41.

[4] Elisabeth Schüssler Fiorenza, *Jesus: Miriam's Child, Sophia's Prophet* (New York: Continuum: 1994).

[5] John Dominic Crossan, *The Historical Jesus: The Life of a Mediterranean Jewish Peasant* (HarperSanFrancisco, 1991).

[6] "Jesus 2000," *National Catholic Reporter* (December 24, 1999).

Jesus as their personal Lord and Savior. Many Evangelicals address him as Lord Jesus or even "precious Jesus" in their prayer and look forward to his Second Coming.

Starting Points for Christology

So who is the real Jesus? What is the best starting point for a contemporary Christology? There are various possibilities. Let us consider some of them.

The New Testament

While the New Testament is the most important source for our knowledge of Jesus, the difficulty with using it as a starting point is that it offers not one Christology, but many. The Synoptic Gospels present a very different Jesus than the one that emerges in John. In general, the Synoptic Jesus says very little about himself; he is much more concerned with the coming of God's kingdom. Furthermore, the three Synoptic authors differ considerably among themselves. Mark's Gospel identifies Jesus as the "Son of God" (Mark 1:1), but as it begins without the traditional Christmas story, it is difficult to see this as having any more than an adoptionist sense; Jesus is declared God's son at his baptism (Mark 1:11). Mark generally sees Jesus as the Messiah and Son of Man who must suffer, probably based on the suffering Servant of Isaiah 52:13–53:12. Only the evil spirits seem to grasp the true identity of Jesus as the holy one (Mark 1:24) or Son of God (Mark 3:11; 5:7).

The Christology of Matthew and Luke is more developed. Both present Jesus as Son of God from the time of his virginal conception. Luke's reflection on the mystery of Jesus extends back to the events preceding his birth and includes what is known as the "infancy narratives." The story of Jesus in the Temple at the age of twelve suggests an effort to pierce the veil of his "hidden life," something that has fascinated Christians from the earliest days of the Church. Luke also represents people addressing Jesus as "Lord" even during his public life, though it is more likely that this title was applied to him only after his death. Matthew's high Christology is evident in his adding to Peter's confession, "You are the Messiah" (Mark 8:29) the words, "the Son of the living God" (Matt 16:16) and in his use of the title Emmanuel, "God is with us," for Jesus (Matt 1:23).

The Fourth Gospel begins by presenting Jesus as the incarnate Word of God (John 1:14) and ends with Thomas' Easter confession, "My Lord and my God" (John 20:28). The Johannine Jesus speaks in long discourses, not parables. He proclaims himself as the Messiah (John 4:26) and only-begotten Son coming from the Father (John 3:18), existing before Abraham (John 8:58). He frequently speaks of himself using the formula, "I AM" (John 6:35; 8:28; 10:11, 14; 11:25), used in the Old Testament and rabbinic tradition for the divine name of Yahweh. And these examples only scratch the surface; there are yet other Christologies in the epistles.

Thus the New Testament gives us a number of different Christologies, and raises a number of questions. Should we start methodologically with those Christologies which emerged by the end of the New Testament period, or with those in the earliest books, or with those even earlier that may lie behind the written texts? Was belief in Jesus' preexistence a late development, or can it be found earlier in the tradition? Were the first disciples aware of what the later Church would call his divinity? Should John's view of Jesus be considered more accurate than Mark's, or do we need to make room for both? And is it enough to base a Christology simply on the Christian confession of the inspired nature of the New Testament texts?

The Creeds and Dogmas of the Church

A second possible starting point could be the creeds and dogmas of the Church. The so-called Nicene Creed, actually a revision of the creed of Nicaea (325) by the First Council of Constantinople (381), still recited at Mass every Sunday, affirms the following:

> I believe . . . in one Lord Jesus Christ, the only begotten Son of God. Born of the Father before all ages. God from God, Light from Light, true God from true God. Begotten not made, consubstantial with the Father: through whom all things were made. Who for us men and for our salvation came down from heaven. And was incarnate by the Holy Spirit of the Virgin Mary: and was made man.

The creed is an official statement of the belief of the Church. It is normative for the Church's faith. Joseph (now Cardinal) Ratzinger chooses the Apostles' Creed as the basis for his approach to Christology in his *Introduction to Christianity*, as it mediates between two extremes, on the one hand, the reduction of Christology to history and on the other, abandoning history as irrelevant to faith. The first approach, symbolized by Harnack, purifies the faith of doctrine and creed, making the reconstruction of the historical Jesus determinative for Christology. The other, symbolized by Bultmann, makes faith in the Christ alone important.[7] We will consider these approaches below.

[7] Joseph Ratzinger, *Introduction to Christianity* (New York: Herder and Herder, 1971) 144–47.

But there are methodological problems with using the creeds as a start-ing point for Christology. Such an approach does Christology "from above." It presumes precisely what needs to be established, namely, that the Church's christological faith, including its profession of the divinity of Jesus, is rooted in some way in the actual Jesus of history. In other words, the Church's christological faith needs a critical foundation. Christology needs to be established "from below," to be grounded in the words and deeds of the Jesus of history.[8] Short of this, it remains vulnerable to the often heard charge that it represents a later "Hellenization" of Christian faith, that Christians of a later generation turned their savior into a god, divinizing the figure of the carpenter of Nazareth.

The Faith of Christian People

A third possible starting point could be the faith of Christian people. What do contemporary Christians say and believe about Jesus? How do they apprehend him in faith? That faith is an important but insufficient source. Contemporary Christians are often divided as to their christological faith. Some no longer accept the divinity of Jesus. Others, particularly conservative Christians, believe in a Jesus who knew he was God's only begotten Son from his earliest days. They confess without hesitation the divinity of Jesus. Occa-sionally this emphasis on the divinity of Jesus overshadows the distinction between the Son and the Father. For others, the theology implicit in their faith leaves little room for the humanity of Jesus.

The idea that Jesus had been confronted with the same struggles faced by each of us is for many Christians difficult to grasp. They find it hard to be-lieve that he had to face real temptation, that he had to struggle to integrate his sexuality, discern God's will for himself, and discover his own vocation. They have been accustomed to imagining Jesus primarily from the stand-point of his divinity. Such an approach suggests that Jesus has only a divine nature. Thus it has been characterized as a "practical Monophysitism," a functional version of the early heresy of Monophysitism which maintained that Jesus had only one nature, a divine rather than a human one. For con-temporary Christians, it is very difficult to relate to such a Jesus as an ex-emplar or to practice the *imitatio Christi*, the imitation of Christ which has always been at the center of Christian life.

---

[8] For a discussion of these two approaches see Karl Rahner, "The Two Basic Types of Christology" in his *Theological Investigations* 13 (New York: Seabury, 1975) 213–23.

Historical-Critical Approach

A fourth possibility would be to follow a strictly historical-critical approach, perhaps best symbolized by John P. Meier at the beginning of his massive three-volume work on the historical Jesus:

> Suppose that a Catholic, a Protestant, a Jew, and an agnostic—all honest historians cognizant of 1ˢᵗ century religious movements—were locked up in the bowels of the Harvard Divinity School library, put on a spartan diet, and not allowed to emerge until they had hammered out a consensus document on who Jesus of Nazareth was and what he intended in his own time and place. An essential requirement of this document would be that it be based on purely historical sources and arguments.[9]

The kicker here is the phrase, "based on purely historical sources and arguments." The Gospels and other New Testament documents are written in the light of the Resurrection and of the disciples' Easter experience of new life in Jesus; they are products of Christian faith. Though there is considerable historical memory enshrined in the texts, as we shall see later, they do not count as historical writings in the modern sense. They were written to proclaim faith in the risen Jesus present in the Christian community and in the lives of his disciples, not to document the story of his life as a modern historian might do.

On the one hand, a critical Christology must be based on historical-critical scholarship. As Walter (now Cardinal) Kasper argues, "church belief has in the earthly Jesus, as he is made accessible to us through historical research, a relatively autonomous criterion, a once-and-for-all yardstick by which it must continually measure itself."[10] The Church needs always to check its doctrine against the historical events on which it is based. Otherwise it remains ungrounded, disconnected, with the risk of being a mythological or ideological construction.

On the other hand, historical-critical research by itself is not sufficient. First, some elements at the center of the Jesus story, for example, his resurrection, are not accessible to historical research, or are only obliquely so. A purely historical approach can tell us a great deal about the Jesus of history. It cannot, however, "prove" the resurrection, nor can it establish the truth of the miracle stories, though it can say whether or not these accounts are deeply rooted in the Jesus tradition or are later additions.

---

[9] John P. Meier, *A Marginal Jew: Rethinking the Historical Jesus*, Vol. 1 (New York: Doubleday, 1991) 1.

[10] Walter Kasper, *Jesus the Christ* (New York: Paulist, 1976) 35.

Second, a "strictly historical" approach does not necessarily exclude the presuppositions of those who claim to follow it. They may reject what they consider the "mythological" or "supernatural" in their sources, while remaining blissfully ignorant of how their own supposedly objective historical scholarship is conditioned by their own unrecognized "secular," "modernist," or "postmodern" biases. We will see this approach in looking at nineteenth-century historical Jesus research or the work of the Jesus Seminar at the end of the twentieth.

Finally and most importantly, the "historical Jesus" reconstructed by scholars is not and can never be the living Jesus of Christian faith. What theologians like John P. Meier and Luke Timothy Johnson call "the real Jesus" is the glorified Jesus reigning at the right hand of the Father, present to his people in the Spirit, mediated by Scripture and tradition, encountered in Christian service, discipleship, and liturgy.[11]

A Dialectical Christology

If Christology is to be both critical (using historical and literary disciplines) and at the same time theological (i.e., a reflection on faith), it must do its historical-critical investigation within the parameters of the historic Christian tradition. Walter Kasper speaks of this as a Christology of "complementarity," that is, one that takes fully into account two criteria, "the earthly Jesus *and* the risen, exalted Christ."[12] The earthly Jesus is to a considerable extent accessible through a critical reading of the Christian texts. But revelation in Christ Jesus is not completely given in his historical life. The mystery of the risen, exalted Christ is an essential part of the Jesus story. But this is accessible only to those who are able to see with the eyes of faith.

Our primary access to the mystery of Jesus the Christ, and hence the starting point for Christology, is the Church, through its Scriptures, its creeds, its faith experienced, proclaimed, and handed on through the centuries. New life in Christ and access to him in the Spirit continue to be mediated through the Christian community. We have no story of Jesus without the Gospels, no sense of what his life and death meant for the earliest Christians apart from their Scriptures.

But the Scriptures by themselves are not sufficient. They must be read and interpreted within the community of faith from which they came if they are to remain alive. In the Church of the first millennium, Scripture

---

[11] Cf. Meier, *A Marginal Jew* I:21–24; Luke Timothy Johnson, *The Real Jesus* (San Francisco: Harper, 1996).

[12] Kasper, *Jesus the Christ*, 35.

was always read and understood within the context of the Church's liturgy. In the modern period, too often historical criticism has replaced biblical theology. For Catholic theology, the French *ressourcement* sought to bring the earlier tradition into harmony with more critical, modern approaches.[13] Protestant theology, with its elevation of the Scripture principle, and particularly evangelical theology with its doctrine of biblical inerrancy, has too often isolated the Bible from the historical worshipping community and allowed it to stand alone. The result has been either the loss of the Scripture principle itself on the liberal side, and on the more conservative, a biblical literalism or fundamentalism.

However, christological faith cannot stand solely on the Scriptures and teachings of the Church. Catholic Christianity historically has rejected the "*sola scriptura*" approach. It emphasizes the compatibility of faith and reason. A Christology not grounded in historical reality could easily become an ideology or myth, a idolatrous divinization of the man Jesus. This is not to suggest that reason establishes faith, but it can and should show that the act of faith is itself reasonable.

Therefore a critical Christology must take as its second criterion the earthly Jesus, the Jesus made accessible through historical research which Kasper calls "a relatively autonomous criterion" through which the Church must continue to measure itself and its teaching.[14] In order to be faithful both to history and to Christian faith, we will follow such a bipolar or dialectical Christology.

We will take seriously the work of historical-critical scholarship, motivated by the conviction that a Christology not rooted in the Jesus of history cannot be the basis for the christological faith of the Church. At the same time, Christology can never be an autonomous discipline, nor can the Scriptures stand by themselves, orphaned from the faith and life of the Church. Both make sense only within the context of the Christian community that continues to confess Jesus as Messiah, Lord, and Son of God, which recognizes his presence in the community gathered in his name, in the Word proclaimed, and in the breaking of the bread.

---

[13] Marie Anne Mayeski, "Catholic Theology and the History of Exegesis," *Theological Studies* 62 (2001) 140–53.

[14] Kasper, *Jesus the Christ*, 35.

Chapter 1

The Three Quests for the Historical Jesus

So we return to the question, "who is Jesus?" Today, there are many answers. In 1977, the editor of *Der Speigel*, a magazine that might be described as the German version of *Time*, published a book called *Jesus Son of Man*. The book probes "how the Christian church dares appeal to a Jesus who never existed, to a mandate he never issued, and to a claim that he was God's son, which he never presumed for himself."[1]

Eight years later Robert Funk, at the time a professor at the University of Montana, founded his famous Jesus Seminar. The seminar is a small group of self-selected academics who meet twice a year in the effort to discover the "real Jesus" hidden behind the Gospels and the doctrine of the Church. Their method is to try and isolate the earliest strands of the Jesus tradition; after a discussion, they vote, using color-coded beads, in order to decide on the authentic words and sayings of Jesus.[2] They reject 82 percent of the Gospel sayings of Jesus as inauthentic, including all those that refer to judgment, reward, and punishments beyond death. Similarly, they reject the Gospel of Mark, with its narrative of the life of Jesus, judging it to be determined chiefly by theological interests. From the disconnected sayings that remain the members of the seminar assemble their reconstructions of the "real" Jesus, a non-eschatological Jesus who bears little resemblance to the one Christians are familiar with. What they offer is a Jewish sage, wisdom teacher, or Cynic philosopher who enunciates a countercultural critique

---

[1] Rudolf Augstein, *Jesus Son of Man* (New York: Urizen Books, 1977) 9.

[2] See *The Five Gospels: The Search for the Authentic Words of Jesus*, a new translation and commentary by Robert W. Funk, Roy W. Hoover, and the Jesus Seminar (New York: Macmillan, 1993).

and is killed, "accidentally crucified" according to Funk.[3] Ben Witherington characterizes the Jesus of the Seminar as merely a "talking head."[4]

The two examples we have noted here, developed from an entirely secular point of view, are only a few of many recent efforts to recover the "Jesus of history," thus distinguishing him from the Christ of the Christian tradition. The difference between the two, first noted in the eighteenth century by the German scholar H. S. Reimarus, has led since then to three different quests for the historical Jesus.

The First Quest: Reimarus to Schweitzer

Hermann Samuel Reimarus (1694–1768) was a professor of Oriental languages in Hamburg, Germany. Among the papers found at the time of his death was a manuscript that argued that the message and intention of Jesus was simply different from that of the early Church. Published in part after his death by G. E. Lessing as the "Wolfenbüttel Fragments," Reimarus' work was immediately controversial.

Reimarus argued that the aim of Jesus and that of the disciples was basically different. He had noticed that Jesus' preaching in the Gospels, particularly in the Synoptics, was centered on repentance in preparation for the coming of the kingdom of heaven. Yet because Jesus made no effort to define the kingdom in clear terms, Reimarus assumed that its meaning must have been obvious to those who heard him. Therefore, he concluded that the key to the aim of Jesus was to be found in the usual meaning of "kingdom of heaven" among the Jews of the day. This was to be a temporal kingdom established by the Messiah, Jesus himself, who would free Israel from Roman rule. This was the real aim or intention of Jesus, to call the Jews to a genuine love of God, a love of one's neighbor, and a new righteousness, beyond the external observance of the Pharisees. In this way they would prepare for the coming of the new kingdom. But he died a failure, feeling that God had abandoned him and crying out on the cross, "My God, my God, why have you forsaken me" (Matt 27:46).

The apostles of course were terribly disappointed. Having given up their trades to follow Jesus, they had been supported during his ministry from the common purse. Reluctant to return to their lowly state after his death,

---

[3] Cited by Luke Timothy Johnson, *The Real Jesus: The Misguided Quest for the Historical Jesus and the Truth of the Traditional Gospels* (HarperSanFrancisco, 1996) 12; in the *Washington Post* (12 November 1988).

[4] Ben Witherington III, *The Jesus Quest: The Third Search for the Jew of Nazareth* (Downers Grove, Ill.: InterVarsity, 1997) 42–57.

Reimarus reasoned that they stole his body and claimed that he had been raised from the dead. To secure their own position, they invented the story that Jesus had been a suffering Messiah who had died for the sins of humankind, that he had ascended to heaven and would come again in power and glory to judge the good and the bad. Thus the aim or intention of the apostles was very different from that of Jesus. They were the one who created what became the Christian story.[5]

The anonymous publication of the "Fragments" by Lessing caused a considerable stir in Germany; indeed the Duke of Brunswick intervened in 1778 to prevent him from publishing the complete set of the papers. Reimarus' little book was a classic Enlightenment text, designed to replace revelation with reason and Christianity with a nondogmatic religion. His work was not entirely original; he owed much to earlier writers, particularly the English Deists. Nor was he the first who would attempt to reduce Jesus to an ethical teacher, albeit a mistaken one. Joachim Jeremias says that his "portrayal of the historical Jesus was clearly absurd and amateurish."[6] But Reimarus cannot be simply discounted. He had recognized a difference between the historical Jesus and the Christ proclaimed by the Scriptures and the Church. He had pointed to the difference between history and dogma. He had raised a critical question, who was Jesus of Nazareth? And he had suggested that the "real" or "historical" Jesus could be recovered by using careful, historical scholarship.

The publication of Reimarus' "Fragments" launched the First Quest for the historical Jesus. Before long, a succession of books on the life of Jesus began to appear from scholars like David Friedrich Strauss, Bruno Bauer, Ernst Renan, Julius Holtzmann, William Wrede, and Johannes Weiss. This was a liberal quest. Most of these scholars, like Reimarus, were dominated by the philosophical principles of the Enlightenment. Most were hostile to orthodox Christianity. They assumed that once the overlay of Church preaching and dogma as well as the Jewishness of Jesus was stripped away, the real, historical Jesus would emerge. But in reality, their work was not as objective as they claimed. Their attempt to read the Gospels through the lenses of the Enlightenment resulted in a reconstructed Jesus fashioned in their own image. In these *Leben Jesu* books, Jesus became an ethical teacher or preacher of morality, a friend of the poor and social reformer, the ideal human being, or simply a character of fiction. What George Tyrrell, the English modernist, wrote of Adolf von Harnack could be said of many of

---

[5] See *Reimarus: Fragments*, ed. Charles H. Talbert (Philadelphia: Fortress, 1970).

[6] Joachim Jeremias, *The Problem of the Historical Jesus* (Philadelphia: Fortress, 1964) 5.

these writers: "The Christ that Harnack sees, looking back through nine-teen centuries of Catholic darkness, is only the reflection of a Liberal Prot-estant face, seen at the bottom of a deep well."[7]

But the First Quest was not without some fruit. In 1882 Martin Kähler in his *Der sogenannte historische Jesus und der geschichtliche, biblische Christus* in-troduced a distinction that has become part of the fundamental vocabulary of Christology. Kähler's distinction was actually a double one. He distin-guished both between "Jesus" and "Christ" and between *historisch* (historical) and *geschichtlich* (historic). The key to the second distinction, difficult to con-vey in English, is the fact that the German word *Geschichte* means both "story" and "history," the past *as interpreted*, since it is always told from some point of view. Thus Kähler was distinguishing between the "historical Jesus" and the "historic *(geschichtliche)*, biblical Christ," the Christ proclaimed by the Bible and the Church, what we today call the "Christ of Faith."

The historical Jesus refers to the man Jesus of Nazareth as he can be known through historical research. The Christ of Faith is the Jesus pro-claimed by the first Christians, by their Scriptures, and by the Church; it is therefore Jesus known in light of the resurrection and interpreted by Christian faith which grasps him as Messiah, Lord, and Son of God. Both are important, as we saw earlier in considering a Christology of comple-mentarity. The object of Christian faith cannot be the historical Jesus; it must always be the Christ of Faith, the Jesus who is confessed by the dis-ciples, proclaimed by the Scriptures, and interpreted by the Church. But that faith must be rooted in the Jesus of history, lest it become a mere mythologization of the founder of Christianity.

The End of the First Quest

Albert Schweitzer (1875–1965), theologian, musician, and medical doc-tor, is best known for the clinic he operated in Gabon, Africa, the chari-table work for which he received the Nobel prize. But one of his books, *The Quest of the Historical Jesus,*[8] delivered the *coup de grâce* to the liberal quest. Schweitzer saw the old quest as a single movement, one of the great achieve-ments of German theology, yet flawed because the theologians pursuing it presupposed that Jesus was a modern man, just like themselves. The result was that they tended to portray him in their own image.

---

[7] George Tyrrell, *Christianity at the Cross-Roads* (London: Longmans, Green, & Com-pany, 1910) 44.

[8] ET, Albert Schweitzer, *The Quest of the Historical Jesus: A Critical Study of its Progress from Reimarus to Wrede* (London: Adam & Charles Black, 1963).

Schweitzer rejected this liberal portrait; he argued that Jesus was not a modern man at all; he was for the contemporary age quite "a stranger and an enigma."[9] The key to his interpretation was his recognition of what he saw as an apocalyptic eschatology in the texts. Jesus was an apocalyptic preacher, convinced that the end was near. A key text for Schweitzer was Matthew 10:23: "You will not finish the towns of Israel before the Son of Man comes." Yet the disciples came back from their mission and the world went on as before. So, he argued, Jesus decided to go up to Jerusalem and provoke a final confrontation, to set loose the "messianic woes" which will inaugurate the end time. But all he accomplished was his own death. He died a failure, disappointed in his vision of the apocalyptic establishment of the kingdom.

With Schweitzer the old quest came to an end. Yet in spite of the excesses rooted in its Enlightenment rationalism, it had produced a number of insights and principles that would become part of modern biblical scholarship. Christian Weisse had made the case for the priority of Mark and pointed to another source common to Luke and Matthew, eventually to be called "Q." William Wrede noticed what he called Mark's "messianic secret." Martin Kähler pointed to the distinction between the Jesus of history and the Christ of faith. Reimarus, Johannes Weiss, and Schweitzer emphasized that Jesus must be understood in the context of first-century Palestinian Judaism. Schweitzer had shown that historical studies are not able to fully recover a historical Jesus like ourselves, that his thought world was very different and he remains someone whose significance we are unable to fully grasp. The creative or perhaps more accurately, theological work of the early Church in interpreting the Christ event had been noted.

The New Quest: Käsemann to Schillebeeckx

In 1953 Ernst Käsemann, a New Testament professor at Tübingen in Germany and former student of Rudolf Bultmann, gave a programmatic lecture at Marburg entitled "The Problem of the Historical Jesus."[10] In it, he called for a new quest, arguing that such a quest, unburdened by the presuppositions of the first, was now possible, using the new methods of historical-critical scholarship—source criticism, form criticism, and redaction criticism. Furthermore, he had some apologetic interests; he argued that

---

[9] Ibid., 398.

[10] Ernst Käsemann, *Essays on New Testament Themes* (Philadelphia: Fortress, 1982), "The Problem of the Historical Jesus," 15–47.

such a quest was necessary to keep Christian faith firmly tied to the life history of Jesus. The question of the continuity between the historical Jesus and the Christ of faith could not be ignored, as it was in the works of scholars such as Bultmann and Karl Barth. Bultmann, who had been Käsemann's mentor, maintained that knowledge of the historical Jesus was not really attainable and in any case, was not really important, as we noted earlier. It was this view that Käsemann was challenging. As he put his argument in a "nutshell" in a later essay: "does the New Testament kerygma (proclamation) count the historical Jesus among the criteria of its own validity? We have to answer this question roundly in the affirmative."[11]

The new, "Second" quest was different from the old in that it was no longer burdened by the rationalist, secular presuppositions of the Enlightenment. Walter Kasper notes three historical and theological principles of Käsemann's New Quest. First, it means recognizing that the Gospels, while not themselves "histories," contain more historical material than had previously been acknowledged. Second, it rejects both myth and Docetism, meaning that Christology must remain focused on the identity of the exalted Lord with the earthly Jesus and on the primacy of Christ before and over the Church. Faith cannot focus only on the kerygma or preaching of the early Church. Finally, the New Quest does not bypass the kerygma, as a purely historical approach would do. Rather it proceeds through the medium of that preaching, so that the historical Jesus is interpreted through the kerygma while at the same time, the historical Jesus helps us to interpret the kerygma.[12]

Once again, a host of books on the historical Jesus and Christology followed. Protestant commentators included G. Bornkamm, E. Fuchs, H. Conzelmann, H. Braun, J. Robinson, G. Ebeling, F. Gogarten, W. Marxsen, and W. Pannenberg, among others, while J. R. Geiselmann, A. Vögtle, H. Schürmann, F. Mussner, R. Schnackenburg, H. Küng, J. Blank, R. Pesch, W. Kasper, J. Sobrino, and E. Schillebeeckx were among the Catholic scholars. Note that most of them were Europeans, particularly Germans.

One of most influential works was the Belgian Dominican Edward Schillebeeckx's massive two-volume work, *Jesus* and *Christ*, coming at the end of the Second Quest.[13] Schillebeeckx (1914–), a dogmatic theologian,

---

[11] Ernst Käsemann, *New Testament Questions of Today* (Philadelphia: Fortress, 1969), "Blind Alleys in the 'Jesus of History' Controversy," 48; see also James M. Robinson, *A New Quest of the Historical Jesus* (London: SCM Press, 1959).

[12] Walter Kasper, *Jesus the Christ* (New York: Paulist, 1976) 33–34.

[13] Edward Schillebeeckx, *Jesus: An Experiment in Christology* (New York: Seabury, 1979); *Christ: The Experience of Jesus as Lord* (New York: Seabury, 1980).

set aside more than three years to immerse himself in critical New Testament studies before beginning his work on Christology. His *Jesus* book is one of the better works on the historical Jesus, insightful in its treatment of how Jesus approached his death and useful for establishing what critical research is able to affirm about his life and ministry. Some find his approach "hypercritical," for example, too reliant on the hypothesized multiple levels of the "Q" community.[14] But with that caution noted, the book remains helpful for establishing a critical minimum in regard to the life and preaching of the historical Jesus.

The New Quest, with its rediscovery of the kerygma, broke with the rationalist liberalism of the Old Quest, with its distaste for Christian doctrine and its pretense of historical objectivity. But many of its practitioners still remained half liberal in their presuppositions. They too easily dismissed the miraculous as mythological, and had difficulty with the eschatological and the prophetic. In this sense, the New Quest was still very much a product of modernity.

The Third Quest

In the early 1980s scholars began speaking of a "Third Quest" for the historical Jesus.[15] Its effort to recover the historical world of Jesus is distinguished by its use of properly historical methods and, increasingly, the social sciences rather than simply the literary disciplines such as form criticism, redaction criticism, and tradition criticism so relied on by the practitioners of the Second Quest. For Third Quest scholars, research into Second Temple Judaism has helped to better understand Jesus in his own historical context as a first-century, Palestinian Jew. Ancient sources such as Josephus, a first-century Jewish historian long ignored by scholars, the documents of Qumran, and the apocalyptic writings are being used to give depth to that context. The use of the social sciences has helped appreciate the social, cultural, and anthropological factors that effected first-century Palestinian Judaism and particularly, the social fabric of Galilean life. Thus, Third Quest scholarship investigates the structure of Galilean family and social relationships, the position of women, the religious milieu, including the ways in which the tradition was passed on and communally expressed, the extent of Hellenistic Greek influence, the impact of the Roman domination and its system of taxation. What was the social climate within which Jesus preached?

---

[14] For N. T. Wright, who is quite critical, it shows the barrenness of the new quest just as Schweitzer's work did for the old; *Jesus and the Victory of God* (Minneapolis: Fortress, 1996) 25.

[15] Cf. Witherington, *The Jesus Quest*; Wright, *JVG*, 83–124.

To what extent, if any, was it possible to separate religion from politics? Who were the ruling elites and where did Jesus and his disciples fit in the social hierarchy? What did "holiness" mean in this period?

A number of those involved in the Third Quest, while emphasizing the historical, also move beyond the closed rationalist system of secular modernity. For example, they take seriously the eschatological context of first-century Palestinian Judaism. What this means is that with the coming of the Third Quest, the Enlightenment worldview has lost its hegemony. Scholars involved in the Third Quest include B. F. Meyer, A. E. Harvey, E. P. Sanders, J. P. Meier, N. T. Wright, Ben Witherington as well as more radical critics such as Elisabeth Schüssler Fiorenza, Richard Horsley, and the members of the Jesus Seminar. Note that most of them are now Americans, with the exception of Schüssler Fiorenza and Wright.[16] Meier and the Jesus Seminar deserve special notice.

John P. Meier's massive three-volume work, *A Marginal Jew*,[17] has been described by Raymond E. Brown as the "most ambitious modern reconstruction of the historical Jesus."[18] Meier is open to all sources, though he (unlike the Jesus Seminar's John Dominic Crossan) does not find the apocryphal gospels helpful. Although Meier uses purely historical sources and arguments, as he makes clear in the introduction to Volume One, he does not exclude the miraculous on a priori grounds as more secular critics might. For example, he argues that the notion "that Jesus acted as and was viewed as an exorcist and healer during his public ministry has as much historical corroboration as almost any other statement we can make about the Jesus of history."[19] Meier sees Jesus as greatly influenced by his predecessor, John the Baptist. He was originally one of John's circle, and though he ultimately broke with him, his own eschatological preaching was in many ways influenced by John.

The Jesus Seminar

I mentioned the Jesus Seminar at the beginning of this chapter. Not all would include it in the Third Quest. N. T. Wright places John Dominic

[16] Witherington considers the work of many of these scholars in his *The Jesus Quest.*

[17] John P. Meier, *A Marginal Jew: Rethinking the Historical Jesus*, Vol. One, *The Roots of the Problem and the Person* (New York: Doubleday, 1991); Vol. Two, *Mentor, Message, and Miracles* (New York: Doubleday, 1994); Vol. Three, *Companions and Competitors* (New York: Doubleday, 2001).

[18] Raymond E. Brown, *An Introduction to the New Testament* (New York: Doubleday, 1997) 826.

[19] Meier, *A Marginal Jew*, II:970.

Crossan and Burton Mack in the Second Quest, with Marcus Borg bridging it with the third.[20] In spite of their rejection of eschatology, I prefer to identify the seminar members with the Third Quest because their interests are strictly historical rather than theological, though I grant some genuine religious interests on the part of Borg.

The Jesus Seminar claims to be an effort to find the "real" Jesus hidden behind the theology of the evangelists and the dogma of the Church. The seminar's founder Robert Funk charges the Church with keeping the faithful in ignorance. While he often blames fundamentalist Christians and the television evangelists for this, it is really the Christ of Christian faith that he objects to. In 1994 he told the *Los Angeles Times* that the Seminar wanted to "liberate" Jesus: "The only Jesus most people want is the mythic one. They don't want the real Jesus. They want the one they can worship. The cultic Jesus."[21] In the first edition of the Seminar's report, *Forum*, he wrote: "The religious establishment has not allowed the intelligence of high scholarship to pass through pastors and priests to a hungry laity."[22] But whether or not "high scholarship" is the goal of the seminar is highly debatable.

John Dominic Crossan, the Seminar's co-chair, is one of its most prolific members. N. T. Wright generously describes him as "one of the most brilliant, engaging, learned and quick-witted New Testament scholars alive today," while judging that his book, *The Historical Jesus* is "almost entirely wrong."[23] The sources for Crossan's reconstruction of the historical Jesus are problematic. Much of it is based on noncanonical texts such as the Gnostic Gospel of Thomas, the Gospel of Peter, and the secret Gospel of Mark, apocryphal works he dates before the year 60 and considers to be of equal or greater importance than the canonical Gospels.[24] Like other members of the Seminar and William Wrede before them, Crossan rejects the Gospel of Mark as the product of theological interests. For his reconstruction of the world of Jesus, he relies heavily on social anthropology. Rather than trying to understand Jesus against his own religious tradition, history,

---

[20] N. T. Wright, *JVG*, 75.

[21] Robert Funk, in the *Los Angeles Times*, View Section (24 February 1994); cited by Luke Timothy Johnson, *The Real Jesus: The Misguided Quest for the Historical Jesus and the Truth of the Traditional Gospels* (HarperSanFrancisco, 1996) 7.

[22] Robert Funk, "The Issue of Jesus," *Forum* 1/1 (1985) 8.

[23] Wright, *JVG*, 44.

[24] John Dominic Crossan, *The Historical Jesus: The Life of a Mediterranean Jewish Peasant* (HarperSanFrancisco, 1991); *Jesus: A Revolutionary Biography* (HarperSanFranciso, 1994); *The Essential Jesus* (HarperSanFrancisco, 1994). For a critique of this position, see Meier, *A Marginal Jew*, I:116–66; also Philip Jenkins, *Hidden Gospels: How the Search for Jesus Lost Its Way* (New York: Oxford University Press, 2001) esp. 54–81.

and Jewish Scriptures, "Crossan defines Jesus within a 'secular,' social and cultural matrix characterized by class, other social distinctions, and the political dynamics of colonization and occupation."[25]

For Crossan, Jesus is a Jewish cynic philosopher and "magician," not a miracle worker in the traditional sense. He rejects the idea that Jesus addressed God as "Abba," chose from his disciples an inner group of twelve, or spoke of a future coming of the kingdom. His practice of "open commensality," sharing meals with all people without regard for Jewish purity laws, social conventions, or traditional family structure, is evidence that he advocated a radical egalitarianism, a "kingdom of nuisances and nobodies" that challenged established structures and hierarchical power. Though N. T. Wright applauds Crossan for his innovative use of the social sciences, he also wonders if his own analysis and selection of materials is not ideologically driven.[26]

Crossan claims that "early Christianity knew nothing about the passion of Jesus beyond the fact itself."[27] He argues that Jesus was executed by the Romans, not by the leaders of the Jews, and that his body was probably eaten by the dogs who scavenged beneath the cross. The first passion narrative and source for Mark's he attributes to a hypothetical "Cross Gospel," an early version of the apocryphal Gospel of Peter. Crossan sees this Cross Gospel as an "historicization" of early passion and parousia prophecies.[28] In his view, the passion account should not be understood as history remembered; it was created by early Christian writers on the basis of Old Testament models. Similarly, he sees the resurrection stories as legitimations of the authority of early Church leaders.

Burton Mack's approach is even more radical. Building largely on a highly hypothetical reconstruction of the community lying behind the Q source, Mack reconstructs Jesus as a wisdom teacher who set in motion a "social experiment," only to have some communities loosely associated with him retell his story sometime after his death in terms of divine power.[29] He sees Mark as the real founder of Christianity. Like Crossan's Jesus, Mack's Mark sounds like a university professor. His Gospel, which Mack dates after 70, was not "a pious transmission of revered tradition"

---

[25] Roger Haight, *Jesus: Symbol of God* (Maryknoll, N.Y.: Orbis, 1999) 67.

[26] Wright, *JVG*, 54.

[27] Crossan, *The Historical Jesus*, 387.

[28] Ibid., 385.

[29] Burton L. Mack, *A Myth of Innocence: Mark and Christian Origins* (Philadelphia: Fortress, 1988) 76; see also *The Lost Gospel: The Book of Q and Christian Origins* (HarperSanFrancisco, 1993).

but "composed at a desk in a scholar's study lined with texts and open to discourse with other intellectuals."[30] It was Mark who invented the story of the conflict between Jesus and the Jewish leaders of his day, making them the villains. This "myth of innocence," Mack argues, has had disastrous effects on Western culture, particularly American culture where it has given rise to another myth of America as "the innocent redeemer of the world."[31]

Marcus Borg is the most sympathetic to the religious dimension of the Jesus story and he writes movingly of his own spiritual journey. He presents Jesus as a charismatic sage and healer, a spirit person, social prophet, wisdom teacher, and movement founder.[32] Though his portrait of Jesus is quite Jewish, he does not find the title "messiah" appropriate. For him, Jesus, like Moses, Ezekiel, Paul, and the Lakota shaman Black Elk, was a spirit person, "one of many mediators of the sacred."[33] As a social prophet, he challenged the prevailing "politics of purity" of the ruling elites with a "politics of compassion." He was put to death because his social vision threatened the dominant classes of the day.

Borg eliminates any talk of the eschatological future from Jesus' preaching and he does not deal at length with the Resurrection. Though he grants that the conviction that "God raised Jesus from the dead" is widespread in the New Testament, he remains by his own admission something of an "agnostic" about an afterlife. The testimony about "near death experiences" suggests to him the inadequacy of a materialistic worldview. But he generally seems reluctant to move beyond the very general affirmation that there is something beyond death.[34]

Few scholars take the work of the Jesus Seminar seriously. Luke Timothy Johnson, in one of the most critical reviews of its work, dismisses it as a entrepreneurial venture guided by Funk which "does not . . . represent anything like a consensus of scholars."[35] Richard Hays judges the Seminar's methodology as problematic for its questionable selection and dating of

---

[30] Mack, *A Myth of Innocence*, 322–23.

[31] Ibid., 371.

[32] Marcus J. Borg, *Jesus a New Vision: Spirit, Culture, and the Life of Discipleship* (San Francisco: Harper & Row, 1987); *Meeting Jesus Again for the First Time: The Historical Jesus and the Heart of Contemporary Faith* (HarperSanFrancisco, 1994); *Jesus in Contemporary Scholarship* (Valley Forge, Pa.: Trinity Press International, 1994).

[33] Borg, *Meeting Jesus Again*, 37.

[34] Marcus J. Borg, *The God We Never Knew* (HarperSan Francisco, 1997) 171–72; in the HarperCollins sponsored Internet Debate with Crossan and Luke Timothy Johnson, Borg stated: "I affirm that the resurrection of Jesus really happened"; Marcus J. Borg <Marcus_Borg@info.harpercollins.com> 3/25/96.

[35] Johnson, *The Real Jesus*, 2.

sources, its use of the criterion of dissimilarity for assessing the authenticity of the Jesus tradition, its insistence on finding a non-eschatological Jesus, and its attempt to assess the sayings of Jesus in isolation from a more comprehensive reconstruction of his life, ministry, and death.[36] Raymond E. Brown summarizes the "devastating judgment" of responsible New Testament scholars: "only a small ripple in NT scholarship; results representing the Jesus the researchers wanted to find; the pursuit of a specific confessional agenda; and dangerous in giving a false impression."[37] The Jesus Seminar has produced a lot of headlines but it has not added much to our knowledge of the historical Jesus.

Conclusion

At the end of this chapter we might ask, are we any closer to answering the question, "who is Jesus," after three quests and more than two hundred years of research into the historical Jesus? There is much to be learned from the different quests we have considered. Though the First Quest was fatally flawed by its Enlightenment presuppositions, still from it came many of the distinctions and concepts which would become part of the vocabulary of Christology, including the distinction between the Jesus of history and the Christ of faith, the priority of Mark, and the "Q" hypothesis.

The Second Quest which began with Käsemann's famous lecture moved beyond the Enlightenment presuppositions of the First Quest and sought to show the *continuity* between the historical Jesus and the Christ of faith. While seeking to recover the historical material contained in the Gospels, Second Quest scholars recognized that historical Jesus scholarship could not simply bypass the kerygma. Their effort to interpret Jesus through the medium of his preaching meant taking much more seriously the Palestinian Jewish background of Jesus, and by implication, the Jewish religious tradition which shaped his own religious identity and imagination. They have refined the tools for the historical-critical study of texts and their research has expanded immeasurably our knowledge of the way the New Testament traditions developed. They also took seriously the meaning of the preaching of Jesus for his own time.

The Third Quest has led to a much greater appreciation of the world of Jesus. Historical studies have led a more accurate picture of movements and currents in his world, while the application of the social sciences has

---

[36] Richard Hays, "The Corrected Jesus," *First Things* 43 (May 1994) 44–46.
[37] Brown, *Introduction*, 821–22.

suggested a more radical dimension to his words and deeds. Thus we have learned a great deal about the life of Jesus, his preaching, the "very words" (*ipsissima verba*) he spoke, the imagery he used, the world he lived in, and his fate, as we shall see in subsequent chapters.

Some, like the members of the Jesus Seminar, argue that the canonical Gospels cannot be taken as reliable sources for our knowledge of Jesus. But Luke Timothy Johnson, in a brilliant chapter entitled "What's Historical About Jesus?" shows how the main details of the "narrative spine" provided by Mark can be corroborated by other, non-narrative New Testament writings as well as by non-Christian writings (NCW). I compress here his summary: Jesus was a human person and a Jew (Paul, Hebrews, NCW), of the tribe of Judah (Hebrews) and a descendant of David (Paul). His mission was to the Jews (Paul, NCW); he was a teacher (Paul, James, NCW), was tested (Hebrews), and prayed using the word Abba (Paul). He prayed for deliverance from death (Hebrews), suffered (Paul, Hebrews, 1 Peter), and interpreted his last meal with reference to his death (Paul, and by implication, Tacitus and Josephus). He underwent a trial and appeared before Pontius Pilate (Paul, NCW); his end involved some Jews (Paul, NCW). He was crucified (Paul, Hebrews, 1 Peter, NCW) and was buried (Paul). After his death he appeared to witnesses (Paul).[38]

Still, the historical Jesus by itself is never sufficient. The historical Jesus cannot simply be identified with the "real" Jesus. John P. Meier has emphasized this point. He distinguishes between the historical Jesus or the Jesus of history and the real Jesus. The historical Jesus is in the final analysis "a modern abstraction and construct," a "fragmentary hypothetical reconstruction of him by modern means of research."[39] The "real" Jesus continues to escape us, "whether we mean his total reality or just a reasonably complete biographical portrait."[40] Most of his life remains veiled to us, and our sources are of necessity selective.

Nor can the historical Jesus be the object of Christian faith. Martin Kähler and Rudolf Bultmann have stressed this and Luke Timothy Johnson has emphasized it again in reaction to the efforts of the Jesus Seminar to identify the real Jesus with the Jesus of their reconstruction. Johnson stresses that Christian faith is directed to the living person, the "real Jesus" whom God has raised up and made both Lord and Christ.[41] He poses in a powerful

---

[38] Johnson, *The Real Jesus*, 121–22; see also his *Living Jesus: Learning the Heart of the Gospel* (HarperSanFrancisco, 2000) 105–08.

[39] Meier, *A Marginal Jew*, I:25, 31.

[40] Ibid., I:24.

[41] Johnson, *The Real Jesus*, 141–42.

way the problematic nature of establishing the meaning of a person by means of critical historiography alone, and the adequacy of history as a basis for faith.

Johnson's point about the insufficiency of the historical Jesus is well taken. He is right to insist that history cannot be normative for *faith*, but he needs to give more attention to its importance for *theology*. If the Church's christological doctrine is to withstand the charge of being nothing more than a Hellenization of Jewish mythopoetic language or merely the product of patriarchal and hierarchical interests, it must be able to be grounded in the Jesus of history as well as in the faith of the Church. Furthermore, to claim that it is "silly" to debate questions such as whether the Jesus of history predicted his return[42] leaves us vulnerable to the varieties of fundamentalist apocalypticism, rapture theologies, and millennialisms which still trouble Christian communities today.

For a solidly grounded Christology, the historical Jesus is crucial. Without it, Christian faith and its Christology remain open to the accusations of divinizing Jesus and falsifying his message that have been heard in the quest for the historical Jesus from the time of Reimarus down to the present-day members of the Jesus Seminar. In the following chapters we will see what current scholarship can tell us about the historical Jesus. But first, we need to look more closely at how the historical-critical method works.

[42] Ibid., 145.

Chapter 2

Methodological Considerations

The various quests for the historical Jesus have demonstrated that there is at least some difference between the Christ proclaimed by the Christian tradition and the Jesus of history. This means that Christology today needs to be done critically, using the literary and historical disciplines that have been developed in the last two hundred years. In this chapter, we need to consider first, the transition from a precritical to a critical Christology. Second, we will look at the stages in the development of the Gospel tradition. Finally, we will outline some criteria for discerning the historical Jesus within the Gospel tradition.

From Precritical to Critical Christology

While the Church has brought critical reflection to bear on the biblical presentation of its faith from the beginning, the Bible itself was not challenged as a source. It was God's word. As sacred history, it provided a record of God's saving acts, from the creation through redemption in Christ and the establishment of the Church. The biblical story in its entirety functioned as a prescientific worldview that was taken literally; those who challenged any part of it were disciplined by the Church or rejected by the believing community. The names of Copernicus, Galileo, and Darwin come immediately to mind. The Bible also functioned as the basic Christian symbol system, "the meta-story into which each individual and communal Christian story is patterned."[1]

Some early scholars and theologians tried to bring a more critical or "scientific" approach to their exegesis and interpretation. Marcion (ca. 150) rejected the Old Testament on the basis of his theological view of God and tried to reduce the four Gospels to one. Tatian (ca. 175), recognizing the

[1] Sandra M. Schneiders, "The Study of Christian Spirituality: Contours and Dynamics of a Discipline," *Christian Spirituality Bulletin* 6/1 (1998) 4.

differences in chronology and detail in the four Gospels, attempted in his *Diatessaron* to harmonize them into one continuous narrative. Origen (185–254) made the first attempt at textual criticism of the Old Testament. His emphasis on an allegorical reading of biblical texts shows his recognition of the importance of hermeneutics or theory of interpretation. Augustine (354–430) in his *De consensu evangelistarum* recognized that the order of the Gospel narratives was based on recollection rather than strict chronological history and that the words of Jesus were not always reported verbatim. But in spite of these early efforts at a more critical interpretation, modern biblical scholars generally characterize biblical scholarship up to the seventeenth century as "precritical."[2]

While a French Oratorian priest, Richard Simon (1638–1712), is usually considered the father of modern biblical criticism, the discipline remains very much a product of "modernity," the mentality at the basis of modern culture. Modernity has its roots in the scientific revolution of the seventeenth century, with its demand for empirical verification, and the Enlightenment of the eighteenth, which gloried in an autonomous reason, freed from the constraints of biblical supernaturalism, theological dogma, and Church authority. The result of the application of Enlightenment rationalism and the scientific method to the Bible was the historical-critical method. Reimarus foreshadowed this approach. But it was his successors in the universities of Germany, particularly Tübingen, who were to develop the various historical and literary methods of investigating biblical texts (form criticism, redaction criticism, source criticism, text criticism, and so forth).

Modern Biblical Scholarship and the Catholic Church

The Catholic Church perceived the Enlightenment as an attack on the Church and on Christianity in general; thus it rejected the new scholarship coming out of Germany as one of its fruits. In the words of Ben Meyer, "Catholic theology retired into a dogmatic corner, while avant-garde Protestant theology allied itself with the spirit of the time."[3] The so-called "Modernist crisis" at the beginning of the twentieth century only served to harden the Catholic Church's attitude. In 1902 Pope Leo XIII founded the Pontifical Biblical Commission (PBC), a Roman congregation charged with

---

[2] Cf. John S. Kselman and Ronald D. Witherup, "Modern New Testament Criticism," *The New Jerome Biblical Commentary*, ed. Raymond E. Brown, Joseph A. Fitzmyer, and Roland E. Murphy (Englewood Cliffs, N.J.: Prentice Hall, 1990) 1130–45.

[3] Ben F. Meyer, *The Aims of Jesus* (London: SCM Press, 1979) 57.

overseeing the use of the Bible in the Church. Between 1905 and 1915, the PBC issued a series of decisions requiring Catholic scholars to hold positions that the new scholarship was challenging, including the substantial Mosaic authorship of the Pentateuch, the historical nature of the first chapters of Genesis, the single authorship of Isaiah, the priority of Matthew, and Paul as the author of Hebrews. But the attitude of the Church was to change radically in the last half of the twentieth century, following Pope Pius XII's encyclical, *Divino Afflante Spiritu*. It would be helpful to call attention to the official documents that signaled the Catholic Church's eventual recognition of the value of historical-critical scholarship.

Divino Afflante Spiritu (1943)

This encyclical of Pope Pius XII has often been called the *Magna Carta* of Catholic biblical scholarship. It instructed Catholic scholars to base their translations on the original Hebrew and Greek texts, rather than on the Latin of the Vulgate, and encouraged them to use the new historical and literary methods in their study of these texts. In others words, the Church was now telling its biblical scholars and theologians that they were free to use a "scientific" approach to biblical scholarship, even though many more conservative scholars feared that this would lead to a rationalism harmful to the faith.

The Pope also warned Catholics about being overly fearful of new ideas: "They must avoid that somewhat indiscreet zeal which considers everything new to be for that very reason a fit object of attack or suspicion."[4] With this green light from Rome, Catholic biblical scholarship began to show a new energy and vitality. In 1955, the secretary of the PBC said that Catholic scholars had "complete freedom" in regard to those conservative decrees of 1905–15, except where they touched faith and morals.

Instruction on the Historical Truth of the Gospels (1964)

Of crucial importance for Christology, this 1964 instruction of the PBC stresses that the Gospels are not literal, chronological accounts of the words and deeds of Jesus.[5] They are the products of a three-stage development that moves from the ministry of the historical Jesus, through the oral preaching of the apostles, and finally to the actual writing of the Gospels

[4] Pius XII, *Divino Afflante Spiritu*, no. 49; text from Catholic Truth Society (London, 1943).
[5] For a translation and commentary see Joseph A. Fitzmeyer, *Theological Studies* 25 (1964) 386–408.

by the evangelists. The instruction teaches that words and deeds attributed to Jesus may really come from the preaching of the early Christian communities or from the particular evangelist who selected from, synthesized, adapted, and explicated the material he received. This does not however mean that the Gospels are not reliable sources: "The truth of the story is not at all affected by the fact that the Evangelists relate the words and deeds of the Lord in a different order, and express his sayings not literally but differently, while preserving (their) sense" (no. XI).

Dei Verbum (1965)

The following year the fathers of the Second Vatican Council approved and promulgated the Dogmatic Constitution on Divine Revelation, *Dei Verbum*. The constitution understands revelation, not as abstract truths expressed in dogmatic propositions, but as God's self-communication in history which reaches its fullness in the person of Jesus and through life in the Spirit offers men and women a share in God's own divine nature (DV 2). Thus its approach is personal rather than propositional. The Church's understanding of revelation continues to develop in history: "This tradition which comes from the apostles develops in the Church with the help of the Holy Spirit. For there is a growth in the understanding of the realities and the words which have been handed down" (DV 8).

Dei Verbum affirms that the Scriptures are inspired; but it also emphasizes that the biblical writers are "true authors," making use of their own powers and abilities (DV 11). Since God speaks through these men "in human fashion," biblical interpreters must carefully seek out the meaning that the authors had in mind, paying attention to the "literary forms" used:

> For truth is proposed and expressed in a variety of ways, depending on whether a text is history of one kind or another, or whether its form is that of prophecy, poetry, or some other type of speech. The interpreter must investigate what meaning the sacred writer intended to express and actually expressed in particular circumstances as he used contemporary literary forms in accordance with the situation of his own time and culture. For the correct understanding of what the sacred author wanted to assert, due attention must be paid to the customary and characteristic styles of perceiving, speaking, and narrating which prevailed at the time of the sacred writer, and to the customs men normally followed at that period in their everyday dealings with one another (DV 12).

The Interpretation of the Bible in the Church (1993)

Toward the end of the century the PBC published another important document, "The Interpretation of the Bible in the Church," reaffirming the necessity of historical-critical study of Scripture.[6] The document is interesting for its evaluation, both positive and negative, of a number of contemporary hermeneutical theories as well as liberationist, feminist, and fundamentalist approaches to biblical interpretation.

The document is particularly critical of fundamentalism. While acknowledging that fundamentalism is correct to insist on the divine inspiration of the Bible and the inerrancy of the word of God, it asserts that "its way of presenting these truths is rooted in an ideology which is not biblical."[7] It finds problematic fundamentalism's failure to take into account the historical character of biblical revelation, its "undue stress on the inerrancy of certain details in the biblical texts, especially in what concerns historical events or supposed scientific truths," its tendency to confuse "the final stage of the tradition (what the evangelists have written) with the initial (the words and deeds of the historical Jesus)." Here the text echoes the earlier "Instruction on the Historical Truth of the Gospels."

In addressing the specific character of Catholic biblical exegesis, the PBC document points, not to some special scientific method, but to the fact that Catholic exegesis always takes place within the living tradition of the Church. "Catholic exegetes approach the biblical text with a pre-understanding which holds closely together modern scientific culture and the religious tradition emanating from Israel and from the early Christian community."[8] Thus biblical scholarship cannot be reduced to the scientific exegesis of historical documents. The Bible must be received as the Word of God and interpreted within the life of the Church.

The conclusion emphasizes once again that "the very nature of biblical texts means that interpreting them will require continued use of the *historical-critical method*." Other "synchronic" approaches (rhetorical, narrative, semiotic, feminist, etc.) can also make a contribution. But Catholic biblical scholarship should avoid a "professional bias" which would blind it to the great tradition of the Church to which the Bible is witness. The PBC document warns against exegesis becoming lost, "like a stream of water, in the sands of a hypercritical analysis."[9] In this way, it points to the

---

[6] "The Interpretation of the Bible in the Church," *Origins* 23/29 (1994) 497–524.

[7] Ibid., 509–10.

[8] Ibid., 513.

[9] Ibid., 524.

dialectical relationship that should exist between historical-critical scholarship and the faith of the Church; each has a role to play in the interpretative task, and each challenges the other. We saw this earlier in speaking about a Christology of "complementarity," one that considers both the historical Jesus of scholarly retrieval and the risen Christ of Christian faith.

In summary, to say that Jesus is the Christ is to invoke both faith and history. A critical Christology needs to do both. We can express the presuppositions of such a Christology in five principles.

1. The Gospels are testimonies of faith, not histories or biographies in the modern sense.
2. The Gospels contain historical material; but to recover that material, they must be read critically, using the historical-critical method.
3. The context for Christology must remain the faith of the Church, expressed in its Scriptures, its creeds, and its liturgy, for without that faith, the story of Jesus is incomplete.
4. The Church's christological faith must be grounded in the historical Jesus; therefore the historical-critical method is essential for the task of Christology.
5. The historical Jesus must be understood from the perspective of the Jewish religious tradition which grounded his religious worldview and shaped his religious imagination.

The Development of the Gospel Tradition

The four Gospels represent the end products of a long process of development extending over some sixty or more years of Christian preaching, catechetical instruction, teaching, worship, and theological reflection on the life, death, and resurrection of Jesus. Deepened by constant reflection on the meaning of the Christ event for the community of disciples, the process also reflects different moments in the faith and life of the early Church.

The Gospels represent the preaching of the early Christian communities in written form. They cannot be taken as histories or biographies in our modern sense. Like good preachers, the evangelists often reshaped the Jesus tradition they received in light of the needs of their respective communities. Each author drew on his own particular Christian experience, shaping his account according to his own insight and point of view.

At the same time, the evangelists evidence a respect for the tradition they received and hand on. For example, in discussing why Luke could use a feminine form of *mathētēs*, the Greek word for disciple, in Acts when he did not use it in his Gospel, John P. Meier says: "Apparently, Luke did not feel authorized to introduce the feminine form into the relatively fixed Gospel tradition, while he did feel free to do so in his new kind of composition, the Acts of the Apostles, where he was not so tightly constrained by a normative tradition and the usage of previous Christian documents (e.g., Mark and Q)."[10]

There was obviously a development in the Church's understanding of the mystery of Christ. We know that the disciples did not perceive the divinity of Jesus during his public ministry and that the earliest Christian communities did not immediately proclaim Jesus as the eternal Son of God. Similarly, comparing the very different Fourth Gospel with the Synoptics, it is highly unlikely that Jesus openly claimed to be the messiah from the beginning of his ministry (John 4:26), or proclaimed his divinity with statements such as "before Abraham came to be, I AM" (John 8:58), or gave long theological lectures on the meaning of the Eucharist even before he had instituted it (John 6:52-59).

The New Testament books developed over some seventy or more years. The first texts were the authentic letters of Paul—1 Thessalonians, 1 and 2 Corinthians, Galatians, Philippians, Romans, and Philemon, written in the 50s. James might be as early as the mid 60s. Mark, written about 68, was the first Gospel and primary source for Matthew and Luke. Colossians, Ephesians, and 2 Thessalonians are most probably "Deutero-Pauline," written by a disciple of Paul. The Pastoral Letters, 1 and 2 Timothy and Titus, are even later. Hebrews may have been written in the early 80s, Matthew and Luke in the mid 80s. John is usually dated in the mid 90s, with the Johannine epistles following later, and 2 Peter is dated somewhere between 100 and 110. See the chart on the following page.

---

[10] John P. Meier, *A Marginal Jew*, Vol. III (New York: Doubleday, 2001) 79.

The Development of the New Testament

33   Apostolic Preaching
–
–
–
–
40
–
–
–
–
50
–   1 Thessalonians, 1 & 2 Corinthians
–   Galatians, Philippians,
–   Philemon, Romans
–
60
–
–
–   James
–   MARK
70
–
–
–   Colossians (?)
–
80
–
–   1 Peter 1–4:11
–   Ephesians, Hebrews (?)
–   MATTHEW, LUKE, Acts
90
–   Jude
–   JOHN, Revelation
–   1 & 2 Tim, Titus
–   1, 2, 3 John
100 1 Peter 4:12–5:14
–   2 Peter

The Synoptic Problem

Matthew, Mark, and Luke are known as the "Synoptic" Gospels (Gk. *syn* + *optic* means "seen together") because of their common perspective. But there are also some significant differences. Matthew and Luke include a number of "sayings" of Jesus not contained in Mark, and each has material unique to itself. Explaining the interrelationship of the three Gospels has been called the "Synoptic Problem."

While the traditional order of the Synoptics was Matthew, Mark, and Luke, a tradition that goes back as far as Papias in the second century, the priority of Mark was first suggested at the end of the eighteenth century. Today it is almost universally accepted that Mark was the first written Gospel, and that it served as a principle source for Matthew and Luke. Of Mark's 661 verses, Matthew includes all but 40–50 (80 percent) and Luke about 350 (about 65 percent). The expression "Triple Tradition" is used of the material common to all three Synoptic evangelists.

There are also some 220 verses common to Matthew and Luke but not found in Mark. This "Double Tradition," much of it in the same order, is usually identified as "Q" (from the German "*Quelle*," source), a hypothesis to explain the source for these sayings (found also in the Gnostic Gospel of Thomas). Q consists of the sayings of Jesus, including the Beatitudes, the Sermon on the Mount (or Plain in Luke), and the "Lord's Prayer," as well as some parables.[11] The Q source, problem written, is thought to have originated in Palestine or Syria within two generations of the death of Jesus. Some scholars see multiple layers of traditions and theologies in the "Q community": a primary Aramaic phase, a further phase from Greek-speaking Jewish Christians, and a final phase of editorial activity, possibly by a Gentile Christian.[12] Others find this reconstruction "highly debatable."[13] It is difficult to build too great a theological edifice on a text that remains only a hypothesis, even if a sound one.

Finally, each Gospel has material unique to each itself, some 50 verses in Mark, 315–330 in Matthew, and 500–600 in Luke. Luke's special material includes some classical parables and stories such as the infancy narratives, the Good Samaritan, the Prodigal Son, the rich man and Lazarus, the Pharisee and the Publican, Zacchaeus, the Good Thief, and Jesus' prayer for his executioners.

[11] For a table of material attributed to Q, see Raymond E. Brown, *An Introduction to the New Testament* (New York: Doubleday, 1997) 118–19.

[12] Cf. Edward Schillebeeckx, *Jesus: An Experiment in Christology* (New York: Seabury, 1979) 101–02.

[13] Brown, *Introduction*, 120.

Stages in the Development of the Gospel Tradition

Using the framework provided by the 1964 PBC "Instruction on the Historical Truth of the Gospels" (VI–IX), we can trace the development of the Gospel tradition through three stages: the words and deeds of Jesus (approximately 28–30 C.E.), the preaching of the apostles (or of the early Christian communities—approximately 30–70), and the writing of the Gospels by the evangelists (70–100). We will consider briefly each stage.

First Stage: The Words and Deeds of the Jesus of History

The first stage includes the actual words Jesus spoke, the stories and parables he told, and the events of his life. Among the authentic words and sayings of Jesus we can include the earliest form of the Beatitudes and the Lord's Prayer, the word "Abba," the expression "kingdom of God," and a number of sayings, to be considered later. The parables also belong to this stage, though they were often reshaped in later preaching. The disciples Jesus chose were witnesses to his preaching. Of course there is much in this stage that has been lost to history, for example, the actual circumstances of his birth and the story of his childhood and youth—known traditionally as the "hidden life" of Jesus.

Second Stage: The Apostolic Preaching

Christian preaching begins with the proclamation (Gk., *kērygma*) of the resurrection of Jesus. But there is much more than this "Easter kerygma" in this stage of oral preaching. The apostles and disciples repeated the sayings of Jesus, proclaimed his teachings, retold his parables and the stories of his life and death. To be sure, as the PBC Instruction acknowledges, they "interpreted His words and deeds according to the needs of their listeners" and proclaimed Christ with different modes of speaking and literary forms familiar to them from Scripture, "catecheses, stories, *testimonia*, hymns, doxologies, prayers" (VIII). Some examples:

Easter kerygma: the proclamation of the resurrection of Jesus, often with an enumeration of the witnesses (1 Cor 15:3-8; Luke 24:34; Acts 2:32). The point of the kerygma was to bring others to new life in Christ.

Sayings of Jesus: The sayings of Jesus were handed down and grouped in collections such as the Q source. Bultmann distinguished three main groups of sayings: *logia* or sayings in the narrow sense (subdivided into declaratory principles, exhortations, and questions), prophetic and apocalyptic sayings, and laws or community regulations.[14]

Stories about Jesus: Stories about Jesus, his baptism, ministry, choice of the Twelve, his interaction with his disciples and others, and his fate.

Parables: the stories or parables Jesus used to present his message include proverbs, examples, similes, allegories, and the more familiar narrative parables. They were transmitted in the early tradition and grouped together; the evangelists frequently adapted them to reflect their editorial and theological interests and sometimes allegorized them.

Miracle stories: The early communities told stories recounting the miracles of Jesus. As they were passed on, they were frequently magnified, expanded, and gathered into collections. Most of the miracle stories concern healings, particularly those that took place on the Sabbath. Similar stories were passed on about the exorcisms of Jesus. These stories were often shaped according to a three-point pattern for oral transmission; first the circumstances ("a violent squall came up"), then the miracle ("He woke up, rebuked the wind"), and finally the result ("They were filled with great awe"—Mark 4:35-41).

Liturgical formulas: Some Jesus tradition comes from the liturgical and sacramental life of the early communities. The trinitarian baptismal formula attributed by Matthew to the risen Jesus (Matt 28:19) has its original *Sitz im Leben* or situation in life in the baptismal liturgy of the Church. Similarly, liturgical formulas from the Eucharists celebrated by the early communities are incorporated into the story of the Last Supper (Matt 26:26-29; Mark 12:22-25; Luke 22:17-19), the retelling of the miracle of the loaves (Mark 6:41 and plls), and the story of the meal Jesus shared with the two disciples on the road to Emmaus (Luke 24:30).

Easter Stories: There are two kinds of Easter stories, some concerning the discovery of the empty tomb, others about the appearance of the risen Jesus to his disciples. These are distinguished from the short, formulaic Easter kerygma by an abundance of imaginative detail.

Hymns: A number of hymns used by the early communities appear in New Testament documents, for example, the hymn in Philippians (2:6-9), the canticles of Mary (1:46-55) and Zechariah (1:68-79) in Luke, and the Prologue in John (1:1-14).

[14] Rudolf Bultmann, *The History of the Synoptic Tradition* (Oxford: Basil Blackwell, 1963) 69 ff.

Christological Titles: Titles used by early communities for Jesus also appear in the Gospels, among them prophet, Messiah, Son of David, Emmanuel, Son of Man, Lord, Son of God. Each title implied a different Christology.

Thus this preliterary stage of Church tradition is rich in a multiplicity of literary forms emerging from the missionary work of those whom Ephesians calls "apostles, prophets, and evangelists" (cf. Eph 4:11) as well as from the cat-echetical and liturgical lives of the early communities. These communities were fully functioning churches, preaching their faith in Jesus as Messiah, Lord, and Son of God, preparing candidates for baptism, gathering for praise and thanksgiving at the supper held in memory of Jesus. Other evangelists, those we call Mark, Matthew, Luke, and John, would eventually draw on this material in presenting the Jesus tradition in written form.

Third Stage: The Writing of the Gospels

While the evangelists were not themselves eyewitnesses to Jesus' ministry, they had a great deal of tradition to draw upon. Each worked both as an editor, selecting and synthesizing material, and as an author, developing his Gospel according to his own insights and gifts and shaping it according to the needs of the community for whom he was writing. Each had a unique point of view; each had a different background; and each was writing in the light of a different historical situation. Luke Timothy Johnson compares them to different portraits: "The gospels are not simply reportage. Neither are they caricatures dashed off with a bit of charcoal in a few moments. They are portraits thick with a texture resulting from long reflection, frequent repainting, and (in the case of two of them) the use of an earlier rendition."[15]

Mark, the author of the First Gospel, is difficult to pinpoint in terms of locale and audience. He is thought to have been a Jewish Christian with ties to Palestinian Jewish Christianity. His community was clearly facing persecution. Many think his Gospel was written from Rome, or at least within a Latin milieu, before the destruction of Jerusalem. Some however argue for a location in Palestine or Syria, and others for a slightly later date.

Matthew's Gospel was most probably written after the final break between the Jewish Christians and the Jewish community, leading to the excommunication of the former from the synagogue around the year 80. It clearly reflects the conflict between the Jewish Christians and the reform

---

[15] Luke Timothy Johnson, *Living Jesus: Learning the Heart of the Gospel* (Harper-SanFrancisco, 1999) 127.

movement of the Pharisees at Jamnia. Matthew himself may have been a Jewish-Christian scribe (cf. Matt 13:52). Part of his task was to assure the Jewish Christians of Antioch who were rapidly becoming a minority in a Gentile church that their new situation was in fulfillment of what had been spoken by the prophets (cf. Matt 2:15, 17, 23).

Luke is thought to have been a Gentile Christian, by tradition from Antioch. He may have been originally a convert to Judaism, one of the "God-fearers" (cf. Acts 10:2) before his conversion to Christianity. He was familiar with the Septuagint translation of the Jewish Scriptures and of all the evangelists the most polished in Greek. He was able to imitate both classical and Hellenistic Jewish styles. His two-volume work, Gospel and Acts, universal in its conception, was addressed primarily to Gentile Christians related to the Pauline mission either through Paul or his disciples.

John's Gospel in many ways is the most complex. Independent of the Synoptic tradition, it is based on the tradition of the "Beloved Disciple," perhaps originally a disciple of John the Baptist and then a follower of Jesus. But the Beloved Disciple was not a member of the Twelve and thus not John the son of Zebedee. The Gospel itself was the work of a later disciple within the Johannine community, and was probably completed by a redactor who added additional material (cf. John 14:31; 20:30-31).

Recovering the Historical Jesus

How can we discern the historical Jesus across the distance of the centuries and through the various levels of the Gospel tradition? First of all, the story of Jesus must be placed within the religious world of a first-century Palestinian Jew. The efforts of critics like John Dominic Crossan to use cultural anthropology rather than the religious tradition of his people to reconstruct the world of Jesus completely overlooks the fact that Jesus was a member of a community whose worldview was formed by the Hebrew Scriptures. Jesus cannot be understood apart from the religious history of Israel. His story, which opens with his baptism by John, is from the beginning situated within a religious context. The Jesus who appears to us in the Christian Scriptures, his understanding of God, his sense of being part of and in solidarity with a people, the religious imagery, anthropology, and theology implicit in his preaching must be understood in the light of that context. His own religious imagination was shaped by the religious tradition of which he was a part.

Over the years biblical scholars have developed a number of criteria or principles for identifying "authentic" material, words and deeds that go back to Jesus himself. In the following section I would like to review five criteria proposed by John P. Meier and used in his own reconstruction of the historical Jesus.[16]

1. *Embarrassment*

The criteria of "embarrassment" assumes that material about Jesus or the apostles that would prove embarrassing to Jesus or the early Church would have been suppressed or softened by the evangelists. The fact that such material is present is usually a sign that it comes from the first stage of the Gospel tradition and so is authentic. Examples include the story of Jesus the sinless one submitting to John the Baptist for baptism, the saying "why do you call me good" (Mark 10:18), Jesus' admitting that he does not know the exact time or hour of the eschatological judgment (Mark 13:32), and Peter's denial. This criterion needs to be exercised together with other criteria, but it can at times be very useful.

2. *Discontinuity*

Also referred to as the criterion of "dissimilarity," "originality," or "dual irreducibility," this criterion focuses on words or deeds of Jesus that do not reflect the practice of either Judaism or the early Church. The presupposition here is that a saying or action contrary to what was taken for granted by the Jewish community or the Church is probably authentic. Examples might include Jesus' prohibition of all oaths (Matt 5:34, 37), the rejection of voluntary fasting for his disciples (Mark 2:18-22), and his prohibition of divorce (Mark 10:1-12 and plls). This is a useful criterion, but Meier warns against presupposing that it will automatically give what is central or fairly representative of Jesus' teaching (173).

3. *Multiple Attestation*

One of the most important, the criterion of "multiple attestation" or "cross section" holds that words or deeds of Jesus which are reported in more than one independent literary source (Paul, Mark, John) and/or more than one literary form (saying, parable, miracle story) are most probably authentic. For example, Mark, Q, and the special material in Matthew and Luke all show Jesus speaking about the kingdom of God; one finds references to this also in Paul and John, even though both prefer to speak about Jesus' message in other terms. Similarly there are multiple attesta-

[16] John P. Meier, *A Marginal Jew*, I:168–77; see also Schillebeeckx, *Jesus*, 88–100.

tions of Jesus' speaking about the destruction of the Temple, his healing the sick, or dealing with outcasts and sinners.

However Schillebeeckx (95) cautions that something found in only one tradition can still be authentic. He notes this in regard to John's report that Jesus also baptized (John 3:22) and Meier (175) raises it in regard to Jesus' Aramaic invocation of God as "Abba," noted only in Mark 14:36.

4. *Coherence*

Also called "consistency" or "conformity," this criterion can be applied once a certain amount of historical material has been established on the basis of the other criteria. This helps to gradually build up a picture of the historical Jesus. Some sayings attributed to Jesus may have been created by the earliest preachers and evangelists; since these earliest Christians would have been familiar with the preaching of Jesus, these sayings may be consistent with his teaching even if not "authentic" in the technical sense of coming from Jesus himself. Schillebeeckx observes that a saying attributed to Jesus, while not actually spoken by him, may be grounded in his inspiration and orientation (98).

Meier (176) notes that this criterion of coherence should not be used negatively, declaring a saying or action inauthentic because it is judged inconsistent with what has already been established as authentic. For example, it is quite possible that Jesus used both wisdom and apocalyptic eschatology in his preaching. Modern academic standards of consistency should not be imposed on Jesus and his contemporaries, whose Semitic mentality was quite different from our own.

5. *Rejection and Execution*

The historical Jesus, in his preaching and ministry, alienated powerful constituencies. Taking note of Jesus' violent end, this criterion of rejection seeks to find the words or deeds that provoked it. As Meier says, "a bland Jesus who simply told people to look at the lilies of the field" would threaten no one. "A Jesus whose words and deeds would not alienate people, especially powerful people, is not the historical Jesus" (177).

Doubtful Criteria

A number of criteria are judged to be inadequate; Schillebeeckx calls them "frequently employed but invalid" (98); Meier sees them as "secondary (or dubious)" (178). They include:

1. *Traces of Aramaic*

This means judging a saying as authentic on the basis of traces of Aramaic vocabulary, syntax, grammar, or rhythm. While Joachim Jeremias popularized this approach, many scholars today question its validity. Sayings reflecting Aramaic vocabulary or usage could come from Aramaic-speaking Palestinian Christians rather than from Jesus. So-called "Semitisms" in Greek texts may reflect the language of the common people rather than an Aramaic original or the efforts of Greek-speaking Christian writers to imitate the biblical Greek of the Septuagint.

2. *Palestinian Environment*

Similarly, judging sayings of Jesus as authentic because they contain "local color," reflecting first-century Palestinian conditions, is dubious. Such sayings may come from early Christians living in Palestine. The criterion works better when applied negatively. A saying that reflects conditions, theological concerns, or customs that are found outside Palestine or only after the death of Jesus are probably post-Easter creations.

3. *Sayings with Formulas*

Sayings distinguished by formulas such as "truly, truly I say to you" or "but I say to you" are not necessarily authentic. Such formulae were frequently used in Hellenistic-Jewish apocalyptic writings.

4. *Abba Sayings*

Though "Abba" is an authentic Jesus word, not every saying containing the word "Abba" is necessarily authentic.

5. *Vividness of Narration*

The fact that a story is vividly told with concrete detail not directly relevant to the point of the story should not be taken automatically as a sign of authenticity. The vividness of the account may simply reflect the skill of the storyteller.

Conclusion

In a culture so influenced by modernity and postmodernism, Christology must be approached in a critical way. In an earlier, prescientific age, the

Bible supplied not just the narrative of faith; it also provided the view of the natural world that was considered normative. Some Christians still approach the biblical text from this supernaturalist perspective. But such a view is increasingly difficult to sustain.

The knowledge explosion brought on by the scientific revolution with its use of the empirical method as well as the triumph of historical consciousness over more classical ways of thinking has forced such Christians to take refuge in a theory of biblical inerrancy that holds that the Bible is absolutely without error. Scripture is inspired, literally "God-breathed" (2 Tim 3:16), and since God does not breathe falsehood, the text must be considered true in all it affirms, including the miracle accounts, the attributed authors, and the narratives traditionally considered as historical.[17] Such an approach saves the "truth" of Scripture at the cost of raising the Bible over and against modern ways of knowing, against scientific evidence. In the final analysis, it is based on a rather recent doctrine of inerrancy that is philosophical rather than biblical. A Christology done on this basis remains precritical.

Belief will not be intelligible in the modern world without reconciling the division between theology and science, faith and reason. While most Christians hold the Bible to be divinely inspired and witness to God's revelation in Christ, they also recognize the biblical books as historical documents. As such, they reflect the limitations of the times and cultures in which they were written.

Though initially suspicious, the Catholic Church ultimately came to embrace the historical-critical method and today encourages scholars to use it in their work.

In spite of occasional lapses, the Catholic tradition has always taught that faith and reason are complementary and must work in concert. This was reemphasized by Pope John Paul II in his 1998 encyclical *Fides et Ratio*.[18] Throughout the encyclical the Pope stresses the compatibility of faith and reason. The two stand in harmony, "without compromising their mutual autonomy" (no. 48).

The Pope also emphasizes that the magisterium of the Church has rejected "fideism" and "radical traditionalism" as well as "rationalism" and "ontologism" (no. 52). He cautions that "a resurgence of fideism . . . fails to recognize the importance of rational knowledge and philosophical discourse

---

[17] See Harold Lindsell, *The Battle for the Bible* (Grand Rapids, Mich.: Zondervan, 1976) esp. 30–32.

[18] John Paul II, *Fides et Ratio*, *Origins* 28 (1998) 317–47.

for the understanding of faith, indeed for the very possibility of belief in God." One "widespread" symptom of this fideistic tendency is a "biblicism" which appeals to the Bible as the sole criterion of truth, thus eliminating the need for the Church. Another is the neglect of speculative theology and classical philosophy (no. 55). For the Pope, philosophy has an indispensable role in the structure of theological studies and helps the Church enter into the dialogue with modern thought and culture (no. 62) which is so important for the Church's evangelical mission.

A contemporary Christology needs to be critical in approach. This means being able to show how the Christology which develops in the New Testament and post-New Testament periods finds its roots in the Jesus of history. In this study we will presume the criteria developed by critical scholarship for recovering the historical Jesus.

Chapter 3

The Jewish Background

Third Quest scholarship has expanded our ability to construct a picture of the historical Jesus considerably by focusing on the social context of his world—first-century Palestinian Judaism in general and the land of Galilee in particular. Galilean society at the time of Jesus was strongly patriarchal, religiously conservative, and increasingly divided economically.

Jesus clearly challenged the social and religious values of this world, as is evident from his parables. But it would be a mistake to assume that in doing so his critique was simply social rather than religious. First of all, such distinctions would not have occurred to someone in his time. Social issues can be separated out by modern commentators, but for those in Jesus' time, social issues were seen within a culture which was itself pervasively religious.

Second, Jesus cannot be understood apart from the religious tradition that formed his culture and shaped his own religious imagination. We can take it for granted that he was a profoundly religious person. As a Jew, he was a member of a people whose history was the story of their relationship with the God whose name out of reverence they declined even to pronounce. Jesus' education was primarily religious, learning the stories and traditions contained in the Jewish Scriptures, certainly in his home and from the elders in the synagogue school in Nazareth.[1] His own public life begins as a result of a profoundly religious experience, his baptism at the hands of John.

Finally, the religious climate of his time was one of anticipation. The sacred texts of Jesus' people rehearsed a tragic history of covenantal infidelity, social tensions, failed kings, lost sovereignty, religious persecution, exile, and martyrdom, as well as an effort to come to terms with the mystery of suffering, injustice, and death in theological terms. Through it all

[1] John P. Meier argues that "the hypothesis of some formal education in the local synagogue is well grounded"; *A Marginal Jew*, Vol. One (New York: Doubleday, 1991) 277.

remained the hope that the God who promised not to abandon his people would again be shown to be gracious to them. We need to review this history and its impact on the religious literature of the community, both canonical and noncanonical.

The traditions that had emerged through the suffering of the people were still influential in Jesus' time and were used by the early Christians to interpret the story of Jesus. Three of them stand out: the messianic tradition, the sapiential or Wisdom tradition, and the relatively late apocalyptic tradition. We will review these three traditions in this chapter and consider the emergence of a hope for life beyond the grave. Finally, we will consider first-century Palestinian Judaism, in all its diversity.

The Messianic Tradition

The messianic tradition has its roots in the Israelite monarchy, particularly in the person of David who remains the ideal Israelite king. The Israelite monarchy begins with Saul, a warrior from the small and centrally located tribe of Benjamin who became king about 1030 B.C.E. when he was anointed by the prophet Samuel (1 Sam 9:1 ff.).

For several hundred years Israel had been a loose association of tribes, united by their common faith in Yahweh and by a common shrine, probably at Shiloh, although there were other shrines as well. These fiercely independent tribes would come together in times of military threat under a charismatic leader or "judge," leaders accepted not on the basis of office or position, but by reason of their courage, cunning, or force of personality. This period is described in the book of Judges. However as Israel underwent a transition from its seminomadic existence to a more stable, agrarian way of life, the system of federated tribes was less and less able to adjudicate intertribal disputes or prevent the wars that frequently followed them. Under pressure from the growing power of the Philistines, the tribes were ultimately forced to accept a king, though this institution remained foreign to many. One tradition views the election of Saul as a usurpation of Yahweh's rightful role as the true king over Israel (1 Sam 8; 10:17-27).

The kingdom of Saul was a modest one that left the old tribal structures largely intact. It was Saul's successor David, from the southern tribe of Judah and the town of Bethlehem, who united the southern tribes with those of the north. Now ruler of a united kingdom, he drove the Philistines once and for all from the land and seized the Jebusite city of Jerusalem, making it his capital. The choice was a happy one. Located between the northern and southern tribal areas, Jerusalem became the political center for a united Israel. After David brought the ark of the covenant to Jerusalem, it became the religious capital as well.

The Oracle of Nathan

At the roots of the messianic tradition is a promise made to David by the prophet Nathan. According to the story in the book of Samuel (2 Sam 7:1-16), David conceived the idea of building a temple to the Lord in Jerusalem. Nathan at first welcomed the idea, but learned that night in a dream that the Lord did not want David to build this house. David, however, was to be rewarded for his piety. Yahweh promised to build a house for David, and to establish for him an everlasting dynasty through his son. Furthermore, God promised to be a father to this heir, and to treat him as a son:

> The LORD also reveals to you that he will establish a house for you. And when your time comes and you rest with your ancestors, I will raise up your heir after you, sprung from your loins, and I will make his kingdom firm. It is he who shall build a house for my name. And I will make his royal throne firm forever. I will be a father to him, and he shall be a son to me (2 Sam 7: 11-14).

In its historical context, this "Oracle of Nathan" referred to David's son Solomon who did build the Temple in Jerusalem that David had proposed. But it also introduced the idea into the tradition that God's covenant with Israel would now be fulfilled through the house and descendant of David, through some future "anointed" (*mashiah* in Hebrew, *christos* in Greek, messiah in English) king in the Davidic line. This became the official, court theology of the southern kingdom of Judah (cf. Psalms 2:7; 89:20-38; 132:11-12; 1 Chr 17:4-14), leading to a false confidence, a guarantee of divine favor linked to God's promise to David. It is evident in Jeremiah's warning, "Put not your trust in the deceitful words: This is the temple of the Lord! The temple of the Lord! The temple of the Lord" (Jer 7:4).

Under David's son, Solomon, the Davidic kingdom reached its zenith, but it was not able to survive his death in 922. The unity that David had nurtured collapsed as the traditional tribal divisions reasserted themselves. The result was two kingdoms, Israel in the north with the majority of the people, and the secessionist Judah in the south. The northern kingdom lasted about two hundred years before it fell in 721 to the Assyrians under Sargon. The surviving Israelite population suffered both deportation and intermarriage with the Assyrian invaders. Their descendants were known as the Samaritans.

Israel's traditions (the Elohist tradition), along with the name, passed to Judah in the south. In the next 150 years, in spite of various efforts at reform, the religious life of the kingdom went into a decline. Hezekiah

(715–687) sought to restore strict Yahwism, but the political alliances he made to support his rebellion against Sennacherib earned him Isaiah's disapproval. His son Manasseh was unable to resist the Assyrians and became their vassal, raising altars to their gods in the Temple. Once again idolatry, magic, and other pagan practices were tolerated in Israel, including the ritual prostitution associated with the fertility cult. Another even more extensive reform was attempted under Josiah (640–609), who closed the outlying shrines, centralizing the worship of Yahweh in the Temple of Jerusalem. His successors sought to stabilize the kingdom with various foreign alliances, but Jehoiakim's revolt against Nebuchadnezzar led to a Babylonian siege of Jerusalem. The result was the destruction of the city and Temple in 588. The Babylonians led many of the leading citizens of Judah into exile in Babylon.

Thus the Davidic kingdom came to an end. A long succession of prophets had warned of God's coming judgment on nation and people. For them, it was a matter of life or death. They attributed the nation's fate to the sinfulness of the people, their infidelity to the covenant, forsaking the religion of Yahweh for the gods of their neighbors. Amos, Isaiah, Micah, Jeremiah, Habakkuk, Ezekiel, and Malachi had rebuked the upper classes for their dishonesty, lack of compassion, and mindless pursuit of wealth which trampled on the rights of the poor.

But at the same time, in most of the prophets, from Hosea, First Isaiah, and Micah in the eighth century down to Third Isaiah writing after the Exile in the sixth, there is the promise, variously expressed, that God would remember what Isaiah calls "the remnant of Israel" (Isa 10:20-22), that God's salvation would again be manifested to the people in the future. Perhaps what was most important about the prophets was that they effected a shift in the religious imagination of the people, away from what God had done for them in the past, to the expectation of a new manifestation of the divine saving power in the future. What emerges is a growing expectation of a new and definitive act of God in a future messianic age. In Second Isaiah this shift becomes explicit, even to the extent of forgetting the great event of the Exodus: "Remember not the things of the past, the things of long ago consider not; See, I am doing something new" (Isa 43:18-19a). Since the images that emerge in the prophetic preaching so shaped the Jewish tradition which Jesus inherited, we must consider them here.

The Davidic Messiah

The image of the Davidic messiah is rooted in the Oracle of Nathan (2 Sam 7:14; Ps 89:20-38; 1 Chr 17:4-14).[2] Some of the "royal psalms" dating from before the eighth century, most probably used in the crowning of the king, repeat the idea that the king is begotten by God (Ps 110:3; cf. 89:27) and can be called God's son (Ps 2:7). Thus the title "son of God" can mean "son of David."

From the eighth century on, the image of the "anointed" offspring of David appears frequently in the Prophets. Often the anointed is one who would govern Israel righteously and deliver the nation from its enemies, thus a historical figure in the life of the nation. Micah describes an ideal ruler who will come from Bethlehem (Mic 5:1-5). Jeremiah proclaims the coming of "a righteous shoot to David" who "shall reign and govern wisely" (Jer 23:5).

During and after the Exile, with the loss of the kingship, the anointed or messiah becomes increasingly a figure in the indefinite future through whom God himself would reestablish the Davidic dynasty and bring about a new order of justice, peace, and righteousness. Ezekiel speaks of "my servant David" who will unite the people and bring about a restoration of righteous living (Ezek 37:24). Similar passages such as Amos 9:11 ff., Isaiah 11:1-9, and Jeremiah 30:9, considered by most scholars to have been added during the Exile, represent a messianism which is more eschatological than historical in the sense that they look forward to a decisive intervention of Yahweh in history, manifesting his salvation. Isaiah 11:1-9 is a marvelous illustration of these themes.

> But a shoot shall sprout from the stump of Jesse
>> and from his roots a bud shall blossom.
> The spirit of the LORD shall rest upon him:
>> a spirit of wisdom and of understanding,
> A spirit of counsel and of strength,
>> a spirit of knowledge and of fear of the LORD,
>> and his delight shall be the fear of the LORD.
> Not by appearance shall he judge,
>> nor by hearsay shall he decide,
> But he shall judge the poor with justice,
>> and decide aright for the land's afflicted.
> He shall strike the ruthless with the rod of his mouth,
>> and with the breath of his lips he shall slay the wicked.

[2] For the development of messianic hope, see Raymond E. Brown, *An Introduction to New Testament Christology* (New York: Paulist, 1994), "Appendix I," 155–61.

Justice shall be the band around his waist,
    and faithfulness a belt upon his hips.
Then the wolf shall be a guest of the lamb,
    and the leopard shall lie down with the kid;
The calf and the young lion shall browse together,
    with a little child to guide them.
The cow and the bear shall be neighbors,
    together their young shall rest;
    the lion shall eat hay like the ox.
The baby shall play by the cobra's den,
    and the child lay his hand on the adder's lair.
There shall be no harm or ruin on all my holy mountain;
    for the earth shall be filled with knowledge of the LORD,
    as water covers the sea.

                                        Isaiah 11:1-9

This passage moves from a vision of the future king in David's line governing wisely and bringing justice to the poor to a more distant vision of an ideal future in which the predatory violence of the natural world is replaced by a new harmony among all creatures. Religious artists have often represented this vision as the "Peaceable Kingdom." Finally, it looks forward to a day when all the nations will know the Lord, through the mediation of Israel. Thus, Isaiah 11:1-9 represents the messianic age as a restoration of paradise, a time in which the threefold alienation of humankind from God, nature, and each other which Genesis 3 attributes to the Fall is overcome.

Another passage in Zechariah 9:9 looks to a future king who will bring peace, though here the king is portrayed as meek and humble, like the poor who made up so great a part of postexilic Judaism. In passages like these, a contrast emerges between the righteousness of the future king and the injustice and oppression of the poor practiced by their predecessors, so often condemned in the prophetic preaching. Thus the messianic age will mean justice for the poor and afflicted of the land, a theme echoed in the later books of the Old Testament, particularly in the psalms (Pss 12:6; 18:28; 22:27; 76:10).

In the apocryphal books of late Judaism, the messianic theme has frequently been politicized into an earthly kingdom established by Yahweh, sometimes seen as immediately preceding the consummation of the world. The apocryphal *Psalms of Solomon* (first century B.C.E.) presents a messiah endowed with both political and spiritual power who will bring the Gentiles under his rule. Even if not used by all, the image of the messiah would have been familiar to most Jews in the time of Jesus. His reluctance to accept the title in Mark 8:30 may reflect the fact that in the Palestine of his time the title was often interpreted politically.

A number of other images associated with the messianic future became interwoven with the Jewish tradition through the prophetic preaching.

Day of Yahweh

Appearing for the first time in Amos 5:18-20, the Day of Yahweh is associated with the fall of Israel, thus, with Israel's coming judgment. Isaiah broadens the concept to include others in this coming day of judgment, without excluding Israel (Isa 2:11). The Day of Yahweh will mean judgment for the wicked, but vindication for the just and the poor (Isa 3:10 ff.). In Ezekiel and Zephaniah the image takes on a cosmic dimension; all the earth will be subjected to God's judgment. In some of the postexilic prophets, the Day of Yahweh takes on more strictly eschatological connotations. In Joel 4:14 and Deutero-Zechariah 14:1 ff., the Day of Yahweh is seen as a day of judgment and defeat for the nations and of vindication for a purified Israel.

New Covenant

The word "covenant" does not appear frequently in the classical prophets of the eighth century—perhaps because covenant theology had been transformed into a false guarantee of God's election and favor, the official theology of the Davidic kingdom. But in Jeremiah it appears as a "new" covenant that God would establish with his people. In his view, the former covenant no longer exists; the people had abrogated it by their conduct. He sees God establishing a new covenant in the future, not a covenant of law but one which would work a change in the heart of each individual (Jer 31:31-34).

In a similar way, Ezekiel speaks of Yahweh establishing a covenant of peace (Ezek 27:26; 34:27). He speaks of Yahweh cleansing his people from their sins and placing a new spirit within them, giving them natural hearts in place of their hearts of stone (Ezek 36:24-28). He envisions God's future as an interior purification and regeneration which touches the individual in a way that goes beyond the old covenantal relationship.

Servant of Yahweh

Finally there is the enigmatic figure of the Servant of Yahweh appearing in Second Isaiah (Isa 40–55) in the so-called Servant Songs (Isa 42:1-4; 49:1-6; 50:4-9; 52:13–53:12). In some of these passages, the Servant is clearly a collective figure for the divided people, Jacob and Israel (41:8 ff.; 44:1 ff.; 44:21; 48:20). But in other passages the Servant appears to be a single figure who will gather the people to the Lord (Isa 49:5), and bring his salvation to the ends of the earth (Isa 49:6). Particularly in Isaiah 53:4-5, 12, the Servant is portrayed as taking upon himself the sins of the people, giving his life as an innocent victim. In this final song, the Servant stands apart from the people in his innocence. The picture is of a future in which salvation comes through the suffering of one who offers himself as a victim for sin (Isa 53:10-12).

The Wisdom Tradition

In the postexilic period another tradition takes shape in Israel, a tradition focused on the "good" life, a life that from the Jewish perspective necessarily involves one's relationship to God. Dealing with divine wisdom, the mystery of suffering and death, the plight of the just man (or woman), this sapiential or Wisdom tradition is both existential and speculative. It is very much concerned with the everyday life of the individual, but it also represents a reflection on God's wisdom. Wisdom is both a virtue, something to be sought (Prov 2:4), and a personification of the wisdom of God. The tradition seems to have developed from two sources, one domestic, from the lessons about life handed on in the various families or tribes, the other royal, from the Jerusalem court where young men of noble families were schooled in wisdom. Some of the material in Proverbs may date back to the period of the monarchy. In the postexilic period, this tradition took on literary expression in five books, Proverbs, Job, Ecclesiastes, Sirach, and Wisdom. A number of wisdom themes have a particular importance for Christology.

Wisdom Personified

As a personification of the divine wisdom or an attribute of God, Wisdom (*sophia* in Greek) appears as a feminine figure (Prov 1, 8, 9; Sirach 24; Wis 7–9; Baruch 3:9–4:4). Particularly in Proverbs, Wisdom is portrayed as "Lady Wisdom." Wisdom calls aloud in the streets (Prov 1:20; 8). She is the gracious hostess whose meal of food and wine offered to the simple is contrasted with the meal of bread and stolen water offered by the fickle woman, Folly (Prov 9:1-15).

Comes Forth from God

Wisdom comes forth from the mouth of God (Sirach 24:3); she is begotten before the world was created (Prov 8:22-23), reflects the glory of God, and is an image of God's goodness (Wis 7:25-26).

Present at Creation

Wisdom is portrayed as having a role in creation. She is created before all things (Sirach 1:4; Prov 8:22-24), present at creation (Wis 7:22; 9:9), playing in God's presence:

> Before the mountains were settled into place,
>   before the hills, I was brought forth;
> While as yet the earth and the fields were not made,
>   nor the first clods of the world.
>
> When he established the heavens I was there,
>   when he marked out the vault over the face of the deep;
> When he made firm the skies above,
>   when he fixed fast the foundations of the earth;
> When he set for the sea its limit,
>   so that the waters should not transgress his command;
> Then was I beside him as his craftsman,
>   and I was his delight day by day,
> Playing before him all the while,
>   playing on the surface of the earth;
>   and I found delight in the sons of men.
>
> Proverbs 8:25-31

Has a Mission for God's People

Wisdom also has a mission in the world (Wis 6:12-16; 9:10-18) and particularly toward Israel. In the book of Sirach, Wisdom is sent down from heaven by God to make her dwelling in Israel; it is God who determines the place for her tent (Sir 24:8). There are obvious parallels here with the Prologue of John's Gospel. Wisdom is identified with the Torah (Sir 6:37; 24:22) and active in Israel's history (Wis 10–12). As Ben Witherington says, the personification of Wisdom, "once introduced into the biblical Wisdom tradition, took on a life of its own and grew in importance, in complexity, and in depth as time went on." As Torah, it became the central focus of Israelite faith, and it was to play an even more striking role in the early Christians' language about Jesus.[3]

Sustains the Righteous Sufferer

The mystery of the suffering of the righteous person is another strong theme in the Wisdom literature. The archetypal figure is Job, the just man whose faith is tried by the loss of his family, possessions, and health. Job's fidelity and humble acceptance of his fate is exemplary: "The LORD gave and the LORD has taken away: / blessed be the name of the LORD" (Job 1:21). But when Job finally demands an explanation of God, the only answer the tradition can make is a wonderful, deeply moving affirmation of the mystery or unknowability of the creator (Job 38–41).

But the wisdom tradition continued to wrestle with the question. The outlook in the book of Ecclesiastes is bleak. Despite his desire for wisdom, the wise man and the fool will both perish. In the words of Qoheleth, "all is vanity and a chase after wind" (Eccl 2:17). Sirach presumes the traditional view that God punishes the wicked and rewards the just in this life, though the author is aware that the righteous will suffer (Sir 2:1-6). The book of Wisdom meditates on the plight of the righteous one, plotted against by the wicked (Wis 2:12-24). The just one is obnoxious to the wicked, for he sets himself against their doings and reproaches them for their violations of the Law (2:12). He "styles himself a child of the LORD" (2:13) and "boasts that God is his Father" (2:16). Implicit here is the idea that God will not abandon the righteous one who is called the "son of God":

> Let us see whether his words be true;
>   let us find out what will happen to him.
> For if the just one be the son of God, he will defend him
>   and deliver him from the hand of his foes.
> With revilement and torture let us put him to the test
>   that we may have proof of his gentleness
>   and try his patience.
> Let us condemn him to a shameful death;
>   for according to his own words, God will take care of him.
>
>   Wisdom 2:17-20

---

[3] Ben Witherington III, *Jesus the Sage: The Pilgrimage of Wisdom* (Minneapolis: Fortress, 1994) 50.

What emerges is the view that the relationship of the righteous to the Lord leads to life beyond death, for "God formed man to be imperishable, / the image of his own nature he made him. / But by the envy of the devil, death entered the world" (Wis 2:23-24). Note how close to Paul the language is here.

The Apocalyptic Tradition

Postexilic Judaism also saw the rise of apocalypticism, a particular species of eschatological thinking. The Greek word "*apocalypsis*" means "uncovering," or "revelation." One characteristic of apocalyptic literature is its reliance on highly symbolic or allegorical language such as one finds in the New Testament book of the Apocalypse or Revelation.

As a literary form, an apocalyptic work is represented as a revelation granted to a seer or visionary about what is soon to take place through a catastrophic cataclysm with cosmic dimensions. It looks to a new order, a clean and definitive break with the old. Many have interpreted this as meaning the end of the present world, as indeed the accompanying imagery suggests. Such an outlook frequently results when a society, because of catastrophe or crisis, loses confidence in its own future. N. T. Wright, following George B. Caird, rejects the idea that apocalyptic thinking necessarily involved an expectation of the "end of the world" in a cosmic sense; it meant the end of the present world order.[4] Jewish apocalyptic literature extends from 200 B.C.E. to 100 C.E., thus bracketing the life of Jesus. The first major apocalyptic work was the book of Daniel (168–164 B.C.E.); other examples include noncanonical works such as 1 and 2 Enoch, 4 Ezra, and 2 Baruch.

The catastrophe that found expression in Daniel was the persecution of the Jews that broke out under Antiochus IV Epiphanes. A Seleucid ruler (175–164), Antiochus sought to unify his kingdom by fostering its Hellenization. After a period of worsening relations, he forbade Temple sacrifices, traditional festivals, Sabbath worship, and circumcision (the sign of the covenant). He ordered the destruction of the Torah scrolls and introduced the cult of Zeus in the Temple. While some Jews went along with Antiochus' decrees, others resisted, and were subjected to torture and death (1 Macc 1–2; 2 Macc 6–7).

One expression of Jewish resistance to this persecution was the revolt, ultimately successful, led by Judas Maccabeus and his brothers. Another

[4] N. T. Wright, *The New Testament and the People of God* (Philadelphia: Fortress, 1992) 298–99; see also George B. Caird, *Language and Imagery of the Bible* (Philadelphia: Westminster, 1980).

expression, less violent, was the book of Daniel. The author counseled fidelity to the Law and assured the people that God's intervention was at hand. The second half of Daniel consists of a number of apocalyptic visions in which various beasts, horrifying to behold, make their appearance (Dan 7–12). In the midst of them, one figure appears in human form, the "son of man."

> As the visions during the night continued, I saw
>   One like a son of man coming
>   on the clouds of heaven;
>   When he reached the Ancient One
>   and was presented before him,
>   He received dominion, glory, and kingship;
>   nations and peoples of every language serve him.
>   His dominion is an everlasting dominion
>   that shall not be taken away,
>   his kingship shall not be destroyed.
>
> Daniel 7:13-14

While the beasts come from below, from the great sea which in the ancient creation myth symbolized chaos and evil, the son of man comes from above, from the realm of God. In the context of the vision, the son of man, like the beasts, is a symbol for a kingdom, here, the kingdom of "the holy ones of the Most High" (Dan 7:18). But the image frequently shifts from kingdom to king, to an agent of God's judgment and justice, particularly in the later noncanonical Jewish writings (1 Enoch; 4 Ezra) that are roughly contemporary with the New Testament.

A work called the Similitudes of Enoch (1 Enoch 37–70) presents a figure who combines the attributes of the son of man in Daniel 7:13, the Davidic messiah of Isaiah 11 and Psalm 2, and the servant of the Lord in Second Isaiah. Chosen by God and hidden in heaven before creation (1 Enoch 48:3, 6; 62:7), he sees the place where the dead are kept until judgment (1 Enoch 22). This is probably the first witness to belief in the judgment of individuals after death in the Jewish tradition. We will consider the question of life after death below. A final chapter that may have a different origin describes the son of man as ascending *to* heaven, rather than descending *from* heaven.[5] The work is difficult to date. The majority of scholars favor a date after the beginning of the Christian era. James

---

[5] Delbert Burkett, *The Son of Man Debate: A History and Evaluation* (Cambridge: University Press, 1999) 98–101.

Dunn places it post-70 C.E. at the earliest.[6] From 4 Ezra (also called 2 Ezra) comes a vision of "something like the figure of a man" (13:3) who emerges from the sea, seems to be endowed with divine powers, and will deliver God's creation (13:26). God calls him "my son" (13:32). This work probably dates from the period 90–120 C.E. The late dates for these Jewish non-canonical writings raises the possibility that the identification of the son of man as a particular individual and that individual with Jesus comes from the Christian community or even from Jesus himself.[7]

Life after Death

The idea of life beyond the grave entered very late into the Jewish tradition. For most of the period reflected in the Old Testament, death meant simply the end of life. The spirit (*ruah*) or principle of life and activity departed and the self (*nepes*) went down to Sheol, the underworld or abode of the dead. In the ancient Near East, Sheol is a place of darkness and dust, the final destination of the human person from which there is no release (cf. Job 17:13-16). But in Jewish thought Sheol was not a place of another kind of life but rather a negation of everything that life represents. For those in Sheol, there was no work, no reason, no knowledge, no wisdom (Eccl 9:10), thus no life. Worst of all, those in Sheol could take no part in divine worship (Ps 6:6; 30:10) and no longer have a relationship with Yahweh (Ps 88:6). Like the "pit" (Ezek 32:17-32), Sheol is often used simply as a synonym for death or the grave.

It was only much later, in the Judaism reflected in the intertestamental literature, that Sheol becomes at least in some sources a place reserved for the wicked, though more often Gehenna was seen as the place of torment and punishment. In the New Testament Sheol appears as the Greek "Hades," though the word is not common.

The psalms are a wonderful reflection of the Jewish experience of God; they sing of the joy of living in covenant relationship with Yahweh, of recognizing God's power in the wonders of creation, of praising God's name in the assembly of the people, and all this without any idea of life after death. But from the time of the sixth-century Exile in Babylon, Judaism began increasingly to wrestle with the question of Yahweh's faithfulness in the context of tragedy, evil, and death. The Wisdom tradition wrestles with the question of the suffering of the just, as we have seen. Ezekiel's vision of

---

[6] James D. G. Dunn, *Christology in the Making: A New Testament Inquiry into the Origins of the Doctrine of the Incarnation* (Philadelphia: Westminster, 1980) 78.

[7] Ibid., 95–96.

the dry bones (37:1-14) uses the image of the resurrection of the dead to describe Yahweh's reanimation of Israel itself; it was not referring to the resurrection of individuals.

The so-called "Apocalypse of Isaiah" (Isa 24–27), dated anywhere from the sixth century to the second, is a later addition to Isaiah which speaks of the final days of the earth and the end of death itself. It has some similarities to the apocalyptic writings. One passage speaks of the resurrection of dead: "But your dead shall live, their corpses shall rise; / awake and sing, you who lie in the dust. / For your dew is a dew of light, / and the land of shades [Sheol] gives birth" (Isa 26:19). Does this resurrection imagery refer to the nation or to individuals? Many scholars see the passage as early evidence for an emerging belief in the resurrection of the dead. At the very least it might suggest that some were beginning to ask, could the God of the living, the God who created the heavens and the earth, also bring life to the dead?

It is only in the second century that the first clear evidence of Jewish hope in life beyond the grave appears. We saw above that the first evidence for a belief in a judgment after death appears in 1 Enoch (1 Enoch 22). The idea of a resurrection of the dead (with at least an implied judgment) appears first in the book of Daniel. A little more than 150 years before the time of Jesus, a fierce persecution broke out under Antiochus IV (167–164). Seeking a uniform Hellenistic culture in his Seleucid kingdom (which included Palestine), Antiochus had forbidden the Jews the practice of their religion, as we saw above. Those who defied his orders were put to death (1 Macc 1). This new phenomenon of martyrdom or death for the faith raised a new question for the Jewish community; if faithfulness to Yahweh and to the Law does not save one from torture and death (cf. 2 Macc 6–7), how is God's own righteousness to the faithful of Israel to be manifested? The author of Daniel assured the people that God had not forgotten them; the divine intervention was at hand. In Daniel's vision, the coming apocalyptic judgment would see the faithful dead raised to everlasting life (Dan 12:1-3).

This same hope for a resurrection of the dead appears in other late works. It is clearly present in 2 Maccabees (2:7; 14:46), another book from the same period as Daniel. And it is present in some of the noncanonical apocalyptic books (2 Baruch 49–51; IV Ezra 7:29-37). Finally, the book of Wisdom, written in the last half of the first century, expresses the hope that God will give the just immortality: "The souls of the just are in the hand of God, / and no torment shall touch them" (Wis 3:1). The dualism of soul and body in this Wisdom tradition reflects the influence of Greek culture; but the underlying thought is Jewish; it is God who will vindicate the just (Wis 2:12-20; 5:1-7).

Thus the idea of life after death was a late development in the Jewish tradition, related to the basic idea of God as the Lord of life. The resurrection of the dead was a strong image expressing this belief, but not the only one. Greek-speaking Jews, influenced by Hellenistic culture, thought simply of God's power to deliver souls from the realm of the dead ("Hades"); they would feel "less tied" to the concept of resurrection.[8]

By the time of Jesus, there were varying views on the subject. Some groups like the Pharisees believed in the resurrection of the dead while others like the Sadducees did not (cf. Luke 20:27-38). But both the concept of a new life beyond the grave and a particular image to express it had become part of the Jewish religious imagination. It is important, however, to note that the concept of the resurrection was both a collective and an eschatological notion; it involved the resurrection of *all* the dead that was to take place when the age of salvation dawned. Given this eschatological context, it is easier to understand why many of the early Christians saw in the resurrection of Jesus a sign that the final days were at hand (cf. 1 Cor 7:29).

First-Century Palestinian Judaism

First-century Palestinian Judaism was far more diverse than is generally recognized. Jerusalem, the religious center, was garrisoned by the occupying Roman military power. It was host to a number of groups and parties that differed from each other in theology, religious observance, and political allegiance. Galilee in the north was an agrarian society of some two hundred villages. Referred to as "the district of the Gentiles" as early as Isaiah (8:23), it was a mixed region of Jewish villages and Hellenized peoples centered in the towns of Sepphoris and Tiberias. With the death of Herod the Great, Galilee came under the rule of the Tetrarch Herod Antipas (4 B.C.E.–39 C.E.), which meant practically that it was no longer responsible to the Jerusalem Temple or priesthood. Under Antipas, Galilee enjoyed a period of relative stability. Yet many of the Jews living there were quite nationalistic, and there were various outbreaks of violence, usually in response to what were perceived as provocations. N. T. Wright lists seven of them which occurred under Pontius Pilate's procuratorship (26–36 C.E.).[9]

---

[8] Edward Schillebeeckx, *Jesus: An Experiment in Christology* (New York: Seabury, 1979) 395.
[9] Wright, *The New Testament and the People of God*, 174.

Religious Life

After three hundred years of Hellenistic rule, Jewish religious identity was under threat. This social situation made the Holiness Code in Leviticus, itself a product of the Exile, even more important. Its rituals of purity and exclusion provided a way of maintaining a clear sense of religious and cultural identity. The Pharisee movement also contributed to this religious culture. With their emphasis on domestic rituals, washings, unique dress, and the observance of sacred time, the Pharisees had in a sense expanded the range of the religious realm, of Jewish spirituality, from the Temple to the home.

Scholars are divided on the question of the presence of Pharisees in Galilee during Jesus' public ministry.[10] But the complicated rules of purity and exclusion in his time are evident from even a casual reading of the Gospels. A person could become impure or unclean by birth or behavior, by eating the wrong kinds of food, through sickness or skin disease (usually identified as "leprosy" in the Gospels), or by failing to observe the moral requirements of the Law. If a Jewish male became ritually impure, he was restricted to the court of the women in the Temple compound. Gentiles were considered impure because they did not observe the Law. Those with "leprosy" had to warn others of their approach with a bell; they became outcasts, forbidden to enter Jerusalem and thus excluded from the community. A woman during her period was considered unclean. "Tax collectors and sinners" were considered impure and were to be shunned. Purity was associated with wholeness, while disabilities such as blindness were associated with sin (cf. John 9:2). Those born out of wedlock or with damaged testicles were also considered impure. The result of these rules of purity was the marginalization of whole classes of people.

Social/Economic Life

Socially, male dominance was taken for granted. The laws and customs that surrounded marriage, divorce, property rights, and inheritances all favored men over women. Marriages were generally arranged, though a man could obtain a wife through intercourse or by paying a price to her father. A man could divorce his wife, but a woman could not generally divorce her husband. Men took an active role in the civic life of the community; women's proper role was in the home, but often included helping with the crops.

---

[10] Cf. John P. Meier, *A Marginal Jew*, Vol. III (New York: Doubleday, 2001) 295–96.

In Jesus' time, the plight of the poor was worsening. Economic changes were exacerbating the differences between the poor and the prosperous. During the long reign of Herod the Great (37–4 B.C.E.), many of the small landowners lost their holdings, either to confiscation or forfeiture because of a triple tax structure: a tribute to Rome, a tax to support the king, and a tithing paid to the Temple, though after Herod's death this third tax seems to have disappeared. The practice of tax farming, selling the right to collect taxes, was widespread. At the same time, a self-sufficient agricultural system was shifting to an economy based on foreign trade. As a result of these economic changes, many of the Galilean peasants were reduced to subsistence farming on inadequate land. An increasing population, military campaigns which made exorbitant demands on the peasants, forcing many into slavery, the need to pay tolls when transporting goods (cf. Matt 9:9)—all these factors contributed to increasing social division.[11] As Ben Witherington says, "In such a situation parables about unlucky tenant farmers, day laborers in vineyards, absentee landlords, unscrupulous middlemen and the like would hardly have sounded like pious platitudes. They would have rung true to the realities of life, a social commentary on how the coming Dominion of God would ultimately change the situation."[12]

Parties and Groups

Palestinian Judaism was made up of a number of different groups and parties. Many of them shared an expectation, differently interpreted, that God was about to act salvifically in the life of the community in a new way, though as Wright notes, "there was no single monolithic and uniform 'messianic expectation' among first-century Jews."[13] We need to consider these different groups briefly.[14]

The Sanhedrin or Council was the supreme religious authority in Jerusalem. Consisting of seventy-one members, it was made up of three different classes: the elders, members of the chief families and clans; the high priests, former high priests and representatives of the four priestly families;

---

[11] Seán Freyne, *Galilee From Alexander the Great to Hadrian: 323 B.C.E. to 135 C.E.* (Wilmington, Del./South Bend, Ind.: Michael Glazier, University of Notre Dame Press, 1980) 155–207.

[12] Ben Witherington III, *The Jesus Quest: The Third Search for the Jew of Nazareth* (Downers Grove, Ill.: InterVarsity, 1995) 27.

[13] Wright, *The New Testament and the People of God*, 307; he interprets the fundamental first century Jewish hope as liberation from oppression, restoration of the Land, and a proper rebuilding of the Temple, 299.

[14] For an in-depth treatment, see Meier, *A Marginal Jew*, III, Part II.

and the scribes, most of whom were Pharisees. The ruling high priest whose appointment was political presided over the Sanhedrin. While its jurisdiction in both religious and secular matters was limited to Jerusalem, it was still quite influential. Jewish communities in the Diaspora looked to it for guidance.

The Sadducees whose origins probably trace to Maccabean times, represented the priestly aristocracy of Jerusalem. As a party they had considerable political power, exercised through the Sanhedrin. Along with their patrons among the wealthy families, they supported the Roman authorities on whom they were dependent for their power. Their economic interests led them to favor political stability. Theologically, they were conservative; they accepted only the Pentateuch as authoritative, and rejected later ideas such as angels, demons, and the resurrection of the dead, all of which developed in the postexilic period.

The Pharisees were descendents of the Hasidim or "pious ones." A deeply religious group comprised of both priests and lay people, they sought to extend the holiness of the Temple into everyday Jewish life, as we have seen. Studying the oral traditions of the elders, they sought a theocratic kingdom governed by the precepts of the Mosaic Law, strictly interpreted. Thus they opposed the Hasmonean rulers as well as Herod, though they tolerated the Romans who allowed the Jews considerable freedom to regulate their life in accordance to the Law. More liberal than the Sadducees, they believed in angels and demons, free will, judgment after death, and the resurrection of the dead.

It is highly probable that Jesus engaged in debates with the Pharisees during his public ministry, though they did not seem to have been involved in his arrest or execution.[15] They played a major role in the reconstruction of Judaism after the destruction of the Temple in 70 C.E. and thus in the formation of modern Judaism; their negative portrait in the Gospels is due to the conflict between the Jewish and Christian communities around the year 80 when the synagogues began excommunicating the Jewish Christians.

While there were scribes in Jesus' time, as there were trained writers throughout the Mediterranean world, it would be a mistake to see them as an organized party so early. The portrait of the scribes in the Gospels usually reflects later polemic.[16]

The Zealots, called "*sicarii*" (stabbers) by the Romans, were fanatic Jewish nationalists who used the tactics of terror and assassination against

---

[15] Meier, *A Marginal Jew*, III:639.
[16] Ibid., 558.

those who stood in their way of an independent Jewish state. They interpreted Jewish messianic hope politically. But Meier argues that this radical group did not emerge as a distinct party until the First Jewish Revolt (66–70). In Jesus' time, the term seems to have been used in a broader sense of someone zealous for the strict observance of the Law; some, though not all, may have been willing to use violence to compel their fellow Jews to practice a strict separation from Gentiles.[17] Simon the Zealot (Luke 6:15) seems to have been a member of this group.

The Essenes, like the Pharisees, were descendents of the Hasidim. Their leader seems to have been a priest known as the "Teacher of Righteousness." Unable to accept the Hasmonean usurpation of the office of high priest, they had withdrawn from the mainstream Jewish community and Temple to the desert along the western shore of the Dead Sea at the Wadi Qumran, about an hour by car from Jerusalem. Thus they had become a sect. They lived a quasi-monastic life under a strict rule, described in the *Manual of Discipline,* found with the other "Dead Sea Scrolls" in 1947 in a cave at Qumran.

The theological vision of the Essenes was highly eschatological, if not apocalyptic. They emphasized the strict observance of the Law, ritual purity, and the study of the Scriptures. Joining the sect meant entering into a new covenant relationship with God. Some of them practiced celibacy. As they prepared for what they thought would be the final eschatological war, they awaited two messianic figures, a Davidic messiah and another, priestly figure, the Messiah of Aaron. The later was considered more important, reflecting the importance of the priestly order at Qumran.

The Samaritans lived in the high country between Judea and Galilee, not far from the modern Nablus. They were a mixed people, descendents of survivors of the northern kingdom of Israel and of those people brought in by the Assyrians to resettle the land after 721. Considered heretics and schismatics by other Jews, the roots of the schism may lie deeper in the old tensions between the tribes of the north and the south. Having built their own Temple on Mount Garizim (cf. John 4:20), the Samaritans did not worship in Jerusalem. They accepted only the Pentateuch and looked for a messianic figure they called "the Restorer."

---

[17] Ibid., 565–66.

Conclusion

Jesus can only be understood in light of the religious tradition of which he was a part. While the Judaism of his day was quite diverse, three traditions had been extremely influential in contributing to the ways in which it was experienced and understood. The messianic tradition looked to the coming of a future Davidic king who would restore the religious and national life of the people. Some of the psalms, echoing the oracle of Nathan, speak of the anointed as God's son (Ps 2:7; cf. 110:3; 89:27). After the Exile, the messianic future was often but not exclusively described in eschatological terms.

The Wisdom tradition had long wrestled with the dilemma of the just man whose sufferings seem to belie the existence of a just and compassionate God. According to the book of Wisdom, he will style himself a "son of God" and trust in the one he calls father even unto death (Wis 2:16-20). Wisdom is also personified as an attribute of God, coming forth from God, present at creation, and sent into the world with a mission for God's people.

The apocalyptic tradition despaired of salvation in the present historical order and anticipated a violent break between the old order and the new as the only way that God's salvation could be realized. From Daniel the image of "one like a son of man" (Dan 7:13) enters the tradition, though it was understood collectively until New Testament times, as well as the idea of a general resurrection of the dead (Dan 12:1-3). And there is other evidence to the gradual development of the hope, if not a belief, for a life beyond the grave.

In the Judaism of Jesus' day, some groups like the Essenes were apocalyptic in their eschatology; others were looking forward to a religious renewal under a messianic leader or king, or believed in the resurrection of the dead, like the Pharisees. Still others looked forward to a political liberation. While their theologies differed and often conflicted, eschatological thinking was by no means foreign to them. Many were looking forward to a new divine intervention in the life of the people.

Chapter 4

Jesus and His Movement

What do we know for sure about the historical Jesus? He appears in conjunction with John the Baptist. He gathered disciples around himself and from them chose a symbolic group, "the Twelve." His brief preaching ministry centered on the proclamation of the coming of the kingdom or reign of God. He was executed at Jerusalem.

What was his ministry? Protestants all too often reduce his message to an individualistic doctrine of salvation. Catholics move too quickly from Jesus to the Church. Biblical scholars and theologians tend to focus on the more radical aspects of his movement or on his preaching of the kingdom of God, though too often in either case without sufficient attention to the Jewish background from which Jesus came. Walter Kasper says that Jesus has no program: "There is nothing planned or organized about his career. He does the will of God as he recognizes it here and now. Everything else he leaves with childlike trust to God, his father."[1] But all of this is too simple. Jesus was a real human being, rooted in the religious tradition of his people, as capable as any of those who followed him of finding his own place in that tradition.

Recently some Third Quest scholars have argued that Jesus' intention was to gather and recreate Israel as God's people.[2] In this chapter we will explore this theme. We will consider, first, the relationship between Jesus and John the Baptist. Then we will look at what is often called the "Jesus' movement" as a religious movement within Palestinian Judaism. In the next chapter we will look more specifically at his preaching and ministry.

[1] Walter Kasper, *Jesus the Christ* (New York: Paulist Press, 1976) 69.
[2] For example, N. T. Wright, *Jesus and the Victory of God* (Minneapolis: Fortress, 1996); Gerhard Lohfink, *Does God Need the Church: Toward a Theology of the People of God* (Collegeville: The Liturgical Press, 1999).

Jesus and John the Baptist

John the Baptist

Jesus emerges into history in connection with the man known as "John the Baptist." John was clearly a historical figure. In addition to the important role he plays in the four Gospels, the Jewish historian Josephus mentions him in his *Jewish Antiquities* (ca. 93–94 C.E.). John first appears in the Judean desert in the region of the Jordan River, proclaiming a message of repentance (Mark 1:4). While the Lukan tradition that he was related to Jesus is doubtful, John P. Meier finds plausible both the idea that he was the only son of a Jerusalem priest and that he might have spent time among the Essenes at Qumran or some other Essene community.[3] Qumran was only a short distance away from the Jordan region around Jericho where John carried out his ministry.

The Baptist (the author of the Fourth Gospel refers to him simply as "John") is very much in the tradition of the Old Testament prophets. His message could scarcely be characterized as "good news," for at its heart was a warning about God's coming judgment. But even though the Jewish community in John's time was strongly influenced by apocalyptic thinking, his imagery is much more prophetic than apocalyptic; Meier describes him as "an eschatological prophet tinged with some apocalyptic motifs."[4] Schillebeeckx sees him as standing outside of Zealotism, messianism, and apocalypticism.[5] In a passage coming originally from the Q tradition, his message, his style of preaching, lifestyle, and the recurring images of "fire," "axe," and "winnow" are all in the prophetic tradition:[6]

> You brood of vipers! Who warned you to flee from the coming wrath? Produce good fruits as evidence of your repentance; and do not begin to say to yourselves, "We have Abraham as our father," for I tell you, God can raise up children to Abraham from these stones. Even now the ax lies at the root of the trees. Therefore every tree that does not produce good fruit will be cut down and thrown into the fire (Luke 3:7-9; cf. Matt 3:7-10).

Two themes predominate in John's preaching. First, he calls all that hear him to a profound conversion. God's judgment was immanent and could not be avoided. His baptism was a sign of one's willingness to be converted,

---

[3] John P. Meier, *A Marginal Jew: Rethinking the Historical Jesus*, Vol. II (New York: Doubleday, 1994) 24–27.

[4] Ibid., 31.

[5] Edward Schillebeeckx, *Jesus: An Experiment in Christology* (New York: Seabury, 1979) 135.

[6] Ibid., 127–28.

a baptism "with water, for repentance" (Matt 3:11). The people must change their ways. Jewish descent counts for nothing; being children of Abraham will not save them. Their only hope lies in repentance. Furthermore, they must show their repentance in their deeds. Luke clearly links repentance with charity and justice (Luke 3:10-14).

Second, John points to "one mightier than I" (Mark 1:7) who will come after him. All the traditions witness to this. John merely points to a successor; he does not and presumably could not identify him. But he will be greater than John; the Baptist says he is not worthy to loosen the strap of his sandal. The one to come after him will baptize, not just with water, but "with the holy Spirit and fire" (Matt 3:11; Luke 3:16) or simply "with the holy Spirit" (Mark 1:8; John 1:33).

John's baptism was a sign of one's repentance; it marked a person as belonging to the true Israel which Yahweh would vindicate. N. T. Wright says that "what John was doing must be seen, and can only be seen, as a prophetic renewal movement within Judaism—a renewal, however, that aimed not at renewing the existing structures, but at replacing them."[7] This argument is confirmed by the fact that John's group of disciples remained together after his death (Acts 19:1-7), like the disciples of Jesus, as a distinct group within Judaism.

Jesus

We know almost nothing about Jesus of Nazareth prior to his baptism at the hands of John. He was born shortly before the death of King Herod the Great in 4 B.C.E. His name, *Yesu* in Hebrew, is a shortened form of *Jehosua* or Joshua, the son of Nun who succeeded Moses. He was known as a Galilean, from Nazareth; his birth at Bethlehem probably represents a *theologoumenon*, a theological affirmation, based on Old Testament prophecy to affirm Jesus' Davidic messiahship.[8] However Jesus' Davidic lineage is affirmed in a number of different New Testament traditions, including Paul (Romans 1:3-4), the Synoptics, Acts 2:25-31, Revelation 3:7; 5:5, 22:16, and is at least implied in Hebrews 7:14. Meier says that he was probably recognized as "Son of David" even during his ministry.[9] There is no evidence that he was ever married.

---

[7] Cf. Wright, *JVG*, 160.

[8] John P. Meier, *A Marginal Jew: Rethinking the Historical Jesus*, Vol. I (New York: Doubleday, 1991) 216–17.

[9] Ibid., 219.

The virginal conception of Jesus is affirmed only by Matthew (1:18-25) and Luke (1:26-38), and of course, remains beyond verification. The classic text in Isaiah 7:14, "the virgin shall be with child," cited by Matthew 1:23, is ambiguous. The Hebrew word translated "virgin," *alma*, simply means a young woman; in the Septuagint it is translated by the Greek *parthenos* which often means virgin, but was also used in the less precise sense. There is no proof that Isaiah 7:14 in the Septuagint was understood as referring to a virginal conception prior to the time of Jesus.[10] Some feminist scholars have argued that Jesus was illegitimate[11] or that his mother had been raped.[12] A similar charge was made by a second-century pagan author, Celsus, in a polemic against Christianity written about 178 C.E., but the evidence suggests that what he reports is a dubious Jewish story originating, not in Palestine, but in the Diaspora in the middle of the second century.

Did Jesus have siblings, as the New Testament seems to suggest? John P. Meier offers a careful review of the issues involved: the different views in the early Church, the difficulty of maintaining that the author of Matthew thought of Jesus' "brothers" (Matt 13:55) as cousins; the fact that there is no case in the New Testament where the Greek *adelphos* ("brother") clearly means stepbrother, the reference of the careful Jewish historian Josephus to James as the brother of Jesus. Meier concludes that from a historical perspective, "the most probable opinion is that the brothers and sisters of Jesus were true siblings."[13]

But this is not the only possible conclusion. Mark 15:40 and Matthew 27:56 place at the crucifixion Mary Magdalene and Mary the mother of the younger James and of Joses ("James and Joseph" in Matthew) who are earlier identified as the brothers of Jesus (Mark 6:3; Matt 13:55). If this Mary at the crucifixion is to be understood as the mother of Jesus, it is strange of the evangelists to identify her by reference to her other children, rather than to Jesus. It is also true that to this day in Middle-Eastern cultures, male members of one's extended family are referred to as "brothers." I experienced this several years ago when one of our scholastics, an Egyptian by birth, took his vows, and several distant relatives showed up, identifying themselves as his "brothers."

---

[10] Ibid., 222.

[11] Jane Schaberg, *The Illegitimacy of Jesus: A Feminist Interpretation of the Infancy Narratives* (San Francisco: Harper and Row, 1987).

[12] Marianne Sawicki, *Seeing the Lord: Resurrection and Early Christian Practice* (Minneapolis: Fortress, 1994) 113–15.

[13] Meier, *A Marginal Jew*, I:331.

The language that Jesus spoke everyday would have been Aramaic. In the period after the Babylonian Exile it had become increasingly popular, replacing Hebrew as the common language. Hebrew remained in use as a sacred language, the language of most of the books of the Hebrew Bible and perhaps was still spoken by some. The fact that Jesus could argue a point of biblical interpretation with the scribes and Pharisees over biblical questions suggests that he was literate and had at least a basic knowledge of Hebrew. He would have been instructed in reading biblical Hebrew as a boy. Many scholars believe that he also had some knowledge of Greek; it was the language of the Gentiles and he would have needed some for dealing with them. Therefore it seems clear that Jesus had some religious education, was literate, spoke Aramaic, and had some knowledge of both Hebrew and Greek.

Mark reports the people of Nazareth asking skeptically after Jesus' synagogue teaching, "Is he not the carpenter (*tektōn*), the son of Mary?" (Mark 6:3). Matthew, dependent on Mark, changes this to "the carpenter's son" (Matt 13:55), from which comes the tradition of Joseph as the carpenter. The Greek word might be better translated as "woodworker," a skilled craft, which would have placed Jesus among the Galilean peasant class, a group of small business people, craftsmen, and independent farmers. Many of Jesus' disciples belonged to this group; they were fishermen who owned their own boats. From a socioeconomic perspective, these peasants were better off than the rural poor, the day laborers, tenant farmers, and hired servants who appear in the Gospels, but their lives were simple and hard.

Jesus and John the Baptist

Jesus emerges into view shortly after his baptism at the hands of John, an event that was certainly historical. We can only speculate why Jesus left his home and trade in Galilee and traveled to Judea where he encountered the Baptist. No doubt he had heard that a new prophet had appeared in Israel and, like other religious Jews, he had shown up where John was baptizing to hear his message. Two things seem clear.

First, Jesus' baptism at the hands of John changed his life. While we cannot read too much psychological meaning into the story of his baptism or take the vision described by the evangelists as a literal account of his experience, the encounter must have been significant. Something happened as a result of that meeting that changed the carpenter of Nazareth into the wandering preacher of the reign of God. The later evangelists seem a little uncomfortable with the story of Jesus' baptism. The first account, Mark's, simply mentions that Jesus was baptized by John in the Jordan (Mark 1:9). Luke, reducing the baptism of both the people and Jesus to past participial phrases, emphasizes that Jesus was at prayer; it is in this context that he experiences the vision (Luke 3:21). In Matthew's account, the Baptist immediately recognizes Jesus and seeks to prevent him from coming forward for baptism, suggesting that Jesus should baptize him instead (Matt 3:14). Matthew's Baptist is clearly aware of the superior dignity of Jesus. In John, the last Gospel to be written, the Baptist reports the vision of the Spirit descending on Jesus (John 1:32), but never mentions the actual baptism. The later evangelists seem uncomfortable with the story of Jesus submitting himself for baptism with sinners. Jesus however, was not a modern individualist; he would have seen himself as a member of God's people, the sinful Israel denounced by the Baptist. His coming forward for baptism was a sign of his personal openness to the coming judgment of God announced by the Baptist and of his solidarity with his people.

Second, it is quite possible that Jesus' own public ministry grew out of the time he spent with John and his disciples. Although only the author of the Fourth Gospel suggests this, there is reason to think that his Gospel at this point is historical. As John P. Meier says, "In this one case, many critics are willing to say, at least *sotto voce*, that the Fourth Gospel is right and the Synoptics are wrong."[14] The Fourth Gospel gives the following clues. Jesus first appears in the company of John; his first followers, including Philip, Andrew, and probably Peter and Nathanael, were originally disciples of the Baptist; and at least in the early days of his own ministry, he seems to have baptized others like John. John 3:22 says that "Jesus and his disciples went into the region of Judea, where he spent some time with them baptizing." Yet a few verses later, the final Johannine editor, no doubt aware of the other tradition, breaks the flow of the narrative at 4:2 to argue that Jesus himself did not baptize. The fact that the earlier passage says that Jesus was baptizing fits in with the criterion of embarrassment; it was widely known as part of the original Johannine tradition and could not be omitted, even if a later editor felt a need to correct it.[15]

The similarities between Jesus' preaching and John's also suggest that Jesus was originally part of John's group. Like John, Jesus called people to conversion of mind and heart; there was a note of urgency to his preaching, both for Israel and for the individual; his message was strongly escha-

---

[14] Meier, *A Marginal Jew*, II:118; N. T. Wright notes that the author of Acts also emphasizes that Jesus' followers date their point of origin from John's baptism; *JVC*, 169.

[15] Meier, *A Marginal Jew*, II:118–22.

tological; he gathered disciples about him; and he apparently continued, at least for a while, John's practice of baptizing.

However, at some point Jesus moved off to begin his own ministry. We don't know the precise reason for his departure from John's circle. But a comparison of Jesus' message with that of the Baptist suggests that his religious experience was different; he had a different vision of God and of God's salvation. John's message was a stern warning about God's coming judgment, as we saw earlier. Jesus' message was different; while there remained a strong theme of warning, it was a much more joyful message, literally "Good News" (*euangelium*), the Greek word translated as "Gospel." God's kingdom was already here, at least in some way. So at some point the two parted.

There is some evidence that John remained doubtful about Jesus and his ministry, or perhaps that he had second thoughts about him. The Q source reports that John sent his disciples to ask, "Are you the one who is to come, or should we look for another?" (Luke 7:20/Matt 11:3). Jesus' response can be seen as a summary of his ministry:

> Go and tell John what you have seen and heard: the blind regain their sight, the lame walk, lepers are cleansed, the deaf hear, the dead are raised, the poor have the good news proclaimed to them. And blessed is the one who takes no offense at me.
>
> (Luke 7:22-23; cf. Matt 11:4-6)

Jesus continued to speak of John with great respect. According to the Q tradition, Jesus declares John greater than any born of women, "yet the least in the kingdom of heaven is greater than he" (Matt 11:11; cf. Luke 7:28). In Mark, Jesus challenges the chief priests, scribes, and elders to acknowledge the divine authority behind John's ministry (Mark 11:27-30 and plls). In Matthew 11:7-11/Luke 7:24-28, Jesus declares John to be more than a prophet and yet less than the least in the kingdom of God. But the New Testament gives no hint of how the Baptist responded to Jesus' challenge. Meier sees in this silence a strong argument for the historicity of this tradition, since it serves no apologetic purpose.[16] There is also the evidence in Acts 18:25 and 19:3 that groups of John's followers survived into the period of the early Church. Perhaps John went to his death with his hesitation unrelieved or his doubt unresolved. But he must have played a role that affected not just the first disciples of Jesus, but Jesus himself as well.

What kind of authorization did Jesus have? Clearly his authority was not based on institutional sources; he was not trained in the Law, like the

---

[16] Meier, *A Marginal Jew*, II:135–36.

Pharisees, nor was he a member of the priestly class like the Sadducees. His authority was personal, charismatic. Though he describes himself in the Synoptic Gospels as a prophet (Mark 6:4 and plls), he does not seem to have used the traditional prophetic introduction, "thus says the Lord." John portrays Jesus in the manner of the wisdom teachers of the Old Testament. Ben Witherington finds this category the most adequate for explaining who Jesus was.[17] In more contemporary terms, he was a layman.

The Jesus Movement

If Jesus proclaimed the coming of God's kingdom or reign, as it is often translated, a natural question is where was this kingdom to be found. A kingdom is concrete; it has parameters or boundaries, a particular location. A reign implies an activity, a power exercised. Did Jesus understand the people of the kingdom as embracing all humanity? Was the locus of God's reign Israel, the historic people of God? Or was God's reign to be exercised over a new or renewed Israel?

Like the Old Testament itself, the ministry of Jesus included a blessing for all the nations. But most scholars today agree that Jesus confined his efforts to his own people. If he had reached out to all, rather than to "the lost sheep of the house of Israel" (Matt 15:24), the struggle faced by the post-Easter Church over the admission of the Gentiles reflected in the Pauline letters and the Acts of the Apostles would make no sense. It is possible that Jesus understood God's reign as being exercised over Israel, the people of God, the religious community defined by Torah, Temple, and priesthood. But if he saw the locus of God's reign as a renewed Israel, an eschatological community, there must be discernable some evidence of a break with the old, some effort to establish something new. This raises the question of Jesus as a movement founder or community organizer; it involves issues of symbol and structure, of prophetic action and organization.

In recent years it has become popular to speak of a "Jesus movement," though some scholars seek to separate it from the religious identity of Israel while others argue a radical difference between Jesus and his followers and the later Church. Elisabeth Schüssler Fiorenza describes the Jesus movement as one of a number of renewal movements within Judaism. She sees it as an "*alternative* to the dominant patriarchal structures" of Judaism, a "discipleship of equals," but not as an "oppositional formation" which rejected its values

---

[17] Ben Witherington III, *The Jesus Quest: The Third Search for the Jew of Nazareth* (Downers Grove, Ill.: InterVarsity, 1997) 185.

and praxis.[18] Jesus' followers were the economically disadvantaged, the "poor, destitute, and starving."[19] John Dominic Crossan describes Jesus' "kingdom-of-God-movement" as originally a group of "itinerants . . . like Jesus himself, primarily dispossessed peasant freeholders, tenants, or sharecroppers. They were not invited to give up everything but to accept their loss of everything as judging not them but the system that had done it to them."[20] Finding little or no evidence for this "itinerant" thesis, whether charismatic or "Cynic-like," Richard Horsley argues that the Jesus movement was based in and ordered towards the renewal of communities in the towns and villages of Galilee.[21]

But the issue of a Jesus movement can be raised another way. If a movement grew up around Jesus, what is the relation between this movement and the community of Israel of which Jesus was a part, and how did this movement relate to the later Church? It is too simple to suggest that Jesus was simply a wandering preacher who drew people to himself without any plan or intention. According to John Meier, "Jesus and the Pharisees represented the two major religious movements active among the ordinary Jews of Palestine in the late 20s of the 1st century."[22] There is considerable evidence in the Gospels that Jesus was as familiar with the symbolic as the prophets who proceeded him, and that he acted deliberately to give an identity to his followers. The evangelists distinguish between the "multitude" or "crowd" to whom he ministered (Mark 6:34), "the disciples" (Mark 14:12-16), other friends and supporters who traveled with him (Luke 8:1-3), and an inner group known as "the Twelve." And they speak of a new kind of family, one without traditional bonds of kinship and clan. We will consider this new family, the disciples, and the Twelve, and then ask what they suggest about Jesus' understanding of his ministry.

A New Family

There is considerable evidence in the Gospels that Jesus envisioned a new kind of family in which relationships were based not on clan, kinship, or patriarchy, so important in the Semitic culture of the East, but on one's

---

[18] Elisabeth Schüssler Fiorenza, *In Memory of Her: A Feminist Theological Reconstruction of Christian Origins* (New York: Crossroad, 1985) 107.

[19] Ibid., 123.

[20] John Dominic Crossan, *The Birth of Christianity: Discovering What Happened in the Years Immediately After the Execution of Jesus*, (HarperSanFrancisco, 1998) 281–82.

[21] Richard A. Horsley, *Sociology and the Jesus Movement* (New York: Continuum, 1994) 115–21.

[22] John P. Meier, *A Marginal Jew*: Vol. III; *Companions and Competitors* (New York: Doubleday, 2001) 639.

acceptance of the kingdom of God.[23] A number of the sayings of Jesus reflect this overturning of traditional family values and roles. For example, Jesus tells his disciples, "If anyone comes to me without hating his father and mother, wife and children, brothers and sisters, and even his own life, he cannot be my disciple" (Luke 14:26/Matt 10:37). Jesus foresees the conflict his coming will bring: "For I have come to set / a man 'against his father, / a daughter against her mother, / and a daughter-in-law against her mother-in-law; / and one's enemies will be those of his household'" (Matt 10:35-36). To the man who wanted to bury his father before following him, Jesus said, "Let the dead bury their dead" (Luke 9:60/Matt 8:22). But this was to encourage the violation of one of the most basic familial obligations, that of proper burial for the dead.[24]

Early in his Gospel, Mark tells a story about Jesus experiencing rejection from both family and the religious community.[25] His relatives, thinking him out of his mind, have come to bring him home by force. At the same time, the religious leaders, represented by the scribes, are attributing his work to the evil spirit (Mark 3:21-22). Jesus accuses the scribes of sinning against the Spirit. But his response to his family is equally challenging: "'Who are my mother and [my] brothers?' And looking around at those seated in the circle he said, 'Here are my mother and my brothers. [For] whoever does the will of God is my brother and sister and mother'" (Mark 3:33-35). As Bruce Chilton says, the dynamic of the kingdom is doing the will of God; "blood relatives were 'outsiders', just as the scribes were."[26] In the Fourth Gospel, Jesus, from the cross, gives his mother as mother to the Beloved Disciple, thus establishing the new family of the disciples (John 19:26-27).

The Disciples

From the time of his departure from the company of the Baptist Jesus was accompanied by a group of disciples. The New Testament uses two words to express the concept of discipleship, the noun *mathētēs*, "disciple," and the verb *akolouthein*, "to follow after."

Mathētēs appears more than 250 times in the New Testament, mostly in the Gospels and Acts. It means literally "one who learns." In secular Greek a *mathētēs* was someone bound to another to learn, an apprentice in a

---

[23] Cf., Horsley, *Sociology and the Jesus Movement*, 122–24.

[24] Cf. Wright, *JVC*, 401.

[25] See Lohfink, *Does God Need the Church?* 158.

[26] Bruce Chilton and J.I.H. McDonald, *Jesus and the Ethics of the Kingdom* (Grand Rapids, Mich.: Eerdmans, 1987) 97.

trade or the student of a philosopher. There is no *mathētēs* without a *didaskalos*, a "master" or "teacher." The verb *akolouthein* means to "follow after." Appearing fifty-six times in the Synoptics and fourteen times in John, it sometimes refers to the crowds that followed Jesus (Matt 4:25; 8:1). But when used of individuals, like *mathētēs*, it shows the special characteristics of the disciples in relation to Jesus.

One rarely finds the master-discipleship relationship in the Old Testament, and the Greek *mathētēs* does not appear in the Septuagint. It comes into the Jewish tradition with Rabbinic Judaism, probably under the influence of the Greek and Hellenistic philosophical schools. The New Testament uses *mathētēs* for the disciples of John the Baptist (Matt 11:2) and occasionally for the disciples of the Pharisees (Matt 22:16), though John P. Meier notes that the only example of a Jewish usage of *mathētēs* that comes close to that of the Gospel tradition appears in Josephus' writings, at the end of the first century C.E., that is, considerably later.[27] While there are some important parallels between the disciples of John and those of Jesus, the usage of *mathētēs* in reference to the disciple of Jesus is unique.

First, being a disciple of Jesus was the result of a personal invitation. Unlike the case of discipleship in Rabbinic Judaism, the disciple did not choose the master; rather Jesus chose and called his disciples (Mark 1:17; 2:14). The initiative always came from him. Similarly, while Jesus called all to repent, to act with mercy and love, to forgive as they had been forgiven, to welcome the kingdom, he did not call all to the very personal following that characterized his disciples.[28] It was not an absolute requirement for sharing in the blessings of the kingdom.

Second, there was an inclusive character to Jesus' call to follow him; his invitation was not restricted to the ritually pure, the religiously observant, the poor, or even to men. "The safe marker-buoys were removed; the necessary separation of the holy and the unclean, the righteous and the sinners, 'us and them', was deliberately undermined, for the dynamics of the Kingdom did not respect such parameters."[29] Among those who followed Jesus were "tax collectors and sinners" (Mark 2:15) as well as a group of women (Luke 8:2).

The issue of women disciples raises some questions. While the Gospel tradition make clear that there were women in Jesus' company, it never calls them *mathētēs*. Meier offers the following explanation. In Jesus' time,

[27] Meier, *A Marginal Jew*, III:44.

[28] Martin Hengel, *The Charismatic Leader and His Followers* (Edinburgh: T. & T. Clark, 1996) 61.

[29] Chilton and McDonald, *Jesus and the Ethics of the Kingdom*, 96.

there were no feminine forms of the Hebrew and Aramaic words for disciple (Hb. *Talmîd*/Ar. *Talmîda*), and the Greek Gospels followed Jewish usage in this regard. Luke does use a feminine form of disciple, *mathēria*, in Acts 9:36, though not in his Gospel, probably because he was reluctant to introduce the word into the relatively fixed Gospel tradition. Conclusion: were there women disciples? Not in name, but certainly in reality.[30] There was also a group of men and women such as Martha and Mary, Lazarus, the anonymous host for the Last Supper, perhaps not "complete" disciples as they did not leave home, yet who supported Jesus and his group, offering them hospitality.[31]

Third, Jesus' call to discipleship meant a radical break with the past, both personal and cultural (Mark 10:21; Luke 9:57-62). Those who followed Jesus "left everything" (Luke 5:11). They left behind parents, family and children (Luke 14:26), jobs (Mark 2:14). His disciples shared his poverty and itinerant life (Matt 8:20). They exchanged natural family relationships for membership in a new family with Jesus, as we have seen (Mark 3:34-35). For some it meant celibacy for the sake of the kingdom (Matt 19:11-12). There is also some cultural baggage to be left behind. The new family of those who follow Jesus will be different from the Israel of old. The following text in Mark is instructive:

> Amen, I say to you, there is no one who has given up house or brothers or sisters or mother or father or children or lands for my sake and for the sake of the gospel who will not receive a hundred times more now in this present age: houses and brothers and sisters and mothers and children and lands, with persecutions, and eternal life in the age to come (Mark 10:29-30).

The careful reader will note that the second half of the sentence omits "fathers" from the new family of the disciples. The omission is significant: fathers "represent patriarchy, the old society in which the man alone ruled and decided. In the new family of Jesus into which the disciples are to grow there can no longer be anyone who dominates others."[32] The fact too that there were women among those who followed Jesus (Luke 8:2) also goes against the culture of the times.

Fourth, being a disciple of Jesus was very different from being a disciple of the rabbis. The latter were students, concerned with learning and passing on the teaching of their masters. The disciples of Jesus shared in his

---

[30] Meier, *A Marginal Jew*, III:73–79.
[31] Ibid., III:80–82.
[32] Chilton and McDonald, *Jesus and the Ethics of the Kingdom*, 132.

ministry; he sent them out to heal the sick, to cast out demons, and to proclaim that the kingdom of God was at hand (Mark 6:7-13; Luke 10:2-12).

Finally, being a disciple of Jesus meant sharing his life of service and loving others with a self-sacrificial love. The disciples are to share what they have with others (Luke 6:30); they must be willing to take the last place and serve others (Mark 9:35), placing others first and being willing to bear insult and injury (Matt 5:38-42). In other words, they are to love as Jesus loved. The author of the Fourth Gospel makes this explicit, when Jesus says in his farewell discourse: "This is my commandment: love one another as I love you. No one has greater love than this, to lay down one's life for one's friends" (John 15:12-13). According to Meier the demand for radical commitment that might entail hostility, persecution, even the sacrifice of one's life, is rooted in Jesus himself. He argues convincingly for the authenticity of two sayings about the radical demands of discipleship that appear in Mark together: "Whoever wishes to come after me must deny himself, take up his cross, and follow me. For whoever wishes to save his life will lose it, but whoever loses his life for my sake and that of the gospel will save it" (Mark 8:34-35 and plls).[33]

The Twelve

While not all agree on the role played by the Twelve in the primitive Church, few question the fact that Jesus chose twelve from the larger group of disciples (though Matthew tends to identify the disciples with the Twelve).

> He went up the mountain and summoned those whom he wanted and they came to him. He appointed twelve [whom he also named apostles] that they might be with him and he might send them forth to preach and to have authority to drive out demons: [he appointed the twelve:] Simon, whom he named Peter; James, son of Zebedee, and John the brother of James, whom he named Boanerges, that is, sons of thunder; Andrew, Philip, Bartholomew, Matthew, Thomas, James the son of Alphaeus; Thaddeus, Simon the Cananean, and Judas Iscariot who betrayed him (Mark 3:13-19).

The passage suggests later theological reflection; the word "apostle" (one who is sent) is most likely post-Easter and the author uses the verb *epoiesen*, "he made" or "he appointed," to indicate a formal institution. The later Church does not remember their names consistently, as some lists differ slightly as to who was included. But that Jesus chose "the Twelve" is

---

[33] Meier, *A Marginal Jew*, III:56–67.

not to be doubted; they are mentioned in independent sources such as Mark, John, and probably the special Lukan material and Q, as well as in the ancient creed naming the witnesses to the resurrection cited by Paul in 1 Corinthians 15:1-7.[34]

What does all this mean for Jesus' understanding of his movement? The act of constituting "the Twelve" as the inner core of his band of disciples clearly has eschatological significance. Meier traces a tradition already present in Jeremiah and Ezekiel and even clearer in postexilic Judaism which began to look forward to a regathering of the twelve tribes in God's future. What emerges is the hope of a new or restored, eschatological Israel. Even the sectarian community of Qumran shared in this hope.[35] Against this background, the Jesus movement was not something that just "happened." His disciples constituted a new "family" of those completely given to the reign of God. The meaning of placing a symbolic group of twelve at the center of his movement would have been immediately apparent to the Jews of his day. This was a deliberate action, a prophetic action on the part of Jesus to establish a renewed or eschatological community of Israel.[36] By his appointment of the Twelve, by making them a sign of the immanent restoration of Israel, he was challenging Israel to a decision of faith.[37]

The Jesus Movement and the Church

The enduring temptation of liberal theology, from its classical expression in nineteenth-century Protestant liberalism to its modern incarnation in the Jesus Seminar, is to reduce Jesus to a rather innocuous teacher of ethics, particularly social ethics. The result is to drive a wedge between this now manageable Jesus and all questions of doctrine, ritual, and Church.[38] A classic expression of this is Alfred Loisy's often-repeated phrase, "Jesus preached the Kingdom of God and what came was the church."[39] But such a reduction cannot withstand serious analysis.

It also ignores what a careful study of the Jesus movement indicates. In calling a group of disciples to share his own mission towards Israel and in

[34] Cf. John P. Meier, *A Marginal Jew*, III:141.

[35] Ibid., 148–53.

[36] Wright, *JVC*, 300 and Lohfink, *Does God Need the Church?* 162 speak of "the eschatological restoration of Israel."

[37] Ben F. Meyer, *The Aims of Jesus* (London: SCM Press, 1979) 154.

[38] Ben F. Meyer refers to "the 1880 consensus" in critical biblical scholarship, according to which there were no ties between "Jesus" and "Church" in his *Christus Faber: The Master Builder and the House of God* (Allison Park, Pa.: Pickwick, 1992) 149.

[39] Alfred Loisy, *L'Evangile et l'Eglise* (Paris, 1902) 111.

constituting "the Twelve," symbolic of the twelve tribes, as an inner group at its heart Jesus was symbolically establishing a renewed community of salvation or an eschatological Israel. Some feminist scholars have stressed the egalitarian nature of Jesus' discipleship, terming it a "discipleship of equals." While there is some truth to this, it is clear from the New Testament that there were different "circles" or groups within the discipleship. In addition to the general group of disciples and "the Twelve," Peter, James, and John seems to enjoy a closer or more intimate relationship with Jesus. They alone accompany him at the raising of the daughter of Jairus, the Transfiguration, and the agony in the garden. Peter stands out in all the traditions. He is always first named among the Twelve (Mark 3:16; Luke 6:14; Matt 10:2; Acts 1:13; cf. 1 Cor 15:5-8). All the primary strata of the gospel tradition, with the possible exception of "Q" attest that Peter was the spokesman for the disciples during the lifetime of Jesus.[40] The Gospel tradition that Jesus changed his name from Simon to Peter ("rock") is most probably historical; it was clearly known by Paul who usually refers to him as Kephas, Aramaic for Peter. The Jesus movement was thus a differentiated group; it consisted of the disciples, the Twelve, an inner circle of Peter, James, and John, and Peter himself.

This eschatological Israel or renewed community of salvation also had certain characteristic ritual actions. At least at the beginning, reflecting no doubt the time that Jesus and some of his first disciples had spent with John the Baptist, the disciples of Jesus and perhaps Jesus himself carried out a baptismal ministry (John 3:22). As with the baptism of John, this baptism was a sign of repentance and of personal openness to God's future.

There was also the tradition of the meal, the meals Jesus shared with his disciples and with others, including the "tax collectors and sinners" for which he was so often criticized, welcoming them as a sign of their inclusion in the reign of God. This meal was to take on an entirely new significance through the Last Supper and after Jesus' death as the disciples carried on this tradition (cf. Luke 24:13-35). We will consider the table fellowship tradition in the following chapter. But what all this shows is that during his ministry Jesus gathered his disciples into a community with a particular identity. His disciples shared in his ministry. The community was characterized by certain ritual actions. His establishment of "the Twelve" as an inner core related his followers to a renewed Israel, a renewed community of salvation.

---

[40] *Peter in the New Testament*, ed. Raymond E. Brown, Karl P. Donfried, and John Reumann (Minneapolis/New York: Fortress/ Paulist, 1973) 159.

What is the relation between this renewed Israel and the Church? Daniel J. Harrington says that one can trace "continuities of belief, personnel, and practice between the group gathered around Jesus in his earthly ministry (the disciples) and the group gathered around the risen Lord (the church)." [41] Gerhard Lohfink says that Jesus' action is not immediately directed to the Church; however to the extent that post-Easter *ekklēsia*—even though incomplete because the synagogue is absent—is the eschatological Israel, one can and must say that Jesus laid the foundation for the Church in all his actions. What Jesus founded, when he appointed the Twelve, was not the Church but the eschatological people of God. But in that act of foundation the basis of the Church was prepared. The Church goes back to the actions of Jesus himself. [42]

Conclusion

While Jesus was known as a Galilean, the matrix for his movement seems to have been the movement of John the Baptist in the Judean desert. There were similar themes in the preaching of both men. Both saw Israel as being at a critical juncture, facing God's judgment. Both called Israel the nation and the individual Jew to a conversion of mind and heart. At some point however Jesus broke with John and began preaching himself and gathering his own disciples, some of whom came from John's company.

The Jesus movement was more than a spontaneous gathering around a charismatic preacher. Though Jesus preached to many, he called some to become his disciples, to a close association with him and to a share in his ministry. He saw these followers as constituting a new family dedicated, as he was, to hearing and doing the word of God. The choice of "the Twelve" is the key to his intention; he saw his community of disciples as constituting an eschatological Israel, the restoration of Israel proclaimed by the prophets. From this community came the Church. We must now turn to Jesus' ministry.

---

[41] Daniel J. Harrington, *God's People in Christ* (Philadelphia: Fortress, 1980) 29.

[42] Lohfink, *Does God Need the Church?* 163; see also his *Jesus and Community: The Social Dimension of Christian Faith* (Philadelphia/New York: Fortress/Paulist, 1984).

Chapter 5

The Preaching and Ministry of Jesus

In his sermon in the house of the centurion Cornelius, Peter gives a brief summary of the ministry of Jesus. He reminds his hearers, really Luke's Christian congregations, of "what has happened all over Judea, beginning in Galilee after the baptism that John preached, how God anointed Jesus of Nazareth with the holy Spirit and power. He went about doing good and healing all those oppressed by the devil, for God was with him" (Acts 10:37-38).

The Gospels offer various portraits of Jesus; he is a healer and exorcist, a prophet, the awaited messiah, the Son of Man. Ben Witherington argues that while John the Baptist stands in the line of the classical prophets, Jesus comes across as a prophetic and eschatological sage.[1] In his view, the Wisdom tradition best explains the diverse aspects of Jesus' ministry. Rather than using the prophetic formula, "thus says the Lord," Jesus teaches on his own authority. He spoke in aphorisms, parables, personifications, and beatitudes—typical of Wisdom speech—and called God Father. There is a more universal flavor to his teaching.[2] John Meier sees him as a wandering prophet and miracle worker in the mold of Elijah and Elisha.[3]

If we move from the Gospel texts to the preacher who lies behind them we find three strands of Jesus tradition, his sayings, his parables, and the central image of the kingdom of God. We will consider these three strands and conclude with a note on the miracle tradition.

The Sayings of Jesus

Not all the sayings or "logia" of Jesus come from Jesus himself. Some of those attributed to him by the evangelists may have been popular proverbs

---

[1] Ben Witherington III, *The Jesus Quest: The Third Search for the Jew of Nazareth* (Downers Grove, Ill.: InterVarsity, 1997) 187.

[2] Ibid., 185.

[3] John P. Meier, *A Marginal Jew*, Vol. II, *Mentor, Message, and Miracles* (New York: Doubleday, 1994) 1044.

that Jesus adopted in his preaching; some may have been attributed to Jesus by the early Christian communities. Rudolf Bultmann gives a long list of such proverbs turned into sayings of Jesus by the Church.[4] But he also lists about fifteen that we can take with some confidence as characteristic of Jesus' preaching. They include the following:

1. If a kingdom is divided against itself, that kingdom cannot stand. And if a house is divided against itself, that house will not be able to stand. And if Satan has risen up against himself and is divided, he cannot stand; that is the end of him (Mark 3:24-26).

2. But no one can enter a strong man's house to plunder his property unless he first ties up the strong man. Then he can plunder his house (Mark 3:27).

3. For whoever wishes to save his life will lose it, but whoever loses his life for my sake and that of the gospel will save it (Mark 8:35).

4. No one who sets a hand to the plow and looks to what was left behind is fit for the kingdom of God (Luke 9:62).

5. How hard it is for those who have wealth to enter the kingdom of God (Mark 10:23b).

6. It is easier for a camel to pass through [the] eye of [a] needle than for one who is rich to enter the kingdom of God (Mark 10:25).

7. Let the dead bury their dead (Luke 9:60a).

8. Enter through the narrow gate; for the gate is wide and the road broad that leads to destruction, and those who enter through it are many. How narrow the gate and constricted the road that leads to life. And those who find it are few (Matt 7:13-14).

9. But many that are first will be last, and [the] last will be first (Mark 10:31).

10. Nothing that enters one from outside can defile that person; but the things that come out from within are what defile (Mark 7:15).

11. Amen, I say to you, whoever does not accept the kingdom of God like a child will not enter it (Mark 10:15).

12. For everyone who exalts himself will be humbled, but the one who humbles himself will be exalted (Luke 14:11).

13. You justify yourselves in the sight of others, but God knows your hearts; for what is of human esteem is an abomination in the sight of God (Luke 16:15).

---

[4] Rudolf Bultmann, *The History of the Synoptic Tradition* (Oxford: Basil Blackwell, 1963) 102–04.

14. When someone strikes you on [your] right cheek, turn the other one to him as well. If anyone wants to go to law with you over your tunic, hand him your cloak as well. Should anyone press you into service for one mile, go with him for two miles (Matt 5:39b-41).

15. [L]ove your enemies, and pray for those who persecute you, that you may be children of your heavenly Father, for he makes his sun rise on the bad and the good, and causes rain to fall on the just and the unjust. For if you love those who love you, what recompense will you have? Do not the tax collectors do the same? And if you greet your brothers only, what is unusual about that? Do not the pagans do the same? So be perfect, just as your heavenly Father is perfect (Matt 5:44-48).

These are not the only authentic sayings of Jesus contained in the Gospels. Some are embedded in stories about Jesus or in his parables; others were occasioned by his healings. But these reflect themes characteristic of the preaching of Jesus. We note the following: the centrality of the kingdom of God (4, 5, 6, 11), a final reversal of status (3, 6, 9, 12), struggle or conflict (1, 2, 3, 4, 8), the danger of wealth (5, 6), and the call for a radical change of heart (4, 10, 11, 14, 15). Thus there was something intrinsically challenging about the preaching of Jesus; his language is disturbing, unsettling, a language which afflicted the comfortable and comforted the afflicted and the disadvantaged.

Final Reversal

The saying about a final or eschatological reversal of status, appearing in various forms four times above (3, 6, 9, 12), must have been a consistent theme in the preaching of Jesus. It appears in stories and parables in the expression, "the first shall be last and the last shall be first" (Mark 10:31; Matt 19:30; 20:16; Luke 13:30) and in alternative forms: "For everyone who exalts himself will be humbled, but the one who humbles himself will be exalted" (Luke 14:11; 18:14; Matt 23:12). In the Canticle of Mary, most probably a pre-Lukan hymn modified by Luke to apply to Mary, it appears in poetic form: "He has thrown down the rulers from their thrones but lifted up the lowly. The hungry he has filled with good things; the rich he has sent away empty" (Luke 1:52-53). This theme of reversal may have been even more radically expressed in the original canticle. Perhaps its most dramatic expression is in the Beatitudes.

The Beatitudes

What we are accustomed to refer to as "the Beatitudes" vividly illustrates the disturbing character of Jesus' preaching as well as the theme of final reversal. Drawing on the sayings of Jesus collected in the Q source, the beatitudes appear in Matthew's Sermon of the Mount (Matt 5:1-48) and Luke's Sermon on the Plain (Luke 6:20-49). Because of the similarities in the two accounts, many commentators conclude that both versions reflect a sermon of Jesus containing the beatitudes and a number of specific instructions defining the response of the disciples in terms of love of neighbor.[5] Both evangelists have adapted the received tradition and added some beatitudes of their own composition, given here in brackets. The longest beatitude in both versions (Matt 5:11/Luke 6:22), also from Q, reflects the persecution faced by the early community.

Matthew 5:3-12	Luke 6:20-26
Blessed are the poor in spirit, for theirs is the kingdom of heaven.	Blessed are you who are poor, for the kingdom of God is yours.
Blessed are they who mourn, for they will be comforted.	Blessed are you who are now hungry, for you will be satisfied.
[Blessed are the meek, for they will inherit the land.]	Blessed are you who are now weeping, for you will laugh.
Blessed are they who hunger and thirst for righteousness, for they will be satisfied.	Blessed are you when people hate you, and when they exclude you and insult you, and denounce your name as evil on account of the Son of Man.
[Blessed are the merciful, for they will be shown mercy.	Rejoice and leap for joy on that day! Behold, your reward will be great in heaven. For their ancestors treated the prophets in the same way.
Blessed are the clean of heart, for they will see God.	[But woe to you who are rich, for you have received your consolation.
Blessed are the peacemakers, for they will be called children of God.	But woe to you who are filled now, for you will be hungry.
Blessed are they who are persecuted for the sake of righteousness, for theirs is the kingdom of heaven.]	

---

[5] Cf. Jan Lambrecht, *The Sermon of the Mount* (Wilmington, Del.: Michael Glazier, 1985) 40.

Blessed are you when they insult you and persecute you and utter every kind of evil against you [falsely] because of me.	Woe to you who laugh now, for you will grieve and weep.
	Woe to you when all speak well of you, for their ancestors treated the false
Rejoice and be glad, for your reward will be great in heaven. Thus they persecuted the prophets who were before you.	prophets in this way.]

Luke's version is shorter than Matthew's and is thought to be closer to the original form of the Beatitudes in Q which Meier judges as "among the best candidates for authentic sayings of Jesus."[6] While both versions have been adapted to include the disciples and others, they contain sayings addressed to the poor, the hungry, and those who mourn and thus reflect the emphasis on God's special concern for the poor and the powerless so evident in the prophetic tradition. Meier offers the following as the earliest Q form of the Beatitudes:

1. Happy are the poor,
   for theirs is the kingdom of heaven.

2. Happy are the mourners,
   for they shall be comforted.

3. Happy are the hungry,
   for they shall be satisfied.[7]

But who are the poor?

The Poor

In the Old Testament the word *ani* was often used for the poor; it means literally "afflicted." It connotes those of lower class status who were often oppressed and lacked the power to defend themselves. The related form *anaw* had the same meaning, but often takes on a religious connotation. The *anawim* were the poor of Yahweh, those without material resources or power who could look only to God for their well-being and deliverance, for it is God who remembers their cry (cf. Pss 9–10). Under the monarchy poverty and injustice became a genuine social problem; the prophetic literature is clear witness to this.

---

[6] Meier, *A Marginal Jew*, II:319.
[7] Ibid., 323.

Economic changes and a double or triple system of taxation in first-century Palestine expanded the number of poor in the land, while the exclusionary rules of purity added to those marginalized or excluded from the religious community. Thus in the time of Jesus "the poor" included more than the economically disadvantaged, the subsistence farmers and day laborers, the unemployed or underemployed. It also included public sinners, women, orphans, the illiterate, the mentally ill, those with disfiguring diseases or bodily injuries, and those whose religious practice did not measure up to the strict standards of the priestly class and the Pharisees. As a result, whole classes of people were classed as sinners, marginalized, or excluded from the community. We catch echoes of this larger group of the poor in Gospel phrases such as "the poor and the crippled, the blind and the lame" (Luke 14:21), this "accursed" crowd "which does not know the law" (John 7:49), or in the frequent criticism of Jesus as "a friend of tax collectors and sinners" (Matt 11:19; Mark 2:16).

The Our Father

The Our Father or Lord's Prayer is thought to go back to Jesus himself, with probably an Aramaic original lying behind the Greek of the Q tradition.[8] We have two versions (Matt 6:9-13/Luke 11:2-4), both set in the context of an instruction of Jesus on prayer. Matthew's version has most probably been expanded, but those parts shared with Luke are most likely closer to the original wording. The prayer addresses God as "Father," a usage unique in his time to Jesus who prayed to God as "Abba" (dear Father).

While the Our Father reflects the themes of Jewish prayer, it is different in its brevity and simplicity, its universality, and its order, mentioning the kingdom before human needs. "Bread" means both food for the body and symbolizes our primary needs. "Temptation" (*peirasmos*) has been much discussed; Lambrecht suggests it means not the temptations that will accompany the coming of the endtimes but simply protection from the dangers of sin and apostasy (cf. Mark 14:38).[9]

The Parables of Jesus

Perhaps nowhere else is the disturbing character of Jesus' preaching more evident than in his parables. Read, for example, his parable of the Workers in the Vineyard (Matt 20:1-16). Most of us react to this parable as

---

[8] Lambrecht, *Sermon on the Mount*, 133.
[9] Ibid., 141.

though it were somehow profoundly unfair. It turns our sense of right and wrong upside down. Why should those who came to work at the last moment enjoy the same rewards as those who bore the heat of the day? Shouldn't their hard labor count for more?

Many of Jesus' parables have a similar effect on us. They challenge our customary way of seeing our world, draw us out of our complacency, force us to ask questions, to rethink our values. Consider the Good Samaritan (Luke 10:29-37), the Rich Man and Lazarus (Luke 16:19-35) the Marriage Feast (Matt 22:1-14), the Parable of the Talents (Matt 25:14-30), the Sheep and the Goats (Matt 25:31-46). Others, like the Lost Sheep, the Lost Coin (Luke 15:1-10), and the Prodigal Son (Luke 15:11-32) suggest a new way of imagining God. Eamonn Bredin points out that there is something shocking and subversive about the parables of Jesus: "It is the *Samaritan* who is neighbor, it is the *last* who are first, it is the *lost* who are rejoiced over, the *stranger* who is at table, the *wastrel* son who is embraced and fêted."[10]

From a literary perspective, parables are stories that combine metaphor with narrative. John Donahue observes that Jesus' parables were unlike the fables of the Greeks or the debates of the rabbis; "the raw material of Jesus' language was the everyday world of nature and human activity."[11] The parables are about seeds growing in fields and harvests, merchants and bakers, laborers and fishermen, tenant farmers, debtors, and land owners, travelers on dangerous roads and village wedding feasts. There is an open-ended or polyvalent character to the parables; they invite us into their world and we often find ourselves identifying with different characters in the story. They admit of multiple meanings, sometimes even within the New Testament (cf. The Lost Sheep in Matt 18:12-14 and Luke 15:4-7).[12]

But if the parables cause us to reassess our way of seeing things, they also give us access to the imagination of Jesus and are suggestive of his personal experience of God. Thus they are doors to a deeper reality.[13] Using poetry and metaphor, the parables link the familiar with the unimaginable. In this way they give concreteness and immediacy to the transcendent; those that hear them are brought to face the mystery of God. Or in language more similar to that of Jesus in the Synoptic Gospels, the kingdom of God is breaking into their everyday worlds.

[10] Eamonn Bredin, *Rediscovering Jesus: Challenge of Discipleship*, (Quezon City, Philippines: Claretian Publications, 1986) 40.

[11] John R. Donahue, *The Gospel in Parable* (Philadelphia: Fortress, 1988) 13.

[12] Ibid., 17–18.

[13] Ibid., 8–11; see also Amos N. Wilder, *Jesus' Parables and the War of Myths: Essays on Imagination in the Scriptures* (Philadelphia: Fortress, 1982); Robert W. Funk, *Language, Hermeneutic and the Word of God* (New York: Harper and Row, 1966).

The Kingdom of God

At the heart of the preaching of Jesus is the Good News of the kingdom of God. Jesus himself may well have been the first to use the phrase "kingdom of God," but its roots lie deep in the Old Testament. The idea finds its origin in the notion of the Kingship of Yahweh. Even prior to the establishment of the monarchy, Yahweh was understood as king of Israel (Deut 33:5; 1 Sam 8:7). In later theology, the concept of Yahweh's royal power was expanded, the result no doubt of reflection on his saving deeds as well as on the attributes claimed for the gods of Israel's neighbors. In the Psalms, Yahweh appears not just as the God who reigns over Israel (Ps 95), but as king over the other nations (Pss 22:29; 47; 99), and finally, as a cosmic king ruling over all creation in virtue of his work as creator (Pss 74:12; 93; 95-99). In some of the later prophets (or in later additions to earlier prophets like Isaiah 24:23) Yahweh's rule was seen in an eschatological perspective, the final establishment of Yahweh's reign over Israel when God's salvation would appear in its fullness (Obad 21; Zeph 3:15-20; Zech 14:16-21).

While there is some reference to God's rule or reign in the earlier tradition (Pss 103:19; 145:11-13), the notion of God's kingdom occurs more frequently in the late Old Testament period. It appears in Tobit 13:1, in Daniel who refers both to the throne of God's reign (Dan 3:54) and to the rule or kingdom which will be given to the saints in the apocalyptic future (Dan 7:14, 18, 22, 27), and in Wisdom 6:4 and 10:10. In some of the intertestamental writings, for example, the Assumption of Moses which is contemporary with the New Testament, the kingdom or reign of God is associated with apocalyptic displays of God's power and judgment and with the establishment of Israel's rule over the nations. N. T. Wright argues that within Second Temple Judaism, the theme of God's kingdom evoked a "complete story-line" which envisioned Israel's final return from exile, a correlative return of Yahweh to Zion, as well as Yahweh's victory over evil in the form of Israel's enemies.[14]

Thus the theme of God's kingdom, if not the actual expression, was familiar to the Jews of Jesus' time. Many interpreted it in terms of freedom from Roman rule. For others, it was understood in the broader context of the messianic hope of Israel that we considered earlier.

The kingdom of God is at the heart of Jesus' message; it appears in the Q tradition, in Mark, in the material unique to Matthew and to Luke, and in John.[15] It is the center of Jesus' Sermon on the Mount and the subject of

---

[14] N. T. Wright, *Jesus and the Victory of God*, (Minneapolis: Fortress, 1996) 204–07.

[15] See Wright's Appendix, "'Kingdom of God' in Early Christian Literature," *JVC*, 663–70.

most of his parables. It appears throughout the Pauline corpus. In the preaching of Jesus, the kingdom of God is a polyvalent symbol; as Eamonn Bredin notes, it is "approaching," "coming," "at hand" (Mark 1:15; Matt 10:7; Luke 10:11). One is called to "enter into" (Mark 9:47; 10:23-25; Matt 5:20; 18:3; John 3:5) or "seek" it (Matt 6:33; Luke 12:31). Some are "not far" from it (Mark 12:34). Others fail to enter it (Mark 10:15; Matt 7:21). The kingdom is a secret not revealed to everyone (Mark 4:11); there are "keys" to it given to some (Matt 16:19). Most of all, it "has come upon you" (Matt 12:28; Luke 11:20) or "is in the midst of you" (Luke 17:21).[16]

What did the kingdom of God mean in the preaching of Jesus? Jesus does not explain it, but its meaning emerges from his parables and its coming is illustrated through his ministry. We will consider four dimensions of his preaching of the kingdom.

1. *Event not Place*

First, the expression kingdom of God (*basileia tou theou*) should generally be translated "reign" or "rule" of God. The concept is dynamic; it refers, not to a place but to an event, God's saving power breaking into history in a new way. The early Church would see it as meaning the coming of the messianic age of salvation. Kenan Osborne offers the following phrases as "substitutes" for the symbol of the kingdom of God:[17]

Presence of God	Justice of God
Love of God	Holiness of God
Compassion of God	Goodness of God
Mercy of God	Creativeness of God
Power of God	Grace of God
Forgiveness of God	Relatedness of God

2. *Eschatological Tension*

Second, there is an eschatological tension in Jesus' preaching of the reign of God. It is both present and future. Jesus' break with John the Baptist was at least in part over this issue. From the beginning Jesus proclaimed that the reign of God was in some way already present (Mark 1:15; Matt 4:17). Joachim Jeremias calls this initial presence "the dawn of the reign of God."[18] It means that God is now manifesting his reign, his salvific

[16] Bredin, *Rediscovering Jesus*, 25.

[17] Kenan B. Osborne, *The Resurrection of Jesus: New Considerations for Its Theological Interpretation* (New York: Paulist, 1997) 150.

[18] Joachim Jeremias, *New Testament Theology*, Part I (London: SCM Press, 1971) 96 ff.

activity in the lives of men and women. Jesus illustrates this and makes present this dawning of the age of salvation in his preaching and parables, his miracles and exorcisms, his proclamation of the forgiveness of sins, and in his table fellowship.

The Kingdom of God As Present

The Parables

The parable tradition illustrates that the reign of God is taking place right now. Chapter 13 of Matthew's Gospel includes seven parables about the kingdom. It is the seed that falls on the rocky ground (3–8), the wheat growing slowly with the weeds (24–30), the tiny mustard seed which becomes the large bush (31–32), the yeast mixed in with the flour (33), the treasure buried in the field (44), the pearl of great price (45–46), or the net thrown into the sea (47–50). Thus according to these parables, the kingdom at this moment is accessible, growing, transforming, hidden, found, and gathering.

Miracles and Exorcisms

For Palestinian Jews of the time of Jesus, sickness or infirmity was attributed to demonic power (Luke 13:10-16) and sin (John 9:1-3). Jesus' exorcisms (Mark 1:23-28; 3:23-27) and his healings show that with the arrival of the reign of God the power of evil over human beings was being broken; God's salvific power was becoming effective in the bodies and spirits of the people to whom he ministered. This theme is explicit in the following sayings: Beelzebul and the advent of the reign of God (Matt 12:27 and pl), the kingdom and household divided against themselves (Mark 3:24-26 and plls), binding the strong man (Mark 3:27 and plls), and Jesus sending the disciples out with power over the demons (Mark 3:14; 6:7; Matt 10:7; Luke 9:1). Ben Meyer argues these show that Jesus himself saw his "deeds of power" (*dunameis*) to be signs of the dawning eschaton.[19]

When Jesus is charged with driving out demons by the power of Beelzebul, he responds: "But if it is by the finger of God that [I] drive out demons, then the kingdom of God has come upon you" (Luke 11:20). The saying is almost certainly authentic; J. P. Meier calls this the "star witness" for the presence of the kingdom in Jesus' ministry.[20]

---

[19] Ben F. Meyer, *The Aims of Jesus* (London: SCM Press, 1979) 155–56.

[20] Meier, *A Marginal Jew*, II:399; cf. Meyer, *Aims*, 155.

The Forgiveness of Sins

The proclamation of the forgiveness of sins is more evidence that the age of salvation is at hand. Forgiveness means the remission of debts, liberation from one's past, and the healing of relationships. In Jesus' preaching it means reconciliation with God and with the community. Whether or not he actually said, "your sins are forgiven" in so many words, he proclaimed forgiveness, not only in words and parables (Matt 18:23-35; Luke 15:11-32), but also in deeds. Here especially, the table fellowship tradition is important, as we will see below.

The claim to authority implicit in Jesus' proclamation of forgiveness was recognized by the Pharisees, who objected, "Who but God alone can forgive sins?" (Mark 2:7). But Jesus was also redefining how one shared in the blessings of salvation. For the Judaism of his day and particularly for the Pharisees, those blessings were available through membership in the community defined by Temple and Torah. Jesus was implying something else. The blessings of salvation were available now for those who trusted in him and in the kingdom he proclaimed. Thus Jesus was replacing adherence to Temple and Torah with allegiance to himself.[21]

Table Fellowship

In what is referred to as the "table fellowship tradition," Jesus proclaimed the forgiveness of sins in deeds. Meals played a very important role in the ministry of Jesus; it is interesting how often they are mentioned in stories about Jesus and appear in his parables. According to Luke, much of Jesus' teaching takes place at meals.[22] In a passage deemed authentic by J. P. Meier, Jesus—in what seems to be a moment of irritation with his critics—contrasts his own ministry, including his meals, with the much more austere ministry of John the Baptist: "For John came neither eating nor drinking, and they said, 'He is possessed by a demon.' The Son of Man came eating and drinking and they said, 'Look, he is a glutton and a drunkard, a friend of tax collectors and sinners'" (Matt 11:18-19).[23]

Jesus' practice of table fellowship illustrates the presence of God's kingdom. To share a meal with someone in the Middle East, even today, is a sign of communion. In the Judaism of Jesus' day, to share bread at table

---

[21] Cf. Wright, *JVC*, 274.

[22] Luke 5:31-39; 7:36-50; 10:38-42; 11:37-52; 14:1-24; 22:14-38; 24:20-49; see John Navone, *Themes of St. Luke* (Rome: Gregorian University Press, 1970) 11–37.

[23] Meier, *A Marginal Jew*, II:145–50.

over which the head of the house had asked a blessing signified fellowship with God, while the purity laws forbade associating with those who were unclean or outside the Law. The distinctions between the clean and the unclean as well as between sinners and the righteous found concrete expression in the rules governing table fellowship.[24] Jesus relativized the purity laws by teaching that "Nothing that enters one from outside can defile that person; but the things that come out from within are what defile" (Mark 7:15). His table fellowship had implications for sinners.

Meals with Jesus were joyous occasions; Schillebeeckx says that it was impossible for his disciples to be sad in his presence; they did not fast, even though the Pharisees criticized them for this (Mark 2:18-22).[25] But he received much greater criticism for associating with "tax collectors and sinners," those considered outside the Law by the religious authorities; this is a constant in the Gospels (Luke 7:34; 15:2). In this way Jesus proclaimed in sign the participation of all in the reign of God. God's reign is inclusive; no one is excluded. Meyer points out that Jesus' openness to sinners did not mean that he acquiesced in their sins. But he did reverse the normal pattern, first conversion, then communion. His offer of communion with sinners triggered repentance; thus "conversion flowered from communion."[26]

The Kingdom of God As Future

But if the reign of God is a present reality in Jesus' ministry, there is also clearly a future dimension to it. In the Our Father, the disciples are to pray, "thy kingdom come" (Matt 6:10; Luke 11:2); this expresses in a more abstract phrase the eschatological hope that "God would come on the last day to save and restore his people Israel."[27] The sayings about the Son of Man coming in judgment also underline the future dimension of God's reign. Even if some of these have been reshaped by the post-Easter community, there is general agreement that Jesus spoke about the Son of Man's role in the coming judgment (Luke 12:8-9; Mark 8:38; 13:26-27; Matt 25:31-32). The parables of the kingdom—the farmer and the seed, the mustard seed, the yeast kneaded in the flour, the buried treasure, the lost pearl, the net cast into the sea (Matt 13:1-53)—bring both the present and the future aspects of the reign of God to light.

---

[24] Meyer, *Aims*, 159.

[25] Edward Schillebeeckx, *Jesus: An Experiment in Christology* (New York: Seabury, 1979) 201.

[26] Meyer, *Aims*, 161.

[27] Meier, *A Marginal Jew*, II:299.

After examining the sayings of Jesus on the kingdom of God from a variety of sources (Q, M, and indirectly John and the material special to Luke) and different literary forms, Meier concludes the following: "Across all these strands and forms of the Jesus tradition one point was constantly confirmed: Jesus did understand the central symbol of the kingdom of God in terms of the definitive coming of God in the near future to bring the present state of things to an end and to establish his full and unimpeded rule over the world in general and Israel in particular."[28] Though beyond our focus here, the future dimension of the reign of God takes on new meaning and importance after the resurrection of Jesus.

3. *Call for an Immediate Response*

A third point to notice about Jesus' preaching of the reign of God is that he calls for an immediate response. In Mark, his message is summarized as "repent, and believe in the gospel" (Mark 1:15). The English word "repent," used in the NAB, has the connotation of being sorry for one's sins. But the Greek *metanoeite* suggests much more. It means to think again, to change one's heart, one's mind, one's way of life, to assume a new standpoint. One desiring to enter the kingdom must become like a little child (Mark 10:15; Matt 18:3; Luke 18:17). This image is radicalized in John's Gospel; Jesus says to Nicodemus that "no one can see the kingdom of God without being born from above" (John 3:3). While the context in John's Gospel suggests a baptismal rebirth in water and the Spirit (John 3:5), Evangelical Christianity sees here a positive requirement that a person must be "born again." The Gospels present numerous stories of men and women whose lives were radically changed by meeting Jesus, among them the disciples, the Twelve, Peter, Mary Magdalene, the Samaritan woman, Zacchaeus, and Levi.

The conversion Jesus calls for means more than a sorrow for sins. His sayings and parables bring out the magnitude of the decision and the radical nature of the conversion itself. The parables of the treasure buried in the field and the pearl of great price compare the news of the reign of God to a discovery of something of such great value that a person gladly gives up everything in order to possess it (Matt 12:44-46). Nothing is worth more. The parable of the wedding feast stresses that the invitation is urgent (Matt 22:1-14), while that of the talents teaches in a practical way the need for immediate action (Matt 25:14-30).

---

[28] Meier, *A Marginal Jew*, II:349.

4. *Relation between the Kingdom and Jesus*

A fourth point concerns the relation between the reign of God and Jesus himself. The Synoptic Gospels do not represent Jesus as saying much about himself, unlike John where Jesus is the center of his preaching. Nevertheless, scholars are generally agreed that Jesus' preaching was not just the Good News of God's reign; it also included the warning of an immanent judgment on those who failed to heed his words. N. T. Wright insists that Jesus "constructed his mindset, his variation on the Jewish worldview of his day, on the assumption that he was living in, and putting into operation, the controlling story which the scriptures offered him, which was now reaching its climax."[29] James Dunn argues that the Jesus tradition consistently affirms the eschatological finality of Jesus' mission (Matt 11:5f./Luke 7:22f.; Matt 13:16f./Luke 10:23f.; Matt 12:41f./Luke 11:31f.; Luke 12:54-56).[30] This theme is clearly present in the Q tradition.[31] The sayings about the role of the Son of Man as judge are particularly significant. While many Son of Man sayings have been reshaped by the early Christian communities, many scholars regard the statement in Mark 8:38 as substantially authentic: "Whoever is ashamed of me and of my words in this faithless and sinful generation, the Son of Man will be ashamed of when he comes in his Father's glory with the holy angels" (cf. Luke 12:8-9). Regardless of whether or not Jesus identifies himself here with the Son of Man, as Kasper observes, the effect is the same. A decision for or against Jesus is the same as a decision for or against the reign of God.[32]

Thus Jesus' preaching of the reign of God cannot be reduced to some universal message of the unconditional love of God, to a modern egalitarianism, or to any other interpretation which separates the messenger from the message. There is an incredible claim to authority that emerges in his preaching and ministry, an implicit Christology. To encounter Jesus is to encounter God's reign. His preaching and parables, healings and exorcisms, table fellowship and proclamation of the forgiveness of sins, the new family of disciples built around the Twelve, all this is evidence that in his work and ministry God's saving power is present to Israel in a new and definitive way.

---

[29] Wright, *JVG*, 593; for his list of judgment sayings, see 183–84.

[30] James D. G. Dunn, *Christology in the Making: A New Testament Inquiry into the Origins of the Doctrine of the Incarnation* (Philadelphia: Westminster, 1980) 85.

[31] Earl Richard, *Jesus: One and Many: The Christological Concept of the New Testament Authors* (Wilmington, Del.: Michael Glazier, 1988) 92–94.

[32] Kasper, *Jesus the Christ*, 108–09.

Reinterpreting the Kingdom

The death and resurrection of Jesus transformed the disciples' understanding of the reign of God that Jesus preached. Paul sometimes describes it as present: "the kingdom of God is not a matter of food and drink, but of righteousness, peace, and joy in the holy Spirit" (Rom 14:17). But most often his emphasis falls on the eschatological future, on the immoral and unjust not inheriting the kingdom (1 Cor 6:9-10; Gal 5:21). John refers twice to the kingdom (John 3:3, 5). More frequently he uses "eternal life" to express salvation in Jesus, and again it is both present and future (John 6:54).

The Christian community needs to express the Good News of God's reign in every age. At times the kingdom of God has been improperly identified with the Church. At the same time, overemphasis on the kingdom as realized or present risks turning it into an ideology, identifying it with an ideal political or social order. The Second Vatican Council maintained the tension evident in Jesus' preaching; it taught that the Church receives the mission to proclaim and establish the kingdom, while the Church itself represents its initial budding forth on earth (LG 5).

Contemporary expressions of the kingdom stress God's presence and action becoming manifested in Christ-like compassion and service of others. For Michael Cook, the kingdom "is Jesus' comprehensive term for the blessing of salvation insofar as it denotes the divine activity at the center of all human life," while faith "is his human, experiential term for salvation itself insofar as it denotes the human response, universally valid, of openness, acceptance, and commitment."[33] Albert Nolan sees the kingdom as one of love and service which reveals God as a God of compassion, for it is human compassion which "releases God's power in the world, the only power that can bring about the miracle of the kingdom."[34] For Elisabeth Schüssler Fiorenza, the reign of God is being realized wherever people are being healed, set free from oppression or dehumanizing power systems, and made whole.[35]

A Note on the Miracle Tradition

Most mainstream scholars do not dispute that Jesus was known as a healer and exorcist. According to John P. Meier, "the statement that Jesus

[33] Michael L. Cook, *The Jesus of Faith* (New York: Paulist, 1981) 56–57.
[34] Albert Nolan, *Jesus Before Christianity* (Maryknoll, New York: Orbis, 1978) 84.
[35] Elisabeth Schüssler Fiorenza, *In Memory of Her: A Feminist Reconstruction of Christian Origins* (New York: Crossroad, 1985) 123.

acted as and was viewed as an exorcist and healer during his public minis- try has as much historical corroboration as almost any other statement we can make about the Jesus of history."[36] It is certainly confirmed by the cri- terion of multiple attestation of sources.

However, the so-called "nature miracles," for example, his changing water into wine at Cana, are more complicated. Like many scholars, Meier sees them as creations of the early Church, though he argues that the tra- dition of Jesus raising the dead goes back to some event in Jesus' ministry. He offers a similar argument for the story of the feeding of the multitude.[37] Walter Kasper, while acknowledging the historical core of the tradition of healings and exorcisms, calls the nature miracles "secondary accretions to the original tradition" and thus probably legendary.[38]

How the miracles are to be interpreted is another question.[39] There are two extremes to avoid. One would be the "supernaturalist" or precritical approach that sees miracles as displays of divine power suspending or con- travening the laws of nature. This approach has tended to interpret miracles apologetically. Jesus healed the sick and changed water into wine; therefore he is the Son of God. There are two problems with this approach. First, in defining miracles as divine interventions from "outside," it assumes a God who does not honor the causality of the created order. Such a God would be arbitrary and could equally be held accountable for natural disasters and historical horrors such as the Holocaust. As Kasper says, "If God is to remain God, even his miracles must be thought of as mediated by created secondary causes."[40] Secondly, a divine intervention that overpowered the causality of the created order would compel belief. This would violate the principle that God never violates our human freedom, for in such cases, belief would not be a free response to grace.

At the other extreme, many critical theologians approach Jesus' miracles from the perspective of their original biblical meaning. Kasper notes that the biblical authors do not use the ancient term, *terata*, which implies the miraculous or extraordinary. Instead the Synoptics speak of Jesus' miracles as "acts of power" (*dunameis*); John calls them "signs" (*sēmeia*). In a pre- scientific age, the unexpected is always seen as an act of God. Earthquakes are "acts of God," not the result of tectonic tensions and seismic shifts. It is true that biblical miracles presume and deepen faith. Yet this approach of

---

[36] Meier, *A Marginal Jew*, II:970.

[37] Ibid.

[38] Walter Kasper, *Jesus the Christ*, 90.

[39] I am indebted here to Kasper's analysis, pp. 91–95, though I have expanded it.

[40] Kasper, *Jesus the Christ*, 92.

many critical scholars is ultimately reductive in that it does not acknowledge anything really new. The miracles of Jesus effect a change only in the level of interpretation, not in reality itself.

Kasper's solution to the dilemma of interpreting the Gospel miracles is to move beyond an understanding of science on the basis of particular events, observable facts, and physical causality. He suggests moving to a higher viewpoint, which raises the question of meaning, not of particular events but of reality as a whole. He rejects a deterministic worldview that allows no room for novelty, for "an all determining freedom which we call God." Rejected too is a deism which reduces God to a cosmic architect, no longer active in creation or simply sustaining all things. Instead he proposes the biblical view, a living God in history "who in constantly original ways offers his love to human beings in and through the events of the world."[41] Such a view denies neither the autonomy of creation nor the initiative of the creator. In recognizing a God who acts in and through creation, it also safeguards the role of human freedom, since a miracle can only be recognized in faith and never forces it. Others may not recognize the miracle at all.

Conclusion

Jesus' preaching, with his stress on struggle, conflict, and a final reversal of status that made the last first and the first last, was often unsettling to his hearers. His parables forced them to look at their world and their values in a new way. There was clearly a warning of eschatological judgment for those who disregarded his teaching.

But there was also a joyful element in what he proclaimed. The God of Jesus was a God of compassion who forgave sinners and declared the poor blessed. Like Jesus, his disciples also could address God as "Abba." If God's kingdom had a future dimension, it was also present in Jesus' ministry. His parables proclaimed that God's reign was already active in the world. His exorcisms and healings, his proclamation of the forgiveness of sins, and his table fellowship showed God's saving power transforming the lives of the troubled, the sick, and the alienated, the tax collectors and sinners.

The core of the miracle tradition cannot be denied. Jesus healed the sick and performed exorcisms. If the miracles of Jesus do not compel faith, they presuppose it. It is that openness to the transcendent God at the heart of faith that enables the one healed to recognize God working in and through the ministry of Jesus.

[41] Ibid., 94.

Chapter 6

The Death of Jesus

In the chapel of an ecumenical community of religious women in Switzerland there is a large crucifix unlike any other I've seen. Looking like a figure sculpted by the Swiss artist Alberto Giacometti, it is actually the work of a Central American who was himself tortured. It portrays a man *in extremis*. He is naked, vulnerable, exposed to the world. The face is a rictus of pain. Some find it too much, a sign of despair rather than hope. It is Jesus in his agony.

Jesus' public ministry was brief, perhaps little more than a year, though according to John it was longer. After some time spent preaching in Galilee, he turned towards Jerusalem, the capital, center of the Jewish community with its Temple and its religious leadership. While the early communities have obviously shaped the various predictions of the Passion in the Gospels, Jesus' ministry early on generated opposition from the religious authorities and would have led him to realize that his course of action might well cost him his life. He had not only the fate of the prophets to consider; the death of John the Baptist, given their earlier association, was much closer to home. It would certainly have made an impression on him. From this perspective, his final journey to Jerusalem could not have been made without a suspicion of its ultimate consequences. Once there, he apparently had some confrontation with the authorities. The Gospels speak of a final meal with his disciples and of his death. After a hearing before the representatives of the Sanhedrin, the governing Jewish religious assembly, he was crucified by the Romans, a brutal form of capital punishment reserved for slaves, criminals and those who rebelled against imperial authority.

Why did he die? Were the Roman authorities or the Jewish leaders responsible? Was there a political reason for his death? Was his offense religious? He must have done something that enraged some powerful group or groups in Jerusalem. As we saw earlier, the criterion of rejection presumes that there must have been some significant cause, some offense in the words or deeds of Jesus that led to his death. He was not humiliated and executed merely for proclaiming the compassionate love of God. And there are other questions. How did he understand his death? Did God ask it of him? How did he see his own destiny?

Thus the death of Jesus raises a host of questions, some historical, others theological and personal. In this chapter we will approach the death of Jesus first from a historical perspective; what was the offense that led to his death? Then we must ask, how did the early Christian communities interpret the death of Jesus from a theological perspective? Finally, we will try to approach it from a personal perspective. Can we pierce the veil of time and text, to gain any insight into how Jesus himself saw his death?

The Offense Behind Jesus' Death

So what offense lies behind the death of Jesus? The first account of his passion and death appears in the Gospel of Mark; indeed, scholars judge it to be the oldest part of Mark's narrative. Mark reports a number of accusations against Jesus. At his hearing before the Sanhedrin, those who gave witness against Jesus alleged that he had said, "I will destroy this temple made with hands and within three days I will build another not made with hands" (Mark 14:58). The high priest accused him of blasphemy for claiming to be "the Messiah, the son of the Blessed One" (Mark 14:62). Others mock him, saying "prophesy" (Mark 14:65), implying that he claimed to be a prophet. At his trial before the Roman procurator, Pilate asked him, "Are you the king of the Jews?" (Mark 15:2) and the soldiers mocked him, using this title (Mark 15:18). So a number of charges emerge—a threat to destroy the Temple, blasphemy, the accusation of being a false prophet, and messianic pretensions—which obviously would have been perceived as a threat to the Roman occupiers. The charges are both religious and political. But how to sort out New Testament theology from the history that lies behind the death of Jesus?

I have always been fascinated by the strange accusation in Mark's Passion narrative that Jesus claimed that he would destroy the Temple "made with hands" and build another, "not made with hands" (Mark 14:58). While Mark stresses that the witnesses testified falsely and that their testimonies did not agree, the fact that he shows the passersby at the crucifixion repeating the charge that he would destroy the Temple (Mark 15:29) suggests that Mark did not consider the saying itself to be false. Matthew follows Mark in this (Matt 26:61; 27:40). Luke omits this charge at Jesus' hearing before the Sanhedrin, though he includes it in his story of Stephen's trial (Acts 6:14). John places a variant of it within the story of Jesus cleansing the Temple (John 2:20).

The story of this provocative Temple action is told in all four Gospels, though John places it early in the ministry, rather than at the end as in the Synoptics (Mark 11:15-16; Matt 21:12-13; Luke 19:45-46). Too often it has been interpreted as righteous anger on the part of Jesus over commerce in the sacred precincts, or in some more recent commentaries, as protest against the Jewish purity system.[1] But against the background of Mark's making Jesus' saying about destroying the Temple (literally "sanctuary") the charge at his trial, John's linking Jesus' Temple action with a similar saying about its destruction is significant, as it suggests that there may have been a connection between the Temple action and his death.

Indeed, this seems to have been the case. N. T. Wright states that "One of the chief gains of the last twenty years of Jesus-research is that the question of Jesus and the Temple is back where it belongs, at the centre of the agenda." He says that most scholars now agree that Jesus performed a dramatic action in the Temple, and that this was one of the main reasons for his execution.[2]

Wright's argument can be summarized as follows: he views the Temple action not as a dispute over economic exploitation or purity rules. Jesus' action was aimed, not at cleansing the Temple, but rather at symbolizing its destruction. To drive out the moneychangers and the traders was to cut off the supply of animals needed for sacrifice in the Temple, and thus, at least temporarily, to close down its cult. This was to strike against the very existence of the Temple as the central religious institution of Judaism.[3] Wright sees Jesus' action as "an acted parable of judgment":

> virtually all the traditions, inside and outside the canonical gospels, which speak of Jesus and the Temple speak of its destruction. Mark's fig-tree incident; Luke's picture of Jesus weeping over Jerusalem; John's saying about destruction and rebuilding; the synoptic traditions of the false witness and their accusation, and of the mocking at the foot of the cross; *Thomas'* cryptic saying ('I will destroy this house, and no-one will be able to rebuild it'); the charge in Acts that Jesus would destroy the Temple: all these speak clearly enough, not of cleansing or reform, but of destruction.[4]

---

[1] Cf. Marcus J. Borg, *Meeting Jesus Again for the First Time* (HarperSanFrancisco, 1995) 55.

[2] N. T. Wright, *Jesus and the Victory of God* (Minneapolis: Fortress, 1996) 405; cf. 370; see also Walter Kasper, *Jesus the Christ* (New York: Paulist, 1976) 117; Raymond E. Brown, *The Death of the Messiah*, Vol. I (New York: Doubleday, 1994) 460.

[3] Wright, *JVG*, 423.

[4] Ibid., 416; the Thomas reference is to the Gnostic gospel by that name.

Wright concludes that Jesus' Temple action was a judgment, both symbolic and prophetic, enacted upon the Temple in word and in action. "The Temple, as the central symbol of the whole national life, was under divine threat, and, unless Israel repented, it would fall to the pagans."[5] This of course was too much for the religious authorities in Jerusalem. They saw Jesus as challenging not just the most important symbol of Jewish life, but their own authority as well, based as it was on the Temple cult. They had to conspire against him.

I find Wright's interpretation of the causes for Jesus' death quite persuasive.[6] Wright argues throughout his book that Jesus was a latter day prophet who understood his own mission in terms of the religious tradition of which he was a part. Announcing the end of the present age, he rejected the turn to violence against the Romans as a way of restoring Israel, saying that those who took the sword would perish by the sword. Instead, his proclamation of the coming of the kingdom of God presumed a reconstruction of Israel, without a future role for the Temple.[7] Though more cautious, Raymond Brown takes a similar position. He assigns a high historical probability that something Jesus did or said about the destruction of the Temple was at least a partial cause of the Sanhedrin's decision that led to his death.[8]

The crucifixion was a shattering event for the disciples. It is quite possible that many of them, fearful for their own lives, fled Jerusalem; many of the Easter stories suggest a Galilean venue for the appearances. Though the experience of the risen Jesus restored their shattered faith and brought them together again, the manner of Jesus' death remained a scandal for the disciples. Crucifixion was capital punishment, it was for slaves, criminals, and those guilty of rebellion. In addition, from a religious perspective, Jesus had incurred the judgment proclaimed in Deuteronomy: "God's curse rests on him who hangs on a tree" (Deut 21:23). This again put the disciples at risk, as the followers of one cursed by the manner of his death.

---

[5] Ibid., 417.

[6] Ben Witherington III observes that Wright has "an advantage over many other Jesus questers in that he gives full historical weight to the importance of the last week of Jesus' life in understanding who he was"; "The Jesus Quest and the Christology of Jesus," *The Christian Century* (November 19–26, 1997) 1076.

[7] Wright, *JVG*, 593–95.

[8] Brown, *The Death of the Messiah*, Vol. I, 459–60.

Theological Perspectives

To deal with the stunning shame of Jesus' death and their own embarrassment, the followers of Jesus drew on their own Jewish background, using metaphors, motifs, and symbolic figures from the Hebrew Scriptures even before the earliest Christian writings appeared. How to explain the suffering of Jesus, his tragic and seemingly meaningless death? The tradition of the prophets, those spirit-filled individuals who proclaimed Yahweh's Word to often hostile communities, frequently suffering rejection and even death, had long been familiar to the Jews. It was still current in Jesus' time, most recently, in the fate of John the Baptist. The figure of the just one, the righteous sufferer in the Wisdom tradition who looked to Yahweh for vindication, was another. Finally, even before Paul, another current took a soteriological perspective, seeing Jesus' death as a redemptive, atoning sacrifice. We will consider these briefly.[9]

The Rejected Prophet

A number of texts, appearing in both the Gospel of Luke and the Acts of the Apostles but drawing on early, pre-Lukan tradition, reflect controversies in the primitive community between the Jewish community and the Jewish followers of Jesus. These texts compare Jesus and his persecuted followers with the prophets rejected by Israel (1 Thess 2:15-16; Luke 11:49-51; cf. Luke 6:22-23; Acts 7:51-53). This theme is found in Paul, in Q, and in Mark. Other texts, building on the Jewish theme of the martyrdom of the prophets, contrast Jesus' death at the hands of the Jewish authorities with his exaltation by God. For example, in Acts 4:10 Peter says: "Jesus Christ the Nazorean whom you crucified, whom God raised from the dead." The contrast here is between Jesus, the prophet rejected by Israel in the person of its leaders and God's action in vindicating him (see also Acts 2:22-24; 5:30-31; 10:40).

The theme of Israel killing its prophets, while usually more symbolic than historical, is frequently mentioned in the New Testament. Yet it appears also in Nehemiah 9:26, where it is a more radical expression of a much older tradition, namely, Israel's bringing God's judgment on itself by refusing to heed the prophets' call to repentance and conversion (2 Chr 36; Ezra 9:10-11; 2 Kings 17:7-20).

---

[9] See Edward Schillebeeckx, *Jesus: An Experiment in Christology* (New York: Seabury, 1979) 274–94; also Marinus de Jonge, *God's Final Envoy: Early Christology and Jesus' Own View of His Mission* (Grand Rapids, Mich.: Wm. B. Eerdmans, 1998) 14–33.

The question over the authority of Jesus verses that of the religious authorities of his day is still very evident in the Gospels. Against the traditional view of the prophets, for those Jews still doubtful about Jesus' prophetic authority, the resurrection represents his vindication: "Therefore let the whole house of Israel know for certain that God has made him both Lord and Messiah, this Jesus whom you crucified" (Acts 2:36). But note; in this very early tradition there is no salvific value attached to Jesus' death by itself.[10]

The Suffering Righteous One

Another motif which helped the earliest Christians deal with the shame of Jesus' death was that of the suffering righteous one. This motif too has ancient roots, going back first to the king oppressed by his enemies and also to the prophets so often misunderstood and persecuted. But it is through the psalms[11] and particularly the Wisdom tradition that the theme of the suffering of the righteous became popular in late Judaism. Here the book of Wisdom played a central role. In it, the wicked plot against the just one, offended by his reproaches and his claim that God is his Father, putting him to the test to see if God will defend him, unaware of God's designs (Wis 2:10-22; cf. 5:1-7; cf. Matt 27:39-43). But the theme is also present in Daniel in the stories of the three young men in the fiery furnace (Dan 3) and of Daniel in the lions' den (Dan 6). The story of the falsely accused Susanna in (deuterocanonical) Daniel 13 is another example. By this time, under the influence of the apocalyptic tradition, the themes of the suffering of the just as well as that of martyrdom (Dan 11:33-35) are often combined with that of their vindication by God through the resurrection of the dead (Wis 5:1-7). Thus, a new theme emerges, that of God's final intervention in the affairs of the world.

Schillebeeckx finds traces of the theme of the suffering of the righteous man in the primitive form of the Markan Passion narrative, with allusions to the psalms, the third Servant Song (Isa 50:4-9), and Wisdom 2. "One could say that the primitive form of the Passion story was governed in its conception by the theme of the 'suffering righteous one,' but that even in the Marcan redaction and yet more obviously in Matthew and Luke this motif has moved into the background."[12] Again he points out that in this earliest stage of the Passion narrative, there is no allusion to Isaiah 53, ar-

---

[10] Schillebeeckx, *Jesus*, 275, 282; also de Jonge, *God's Final Envoy*, 17.

[11] Cf. Ps 7:4-10; Pss 22, 25 31, 34, 37, 119.

[12] Schillebeeckx, *Jesus*, 290.

guing against a sense that the suffering and death of Jesus had salvific value. He calls this the "salvation history" scheme of interpretation, a divine plan of salvation discerned through a meditation on Scripture (Luke 24:26; 24:44-46).[13]

A Redemptive Death

A third theme sees Jesus' death as a redemptive sacrifice that atones for sins. This soteriological theme, recognized by the Greek *huper* formula, "for us" or "for our sins," occurs frequently in the New Testament documents. It is present in the pre-Pauline kerygma of 1 Cor 15:3b-5, in Gal 1:4; Rom 4:25; 5:8; 8:32; Eph 5:2; in the cup words in the Last Supper accounts, in the "ransom for many" passage in Mark 10:45; and in 1 Pet 2:21-24. It becomes the governing theme in Paul's Christology, as well as in Hebrews, the Deutero-Pauline letters, John, and the Apocalypse. Marinus de Jonge compares this early Christian interpretation of the death of Jesus to the stories of the martyrs in Maccabees, Eleazar in 2 Macc 6:18-31 and the seven brothers and their mother in 2 Macc 7 whose death for the Law brings about a decisive change for Israel. He finds agreement in terminology (for example, 2 Macc 7:33, 37-38 and Rom 5:6-11), but in Maccabees the eschatological element present in the death of Jesus is missing.[14]

Schillebeeckx argues that in the pre-Synoptic as well as the pre-Pauline material, these "for us" formulae are more sparse. But after a careful analysis, he concludes that the soteriological formulae form "a very old and self-contained complex of tradition, the emergence of which cannot be accounted for either by secondary deduction from other interpretations of Jesus' death or by referring it to Jewish theologies of the martyr's vicarious suffering."[15] At this point he asks, might it be rooted in something Jesus said or did himself in those final days before his death. We will consider this below.

The Stone Rejected by the Builders

A final motif. We saw at the beginning of this chapter that the historical offense behind the death of Jesus was most probably his action in the Temple. An interpretation of the rejection and death of Jesus based on that incident in some ways pulls together some of the themes we have just considered.

[13] Ibid., 291.
[14] De Jonge, *Early Christology*, 26–29.
[15] Schillebeeckx, *Jesus*, 293.

Mark follows his account of the cleansing of the Temple (Mark 11:15-19) with the story of the withered fig tree (Mark 11:20-25), questions about Jesus' authority (Mark 11:27-33), and the parable of the tenants (Mark 12:1-12). Each of these accounts serves as further commentary on the Temple incident. The Temple action is "sandwiched" into the story about Jesus cursing the fig tree. Taken by itself, the story makes little sense; it is the only *destructive* miracle of Jesus. Its meaning emerges only in the context on the Temple action. N. T. Wright notes that scholars today generally accept the story as "an acted parable of an acted parable."[16] Jesus comes to both the fig tree and the Temple seeking fruit, and finds none. What he does to the fig tree is a parable of what will happen to the Temple; both will be destroyed. There is a clear parallel here to Jeremiah's famous "Temple of the Lord" passage, in which he asks in the Lord's name, "Has this house which bears my name become in your eyes a den of thieves?" (Jer 7:11; cf. Mark 11:17). Then, just a few verses later, Jeremiah in Yahweh's name rebukes Israel for her disobedience:

> I will gather them all in, says the LORD:
> > no grapes on the vine,
> No figs on the fig trees,
> > foliage withered! (Jer 8:13).

Both stories, Jeremiah's Temple sermon and Mark's story of the cleansing, juxtapose the Temple as a "den of thieves" with the image of a barren fig tree.

Mark follows the fig tree parable with the parable of the tenants and the vineyard another symbol of Israel, based on Isaiah's "Song of the Vineyard," in which the owner, God, comes looking for fruit and finds only wild grapes (Isa 5:4). At the end of the parable of the tenants, after asking what the owner of the vineyard will do to the tenants after they have abused his servants and killed his son, Jesus says that he will put the tenants to death, and give the vineyard to others (Mark 11:9). Then he asks the religious leaders who have questioned his authority, whether they have read this Scripture passage:

> The stone that the builders rejected
> > has become the cornerstone;
> by the Lord has this been done,
> > and it is wonderful in our eyes (Mark 12:10-11).

The quotation here is from Psalm 118:22-23. The psalm was used in the Temple liturgy, sung as king and people processed into the Temple precincts.

---

[16] Wright, *JVG*, 421.

The verse about the stone rejected by the builders was most probably an ancient proverb; someone thought to be insignificant has triumphed through divine election. Here it is Jesus rejected by Israel's leaders who has become the basis of the new, eschatological Temple. There may well be a play on words between this saying and the parable; "stone" is *eben* in Hebrew, while the rejected "son" in the parable is *ben*.

Many commentators see a link between this quotation of Psalm 118:22-23 and Isaiah 28:16, in which Yahweh says,

> See, I am laying a stone in Zion,
> a stone that has been tested,
> A precious cornerstone as a sure foundation.

The New Testament writers clearly saw the connection between Jesus, the rejected son who became the new foundation of God's people and the stone rejected by the builders in Psalm 118:22; in addition to the Synoptics, the text from Psalm 118 is applied to Jesus in Acts 4:11 and in 1 Peter 2:7. In 1 Peter it is used to argue that the community itself is a new spiritual building built of living stones, a spiritual house and a holy priesthood (1 Pet 2:5), with Christ as the cornerstone, as well as a stumbling block for those who don't believe. The author of 1 Peter quotes Isaiah 28:16 about Yahweh laying a stone in Zion (a variant of this tradition appears in Rom 9:33) as well as Isaiah 8:14, which says that Yahweh "shall be a snare, an obstacle and a stumbling stone to both the houses of Israel." In other words, Jesus is the foundation of the new Temple, the new people of God, as well as the sign of contradiction, the stone on which many would fall.

But where does this interpretation originate? Does it represent an effort on the part of early Church to deal with Jesus' rejection and death? Or does it go back to Jesus himself? Wright believes that it does,[17] though other scholars are less certain. It remains difficult, if not impossible, to give a definite answer to this question. However, as it became increasingly clear that his ministry would cost him his life, we must ask, how did Jesus understand his death?

How Did Jesus Understand His Death?

For all his insight into what led to the death of Jesus, N. T. Wright may attribute more to his self-understanding than a critical reading of the sources will allow. He says that Jesus died because, ultimately, "he believed

---

[17] Wright, *JVC*, 499–501.

that it was his vocation,"[18] that on the basis of his reading of Daniel, Zechariah, and the Psalms, particularly Psalms 110 and 118, he came to see that God's kingdom would come through the true king sharing in the suffering of the people.[19] Wright does not doubt that Jesus was conscious of a messianic role, shaped by his pondering these passages and others such as Isaiah 40–55.

But Wright is not the only scholar to argue that Jesus saw meaning in his death, that he accepted it freely, and that he understood it as part of his ministry. Both Walter Kasper and Edward Schillebeeckx take similar positions. What is interesting is that both scholars find an expression of Jesus' sense of his death as a completion of his life in the story of the Last Supper.

The Last Supper

Schillebeeckx makes the case that a number of texts speaking of Jesus as a servant "appear to have an intrinsic connection with something that happened at the Last Supper shortly before Jesus' death."[20] He considers four texts: Mark 10:45 and Luke 22:27 as well as Luke 12:37b and John 13:1-20. We will consider each text briefly.

1. For the Son of Man did not come to be served but to serve
   and to give his life as a ransom for many (Mark 10:45).

This text establishes a connection between Jesus' life of service (*diakonia*) and his expiatory death. The Greek verb *diakonein* in secular Greek meant waiting at table, though in Hellenistic Jewry it was used for all types of service. In the Hellenistic Jewish-Christian and Pauline Gentile-Christian churches it took on a Christian, ecclesial connotation. What is important here in Mark's usage is that two themes, Jesus' life as service, using the secular Greek sense of *diakonia*, and what Mark sees as the expiatory meaning of his death, owe their combination to the Last Supper tradition. It was from this locus, Schillebeeckx argues, that *diakonia* took on a new meaning of Christian, ecclesial service or ministry (303–04).

2. For who is greater: the one seated at table or the one who serves? Is it
   not the one seated at table? I am among you as the one who serves (Luke
   22:27).

---

[18] Ibid., 593.
[19] Ibid., 601.
[20] Schillebeeckx, *Jesus*, 303.

In this second text on *diakonia*, the shift to an ecclesial, ministerial sense of service has already occurred. Luke places it in the context of the Last Supper, to show that Jesus' example of service is "a model for those who hold office in the Church, 'the disciples', and a guide for the conduct of the local church leaders when celebrating the supper of the Lord" (304). But by placing the text in close proximity to 22:15-20, his account of Jesus identifying the bread and wine with his Body and Blood offered "for you" (vv. 19-20), Luke makes the same connection between Jesus' service and the meaning of his death that we saw in the previous text (Mark 10:45).

3. "Amen, I say to you, he will gird himself, have them recline
   at table, and proceed to wait on them" (Luke 12:37b).
Luke 12:37b is part of a *parousia* parable which shows an identity between the earthly Jesus and the Jesus who is to come on the Last Day. The heavenly meal associated with the Parousia, the eschatological or messianic banquet, is in continuity with the service performed by the earthly Jesus. The text presupposes the tradition of the foot-washing.

4. The Johannine Foot Washing (John 13:1-20). John's story of Jesus washing the feet of his disciples at the Last Supper is the last of the *diakonia* texts. Again the approaching death of Jesus is seen as a service through which his disciples enter into a new covenant or fellowship with him. Schillebeeckx' conclusion is that the salvific interpretation of the death of Jesus is not some secondary development, but is rooted in the way the early Christian churches understood the Last Supper. "The Last Supper tradition, therefore, is the oldest starting-point for the Christian interpretation of Jesus' death as a self-giving on Jesus' part that procures salvation." Then he asks the crucial question: "Did the earthly Jesus himself envisage his death as a 'service performed out of love' and hint at all at this meaning of his death while still living on earth?" (306).

Did Jesus See Salvific Meaning in His Death?

While Jesus did not seek his own death, his determination to bring his message to Jerusalem, no matter the cost, is evidence that he did not let the fear of death deter him from his mission. Schillebeeckx argues that Jesus would have had to confront the meaning of his death in light of his message. And granting that the passion predictions are composed in light of the Easter event, he must have said something to prepare his disciples for the shock of his death (307). Walter Kasper says that "Jesus thought of his death in relation to his message of the coming of the Kingdom of God."[21] To see *how* Jesus thought about his death, both scholars turn to a closer examination of the story of the Last Supper.

Both Kasper and Schillebeeckx recognize that the words of Jesus over the bread and the cup at the Last Supper are heavily colored by the later liturgical tradition of the early Christian communities. But both call attention to a strange saying in the midst of the institution narratives: Jesus says, "Amen, I say to you, I shall not drink again the fruit of the vine until the day when I drink it new in the kingdom of God" (Mark 14:25; cf. Luke 22:16-18). This saying, promising a renewed fellowship with the disciples even in the face of his approaching death, must go back to Jesus himself. Kasper notes that the saying does not reflect the later liturgy and therefore must be authentic.[22] Schillebeeckx says that it states "in a more precise and explicit form" Jesus' promise of a fellowship renewed in the kingdom of God, made in the context of his announcement of his imminent death.[23]

Thus there is evidence that Jesus told his disciples that in spite of his death, or even more, through his death, God's reign would come about. In the very face of death, he offered his disciples a cup of blessing, promising them a renewed fellowship with himself on the other side of death. In Schillebeeckx's words, "Jesus felt his death to be (in some way or other) part and parcel of the salvation-offered-by-God, as a historical consequence of his caring and loving service of and solidarity with people. This is the very least—albeit certain—thing about the 'institution narrative' and the account of the Passion that we are bound to hang on to as a historical core."[24] In later theological terms, Jesus' death would be recognized as a sacrifice, even if he does not say this explicitly, and the renewed fellowship with him he promises would be seen as an eschatological blessing. But from a historical-critical perspective, it is important to note that the saying about drinking again in the kingdom of God comes from the first level of the Gospel tradition, from the words of Jesus himself. His death was tied in with his mission. "There is no gap between Jesus' self-understanding and the Christ proclaimed by the Church."[25]

---

[21] Walter Kasper, *Jesus the Christ*, 120.

[22] Ibid., 117.

[23] Schillebeeckx, *Jesus*, 308.

[24] Ibid., 310.

[25] Ibid., 312.

How Did Jesus See His Own Destiny?

A final question remains. How did Jesus see his own destiny? Did he look forward to the end of the world, as Schweitzer has suggested? Did he anticipate his own resurrection?

It is very difficult to enter into the psychology of another person, even those we know personally. How much more impossible is it for us to enter into the psychology of Jesus. The New Testament evidence is very sparse, and its complexity makes speculation very difficult. As we saw in the last section, we can gain some insight into Jesus' self-understanding, based on a careful reading of the texts. But there is still much that remains mystery. Nevertheless, we can say something about the way Jesus faced his own destiny.

Since at least the time of the Maccabees, there had a current within Israel that cherished a hope for the resurrection of the dead. Jesus may have shared in this hope, as the debate with the Sadducees over the resurrection in the Synoptics suggests (Mark 12:18-27 and plls). But in Jewish thought the resurrection of the dead was an apocalyptic concept, associated with the resurrection of all the dead in the eschatological future (cf. Dan 12:1-3). There is no evidence of a belief in the resurrection of an individual, nor of resurrection apart from the apocalyptic context. N. T. Wright, throughout his book, argues that Jesus neither expected nor proclaimed the end of the space-time universe.[26] Then how did Jesus image his hope?

It is difficult for many Christians to grasp the full horror of Jesus' passion. Popular piety often fails to take the humanity of Jesus seriously. Many start from the belief that Jesus was God and therefore knew what would happen to him. Others put their emphasis on Jesus as a human person like ourselves, and approach his passion from this perspective. Perhaps we might gain some insight here by following a suggestion of Ignatius of Loyola. In his *Spiritual Exercises*, Ignatius invites the retreatant in the Third Week to consider how in the Passion "the divinity hides itself." What would that have meant for Jesus?

At the end, Jesus entered the dark night of the spirit. He found himself vulnerable and alone, deserted by his friends, abandoned even by his God. Mark tells us that on the cross he cried out, "My God, my God, why have you forsaken me?" (Mark 15:34). The saying comes from Psalm 22:2. Some see it as a cry of despair and abandonment. Others point out that the psalm ends with the confidence that Yahweh will hear the psalmist's prayer and give him new life; they say it represents an expression of hope.

---

[26] Cf. Wright, *JVG*, 594.

But the saying raises more questions than it answers. We do not know whether or not Jesus really spoke these words, let alone recited the psalm as he was dying. Unlike Matthew, Luke does not follow Mark in reporting it; he represents Jesus dying with the words, "Father, into your hands I commend my spirit" (Luke 23:46). John's account has a quiet solemnity; at the end, Jesus says simply, "It is finished," bows his head and dies (John 19:30).

It would not be false to say that Jesus in his agony experienced fully the absence of God that all of us feel at times in our lives, and that the dying so often seem to experience, even those of profound faith. Yet he did not despair. Kasper focuses on Jesus calling out to the God he called Father, but who withdraws in his very closeness. "Jesus experienced the unfathomable mystery of God and his will, but he endured this darkness in faith. This extremity of emptiness enabled him to become the vessel of God's fulness."[27]

Similarly, Schillebeeckx looks at Jesus' relationship to God in terms of what he calls his "*Abba* experience," the source and ground of his life and ministry.[28] Few debate today that Jesus called God Abba or that this usage was virtually unprecedented. Abba means "father." While it had long been used of earthly fathers in Jewish family life, its use in prayer to God was not to be found either in late Jewish devotional literature or in the rabbinical texts. It appears only once in the Gospels, in Mark 14:36. Still, there is a cautious agreement among scholars that Abba was an authentic word of Jesus himself, his ordinary form of address to God. It should be seen behind the Greek "the Father," "Father," or "my Father" in the Gospels.[29] The fact that the early Christians also called on God as "Abba" (Gal 4:6; Rom 8:15) suggests that this usage was one they learned from Jesus.

Yet the intimacy with God that Abba implies for Jesus seems to have been different from the experience of Jesus' disciples. The Gospels do not represent Jesus speaking of "our father," with the exception of Matthew 6:9/Luke 11:2 where Jesus instructs the disciples on how *they* should pray. Otherwise he says "my father" or "your father." This convention is present also in John's account of Jesus' appearance to Mary Madgalene, where the strange formulation appears, "I am going to my Father and your Father, to my God and your God" (John 20:17).[30] God is father of both Jesus and Mary, but not in the same way.

At the end of his massive study, N. T. Wright develops a nuanced answer to the question of Jesus' self-understanding. He suggests that Jesus had an

---

[27] Kasper, *Jesus the Christ*, 118–19.

[28] Schillebeeckx, *Jesus*, 256–71.

[29] Ibid., 260; see also Wright, *JVG*, 648–49.

[30] Kasper, *Jesus the Christ*, 109; Schillebeeckx, *Jesus*, 263.

awareness of his vocation, though something far different from what he calls a "supernatural" awareness of himself, or perhaps better, a knowledge that could be formulated conceptually. It was, he says, like knowing that he was loved. Yet Jesus was conscious of "a vocation, given him by the one he knew as 'father', to enact in himself what, in Israel's scriptures, God had promised to accomplish all by himself."[31] Wright's judgment here is a careful one; what we have already seen about Jesus proclaiming God's nearness to a renewed, eschatological Israel implies something quite similar.

Perhaps the most we can say is that sure as Jesus was of his mission, and aware of a closeness to the one he called Father, he faced his own death with all the fear, uncertainty, and doubt that any human being experiences when approaching death. *In extremis*, he clung to his faith in his Abba and continued to hope that Abba would vindicate him. Though the Father did not intervene and it appeared as though his ministry was ending in failure, he did not despair. Jesus had not been mistaken. God's reign was still at hand. The story of the agony in the garden says this symbolically, if not literally.

Conclusion

Why was Jesus executed? Most scholars today believe that his action in the Temple was a primary cause of his death. What he did was far more than a protest against the traders and the moneychangers; it was a symbolic action, a prophetic sign that the Temple itself was to be destroyed. While we cannot be certain that Jesus' saying about the destruction of the sanctuary was cited at his hearing before the Sanhedrin,[32] what he said or did to symbolize the Temple's destruction was remembered and played a major role in bringing about his death.

His death stunned and scattered the disciples; in the post-Easter period they sought to make sense of his death, drawing on the motifs and symbolic figures in their Scriptures. From the prophetic tradition came the image of the rejected prophet. The Wisdom tradition contributed the figure of the suffering just one, persecuted by the wicked but looking to Yahweh for vindication. These developed quite early. But neither attached initially any salvific meaning to the death of Jesus.

Another complex of tradition, earlier than Paul and the Synoptics, interprets Jesus' death from a soteriological perspective; he died "for us," "for our sins." Still another tradition sees Jesus as "the stone rejected by the

---

[31] Wright, *JVG*, 653.
[32] R. E. Brown, *The Death of the Messiah*, Vol. I, 460.

builders." Playing on the Hebrew words "son" *(ben)* and "stone" *(eben)*, the rejected son becomes the new foundation of God's people (Mark 12:10) while the people themselves become the new Temple built of living stones (1 Pet 2:7).

Finally, in raising the question of how Jesus saw his own death, a number of texts speaking of Jesus as "servant" were found to be rooted in the tradition of the Last Supper. A closer examination of Jesus' final meal with his disciples suggests that he saw his death, freely accepted, as part of his life and ministry. This is not the same as attributing salvific efficacy to his death itself. But it seems clear that in spite of the failure his death seemed to represent, he offered his disciples a renewed fellowship with himself beyond it. Thus he died, not despairing, but confident that the God he called Abba would in some way vindicate him, trusting that his mission would not end in failure.

Chapter 7

God Raised Him from the Dead

The death of Jesus was a shattering experience for the disciples. It left them disoriented, terrified for their own safety, unsure of the future. Many of them seemed to have fled Jerusalem and returned to Galilee. Luke suggests something of their confusion and disappointment in the story of the two disciples on the way to Emmaus. Meeting a stranger on the road, they tell him about the one they had followed and his tragic death: "We were hoping that he would be the one to redeem Israel" (Luke 24:21). As the story unfolds, the two disciples come to recognize the stranger as Jesus himself, still with them but present in a different way. The same theme appears in the other "Easter" stories. They tell how Peter, Mary of Magdala, and the others who followed Jesus came to believe that God had delivered Jesus from the realm of the dead and given him new life.

Certainly the conviction that Jesus lives now on the other side of death is at the center of the New Testament; without it, the various books and letters are incomprehensible. The Christian community, the Church, begins with the proclamation that God raised Jesus from the dead. But how did the disciples come to this conviction? How were they able to recognize this new mode of Jesus' presence? Did anything in their tradition prepare them for what has been called their "Easter experience"?[1] What was that experience? And what, if anything, does the Easter experience of the disciples have to say for Christians today? In this chapter we will seek to address these questions.

The Easter Experience

We have already seen that the idea of life beyond death developed late in the Jewish tradition. By the time of Jesus, both the concept of Yahweh

[1] Edward Schillebeeckx, *Jesus: An Experiment in Christology* (New York: Seabury, 1979) 280.

111

bringing the dead to life and the specific image of the resurrection of the dead were part of the Jewish religious imagination. It is within this framework that the Easter experience of the disciples must be understood.

We can't say precisely what the Easter experience of the disciples was. Did they actually see the Easter Jesus with their eyes, hear him speak with their ears, and touch him with their hands? Was their experience some kind of vision or dream? Was it an interior experience, a revelatory experience? The New Testament data is complex; the Easter stories themselves suggest that there is something that cannot be objectified about this manifestation of Jesus to his own. Jesus suddenly appears and disappears; doors or locks do not hinder him; those closest to him do not immediately recognize him. The appendix to Mark's Gospel says strangely that Jesus "appeared in another form" to two disciples (Mark 16:12), suggesting that there was something quite different about the experience.

Opinions among scholars vary considerably. Some, more skeptical, reduce the Resurrection to a subjective experience on the part of the disciples. After his death, the force of Jesus' personality struck the disciples in a new way, and they proclaimed that he was with them still.[2] He lives on. But this makes the Resurrection something that happened to the disciples, not to Jesus. From this perspective, the Resurrection becomes a product of faith.

Others, more mainstream, seek ways to describe the disciples' experience. Reginald Fuller says that the resurrection appearances "involved visionary experiences of light, combined with a communication of meaning. They were not in their inner most essence incidents open to neutral observance or verification, but revelatory events in which the eschatological and christological significance of Jesus was disclosed."[3] James M. Robinson says something similar; on the basis of the story of Paul's conversion in Acts, he suggests that it was an experience of blinding light.[4] Dermot Lane interprets the resurrection stories as an imaginative reaction to a transcendent experience; he argues that the manifestation of the risen Jesus was a revelatory experience, "probably best understood in terms of a visual experience giving rise to new insight."[5] This represents the only possible

---

[2] Cf. Willi Marxsen, *The Resurrection of Jesus of Nazareth* (Philadelphia: Fortress, 1970); for a review of this position see Gerald O'Collins, *Jesus Risen: An Historical, Fundamental, and Systematic Examination of Christ's Resurrection* (New York: Paulist, 1987) 103–07.

[3] Reginald H. Fuller, *The Formation of the Resurrection Narratives* (New York: Macmillian, 1971) 48.

[4] James M. Robinson, "Jesus: From Easter to Valentinus (or to the Apostles' Creed)," *Journal of Biblical Literature* 101 (1982) 5–37, esp. 9–10.

[5] Dermot A. Lane, *The Reality of Jesus* (New York: Paulist, 1975) 49.

way the transcendent reality of the risen Jesus could impinge on the consciousness of the disciples; it does not define that reality itself. "Indeed the appropriateness of attributing in the literal sense physical characteristics such as limbs and senses to the risen Jesus must at least be questioned."[6]

Edward Schillebeeckx speaks of the Easter experience as a conversion process, "a gracious gift of conversion to Jesus *as* the Christ" through Jesus himself "who enlightens, who discloses himself as the risen Christ in and through the grace of conversion."[7] This is Easter experience as grace. But he would insist that the experience is not merely subjective: "after his death Jesus himself stands at the source of what we are calling the 'Easter experience of the disciples.'"[8] Finally, Roger Haight argues that the disciples' basic experience "is that Jesus lives in God's glory," an experience which is essentially accessible to all Christians, though they are dependent on the initial disciples for the knowledge of the historical Jesus which grounds their belief and hope.[9]

What is clear is that those closest to Jesus came to believe without any doubt that the Jesus who had been crucified was alive. But the New Testament evidence is complex, and much of it is more theological lesson, designed to bring others to Easter faith, than historical narrative. Ben F. Meyer distinguished between the disciples' Easter *experience* itself, which could not be shared, and the *truth* of that experience, which was shared, precisely by being "fixed" in formulas to be believed and confessed.[10] We need to look more closely at the New Testament evidence.

The Easter Tradition

The Easter tradition in the New Testament can be broken down into two distinct strands, the Easter kerygma or proclamation and the Easter stories.[11] A careful consideration of the differences between the two can give us some insight into the disciples' Easter experience. It can also help us better understand how the early communities' Easter experience can still speak to Christians of today. We must consider also the New Testament language about Jesus' new life.

---

[6] Ibid., 62.

[7] Schillebeeckx, *Jesus*, 384.

[8] Ibid., 392.

[9] Roger Haight, *Jesus: Symbol of God* (Maryknoll, N.Y.: Orbis, 1999) 129.

[10] Ben F. Meyer, *Christus Faber: The Master Builder and the House of God* (Allison Park, Pa.: Pickwick Publications, 1992) 140.

[11] Ibid., 125.

Easter Language

While the image of a general resurrection of the dead was already part of the Jewish imagination as we have seen, and the disciples' Easter experience is most often expressed in resurrection language, that language is not the only language used to express the mystery of Jesus' new life. Nor does it seem to be the earliest.

Some scholars argue that the very early and widely disseminated *kerygma* of the Q community had no explicit proclamation of the Resurrection. Its equivalent was the idea of the heavenly Jesus actively present in the Christian prophets and coming in the Parousia.[12] The terms "exalted" or "exaltation" are sometimes used in place of "resurrection." Exaltation conveys the idea that Jesus has been brought from the dead and enthroned "at the right hand of God" (Acts 2:33). It appears in the pre-Pauline hymn in Philippians: "he humbled himself, / becoming obedient to death, / even death on a cross. / Because of this, God greatly exalted him" (Phil 2:8-9). Similar language expressing this exaltation or glorification is found elsewhere in the New Testament.[13] An early poetic formulation of the kerygma in 1 Timothy, perhaps a liturgical hymn, says, "Who was manifested in the flesh, / vindicated in the spirit / . . . taken up in glory" (1 Tim 3:16). It appears in the Emmaus story: "Was it not necessary that the Messiah should suffer these things and enter into his glory?" (Luke 24:26). Other passages combine exaltation with resurrection as its consequence (Rom 1:4; Acts 2:33; 5:30-31; 1 Pet 1:2). In the Fourth Gospel, exaltation means being raised both on the cross and to the Father. Kasper notes that Luke in Acts breaks the usual unity of resurrection and exaltation by inserting a forty-day period between the Resurrection and the Ascension.[14] However, in Luke's Gospel, the Ascension takes place on Easter Sunday night.

The most common language to express Jesus' passing from death to life is the language of resurrection. Two terms are used in the New Testament documents, *egeirein*, a transitive verb meaning "to awaken," "to raise up," and *anastanai*, "to arise," or "to raise up." Most often the usage is "he was raised up" (Rom 4:25; 6:4; 7:4; 1 Cor 6:14; 15:4; Mark 16:6); the Resurrection is something that happened to Jesus. It is God's action, God's vindication of Jesus' life and ministry, raising him to new life. Much less frequently is the active usage: "Jesus rose from the dead" (cf. 1 Thess 4:14; John 20:9).

---

[12] Cf. Schillebeeckx, *Jesus*, 416.

[13] Cf. Gerald O'Collins, *The Resurrection of Jesus* (Valley Forge, Pa.: Judson, 1973) 50–53.

[14] Walter Kasper, *Jesus the Christ* (New York: Paulist Press, 1976) 148.

Resurrection language is metaphorical; the comparison is with being awakened from sleep. The new life of Jesus is a mystery that can neither be comprehended nor adequately explained. It is different from the resuscitation of a corpse, as in the raising of the widow's son or Lazarus in the Gospels, both of whom must face death again. Paul's effort to explain the nature of the risen body to the Corinthians (1 Cor 15:35-56) comes close to a breakdown of the language. He runs through several analogies, heavenly and earthly bodies, the transformation of the seed, the first and the last Adam, and contrasts a "natural" with a "spiritual" body, a *sōma pneumatikon* (1 Cor 15:44). But a spiritual body is, to be precise, a contradiction in terms; it is an oxymoron. Kasper notes that *pneuma* in *sōma pneumatikon* means not the "stuff" or substance that constitutes the body, but rather the dimension in which it exists. A spiritual body is in the divine dimension.[15]

The resurrection of Jesus is an eschatological event; Jesus lives now on the other side of space, time, and history; he is completely with God. Our language is conditioned by our bodily experience in a material world. We think in terms of images. Thus we must use metaphorical language to speak about his new life, describing the unknown by comparing it to the known. He has been raised from the dead; he ascended into heaven; he is at the right hand of God; he will again come on the clouds of heaven. The Good News of Jesus' new life was transmitted by two different strands of tradition, the Easter kerygma and the Easter stories.

The Easter Kerygma

The Easter kerygma represents short, formulaic expressions of belief in the resurrection of Jesus deriving originally from early Christian preaching or liturgy. The Easter kerygma dates from the earliest days of the Church; thus it predates the Gospels and even the letters of Paul, the earliest New Testament documents. One of the most important examples of the Easter kerygma appears at the end of the first letter to the Corinthians: it may originate in the community of Antioch in the thirties:

> For I handed on to you as of first importance what I also received: that Christ died for our sins in accordance with the scriptures; that he was buried; that he was raised on the third day in accordance with the scriptures; that he appeared to Cephas, then to the Twelve (1 Cor 15:3-5).

---

[15] Kasper, *Jesus the Christ*, 150.

Note that the tradition Paul reports here is not a dramatic description of an event; it gives no details, is more reportorial or proclamatory than imaginative. The Easter kerygma is not a description of the disciples' Easter experience, but a binding testimony to their Easter faith. It states the belief of the early communities that Jesus has been raised and that there are witnesses. Here are some other examples.

> God raised this Jesus; of this we are all witnesses. Exalted at the right hand of God, he received the promise of the holy Spirit from the Father and poured it forth, as you [both] see and hear.
>
> Acts 2:32-33

> Therefore let the whole house of Israel know beyond any doubt that God has made him both Lord and Messiah, this Jesus whom you crucified.
>
> Acts 2:36

> [A]nd that the Lord may grant you times of refreshment and send you the Messiah already appointed for you, Jesus.
>
> Acts 3:20

> The God of our ancestors raised Jesus, though you had him killed by hanging him on a tree. God exalted him at his right hand as leader and savior to grant Israel repentance and forgiveness of sins.
>
> Acts 5:30-31

> The gospel about his Son, descended from David according to the flesh, but established as Son of God in power according to the spirit of holiness through resurrection from the dead.
>
> Rom 1:3-4

> If you confess with your mouth that Jesus is Lord and believe in your heart that God raised him from the dead, you will be saved.
>
> Rom 10:9

> The Lord has truly been raised and has appeared to Simon.
>
> Luke 24:34

Some of these texts, for example Romans 1:3 and 10:9, are ancient catechetical formulas, confessions of faith. Some like Luke 24:34 probably had their origin in the liturgy. And there are other formulas and hymns (Phil 2:6-11; Acts 10:36-43; 1 Tim 3:16) which are confessions of faith in the resurrection of Jesus. Some of them, for instance Phil 2:6-11, are clearly pre-Pauline. In some of them (1 Cor 15:5; Luke 24:34) Peter has a central role as the first witness.

The Easter Stories

The Easter stories developed later in the tradition. They are quite different. Where the kerygma texts give short statements of belief, the stories are dramatic, imaginative accounts, narratives complete with dialogue and vivid detail about persons, place, and circumstance. There are two types of Easter stories, stories about the discovery of the empty tomb and appearance stories. Originally separate traditions, the tomb traditions originating in Jerusalem, and the appearance traditions perhaps in Galilee, though they often appear combined. They do not always agree in all respects with the Easter kerygma; for example, the women and especially Mary Magdalene play an important role in some of the stories.

Mark 16:1-8 represents the oldest Easter story. It is interesting to note that this First Gospel had only the story of the discovery of the empty tomb; there is no appearance story, though it points to Jesus appearing to the disciples in Galilee. The women at the tomb in Jerusalem are told by the young man they find there, "Go and tell his disciples and Peter, 'He is going before you to Galilee; there you will see him, as he told you'" (Mark 16:7). According to Kasper, the tradition of the empty tomb is an ancient one but not an historical account of its discovery; the text represents a narrative which was the basis of a cultic ceremony, used by the Jerusalem Christian community to honor the tomb of Jesus. However, its cultic nature does not imply that there is not history behind the tradition; indeed, if the tomb had not been empty, a tradition celebrating it would make no sense.[16] The Markan appendices summarize briefly several stories from the other Gospels, reflecting the traditions found in Luke 24 and probably with some influence from John 20.

Matthew's Gospel expands on Mark's. It includes a story of Jesus appearing to the women on their way home from the tomb, another empty tomb story that involves the bribing of the guards, and an appearance to the eleven disciples on a mountain in Galilee. Luke, because of the literary and theological structuring of his two-volume work, transposes the appearances to Jerusalem and its environs. They include the women at the tomb, with the additional detail of Peter running to the tomb (Luke 24:12), the story of the two disciples on the road to Emmaus, an appearance to the eleven and others gathered in Jerusalem, and a brief ascension account.

John's account is quite different from those of the Synoptics. Chapter 20, set in Jerusalem, has the stories of Mary Magdalene finding the tomb empty,

---

[16] Kasper, *Jesus the Christ*, 127; Gerald O'Collins gives an impressive list of scholars who hold the essential reliability of the empty tomb story; see *Jesus Risen*, 123.

Peter and John at the tomb, an appearance to Mary Magdalene, and two appearances to the disciples, one without Thomas. Chapter 21, an appendix added later, is set in Galilee and seems independent of the preceding chapter. It is the story of an appearance of the risen Jesus to seven disciples who are fishing and includes a miraculous catch of fish, the rehabilitation of Peter after his betrayal, and a tradition about the Beloved Disciple.

A careful reading of the Easter stories makes quite evident that they do not agree. There are discrepancies about which women went to the tomb, how many "young men" were there, where the appearances took place, and who was the first to whom Jesus appeared, Peter or Mary Magdalene. Many scholars point out that the two traditions of appearances, Galilee and Jerusalem, show no awareness of each other.[17] Luke and the original Mark are not aware of an appearance to the women before the other disciples. But all this is unimportant; it is not the point. These are not historical accounts of the disciples' encounter with Jesus after his death, but stories, testimonies to their Easter faith written to make that faith available to others (cf. John 20:31). Roger Haight is correct to stress the analogy between the disciples coming to Easter faith and our own.[18] Thus the Easter stories are highly theological reflections on the disciples' Easter experience whose purpose is evangelical. In the following section, we will reflect further on these stories, to see what they might suggest for Christians today.

Reflections on Easter Faith

Historical Event or the Product of Faith?

Some scholars make the Resurrection a product of faith, as we saw earlier. For Rudolph Bultmann, the Resurrection is "not an event of past history with a self-evident meaning." He sees it as "a mythical event pure and simple"[19] used by the early Christians to ground their understanding of Christ as the basis of their new, authentic existence. For Willi Marxsen, it means that the "cause" of Jesus goes on.[20] For him, "*the miracle is the birth of faith.*"[21]

[17] For example, Raymond E. Brown, *An Introduction to New Testament Christology* (New York: Paulist, 1994) 167.

[18] Haight, *Jesus: Symbol of God*, 128–29.

[19] Rudolph Bultmann, "New Testament and Mythology," in *Kerygma and Myth: A Theological Debate*, Vol. I, ed. Hans-Werner Bartsch (London: S.P.C.K., 1964) 1–44, 38.

[20] Willi Marxsen, *The Resurrection of Jesus of Nazareth* (Philadelphia: Fortress, 1970) 126, 183 ff.

[21] Ibid., 128; italics in original.

There are, however, many scholars who accept the resurrection as something real that happened to Jesus and yet will argue that it was not a historical event. In part, what is at issue here is terminology. The accepted definition of a "historical" event is something that is at least *capable* of verification by the criteria of historical investigation. In this sense, the resurrection of Jesus is not something that can be "*proved*." The resurrection is an act of God's power bringing Jesus from the dead; as such, it can not be seen. All that can be seen historically are the results of this act, "the appearances, the empty tomb, and Christianity itself."[22] Even if it could be demonstrated today that the tomb itself was empty, that would not prove that Jesus had been raised; there could be other explanations. Kasper says that the resurrection has a historical dimension in that it happened to the crucified Jesus of Nazareth, but even this is carefully qualified language.[23]

In talking about the Resurrection it is important to avoid two extremes. On the one hand, the Resurrection should not be understood as an "objective," "this-worldly" event. Such events are essentially public; they can be seen by any neutral observer. The witnesses testify to their experience of the risen Jesus; they did not see the Resurrection itself. The Resurrection is a "transhistorical event," one that takes place by definition on the other side of death. There could be no "film at eleven" even if a camera crew had been present. As something that lies outside the conditions of space and time, the resurrection of Jesus is not capable of verification in the way that events in "this world" can be verified. The Easter stories suggest this; the disciples' experience of the risen Jesus was very different from their previous experience of him. Their initial reaction is hesitation, incredulity, fear, even doubt.

On the other hand, it would be a mistake to reduce the Resurrection to a purely subjective event, an interior feeling of the disciples who were the witnesses, as we saw above. The New Testament is familiar with the language of dreams, visions, raptures, and avoids it here. The Easter experience of the disciples is more than a mystical experience of the transcendent God; it is extremely personal process in which Jesus discloses himself as present in a new way. Dermont Lane speaks of it as a "transforming experience." "Those who had followed Jesus in faith now come to recognize him in a different way as risen in light of their transforming experience of his new, real, personal presence."[24] Kasper uses the category "revelation" which he sees as "an entirely personal process which, according to Phil 3:12,

---

[22] Lane, *The Reality of Jesus*, 45.
[23] Kasper, *Jesus the Christ*, 150.
[24] Lane, *The Reality of Jesus*, 61.

consists of Christ's making a person his own." Revelation (*apocalypsis*) is the word that Paul uses describe his own coming to know the risen Jesus, speaking of God who "was pleased to reveal his Son to me, so that I might proclaim him to the Gentiles" (Gal 1:15-16). Paul is the only New Testament author who is both an acknowledged witness to the Resurrection (cf. 1 Cor 15:8) and who actually refers autobiographically to that experience. Thus his language is particularly significant. Notice how different his spare but authentic testimony is from the dramatic account told several times in Acts (9:1-9; 22:3-16; 26:2-18), a much later work; the Acts version is really another Easter story. Paul's language in Galatians is the language of religious experience; not a detailed narrative, but testimony of a transforming inner experience that left an unshakable certainty.

If the resurrection is neither a purely objective, "already-out-there-now real" event, nor a subjective event, then how should we think of it? The Resurrection is properly an eschatological event, that is a real event, but one that takes place on the other side of space and time, death and history. Jesus lives now fully in God's future; his new, eschatological mode of existence is radically different from that of his earthly life. In a felicitous phrase, Kasper says that through "Jesus' Resurrection and Exaltation a 'piece of the world' finally reached God and was finally accepted by God."[25]

Is "Faith" Necessary to Perceive the Risen Jesus?

Why didn't the risen Jesus manifest himself to his opponents, to the chief priests and the members of the Sanhedrin, or to Pilate? Wouldn't this have been more effective? Why is it that Jesus seems to have appeared only to his friends, to those who followed him?

A careful reading of the Easter stories shows that the disciples' Easter experience does not take away their freedom or compel their belief. In all the appearance stories, there is a stress on their initial non-recognition, confusion, doubt, and fear. In the original ending of Mark, the women "fled from the tomb, seized with trembling and bewilderment. They said nothing to anyone, for they were afraid" (Mark 16:8). The disciples doubt the report of Mary Magdalene and the women (Luke 24:9-11; Mark 16:11). The two disciples on the road to Emmaus do not recognize Jesus and must first be instructed and share in the meal (Luke 24:13-35). When they recognize him, he is already gone. The eleven and others gathered in Jerusalem "were startled and terrified and thought that they were seeing a ghost" at Jesus' appearance (Luke 24:37); he had to lead them to believe (Luke

---

[25] Kasper, *Jesus the Christ*, 152.

24:38-42). Even Mary Magdalene who loved Jesus does not recognize him (John 20:14), and Thomas cannot believe without physical evidence (John 20:25). In the Johannine appendix, the disciples do not recognize Jesus standing on the shore (John 21:4). A particularly interesting text, Matthew's story of the appearance of Jesus to the eleven on the mountain in Galilee, says "When they saw him, they worshiped him, but some doubted" (Matt 27:17, NRSV). Commenting on this text, Kenan Osborne observes that according to the New Testament, "belief in the resurrection of Jesus is not an easy matter, either in the case of the disciples or in the case of the early Jesus communities generally."[26]

The cumulative effect of these stories is to suggest that the disciples' coming to believe in Jesus' new life was more a gradual process than an instant recognition, compelling belief. The experience did not overwhelm them, taking away their freedom. It was as though Jesus had to lead them to faith, just as in his ministry he continually insisted on the importance of faith; where it was lacking he could work no miracles (Mark 6:5). He disclosed himself to his own; they had to allow grace to lead them to faith. Osborne uses the category of "religious experience" as the category that describes their response to the "act of God in their lives," bringing them to believe in the resurrection event.[27] Haight speaks of the "transcendent character" of the Resurrection; "it is known as a revelatory religious experience and not in an empirical, historical perception or an objective inference from such an event."[28]

Even more, the risen Jesus manifested himself to his friends and disciples, to those who loved him and had opened their hearts to them, those who had a relationship with him. In other words, he appeared to those who had "faith" in its fundamental sense as an openness to God, however partial. And they had to respond in faith. Those whose hearts were closed could not recognize the risen Jesus; he could not appear to them. Even Paul, the one obvious exception, however misguided and insecure he may have been before his conversion, was honest in his quest and zealous for what he perceived as being in accordance with God's will. Is this so different from our own experience?

---

[26] Kenan B. Osborne, *The Resurrection of Jesus: New Considerations for Its Theological Interpretation* (New York: Paulist, 1997) 55.

[27] Ibid., 117.

[28] Haight, *Jesus: Symbol of God*, 144.

Presence, Empowerment, and Mission

The Easter stories suggest that those to whom Jesus appeared were touched and changed. In other words, the Easter experience of the disciples was transformative. At the very least, these stories show how the disappointed and terrified followers of Jesus were moved, even emboldened, to carry on his movement. From a theological perspective, the disciples experienced forgiveness, acceptance, love, and empowerment. Certainly the male disciples who had deserted Jesus in his hour of need were burdened with guilt. They had abandoned their teacher, one they had followed and loved. But Jesus greets them with a blessing of peace (Luke 24:36; John 20:19, 21, 26). They are forgiven. Peter who had betrayed Jesus three times before a charcoal fire is rehabilitated. Again before a charcoal fire, Jesus asks him three times, "Peter do you love me." Nor is his betrayal held against him. Jesus makes Peter the pastor of the flock (John 21:15-18).

Those who have seen the risen Jesus are missioned to bring the Good News of the resurrection to others. The origin of the word "apostle" is to be found here; *apostolos* means literally "one who has been sent." The eleven are given the Holy Spirit to forgive sins (John 20:22) and sent to preach forgiveness to all nations (Luke 24:47) with power to baptize and teach (Matt 28:19-20). Mary Magdalene is sent to bring the Good News to the apostles (John 20:17; cf. Matt 28:10). The early tradition did not call women apostles because in the Palestinian Jewish culture of the time, the word of a woman was generally not recognized as legally binding testimony[29] and apostles were witnesses to the Resurrection. If women were included among the witnesses by the New Testament authors, they must have played a significant role in the beginning of the post-Easter community. The later tradition did not always honor the memory of women's contributions to primitive Christianity;[30] nevertheless, Mary Magdalene was known as the "apostle of the apostles" (*apostola apostolorum*) from the early centuries of the Church; the title may be as old as Hippolytus of Rome, thus early third century.

The transforming encounters with the risen Jesus are associated with encounters with the Lord in the Church, encounters the later Church would call sacramental.[31] The presence of Jesus is associated with the proclamation of the forgiveness of sins (John 20:22) and with the meal

[29] See Joachim Jeremias, *Jerusalem in the Time of Jesus* (Philadelphia: Fortress, 1969) 374–76.

[30] Cf. Elisabeth Schüssler Fiorenza, *In Memory of Her: A Feminist Reconstruction of Christian Origins* (New York: Crossroad, 1983).

[31] Cf. Dermot Lane, *The Reality of Jesus*, 61.

that the Church would call Eucharist (Luke 24:30-35). Meal language appears in another appearance story, the meal that the risen Jesus offers to the disciples in the Johannine appendix (John 20:21-23). It appears also in the Easter kerygma: "This man God raised [on] the third day and granted that he be visible, not to all the people, but to us, the witnesses chosen by God in advance, who ate and drank with him after he rose from the dead" (Acts 10:40-42; cf. Luke 24:31, 35). Many see here a reference to the eucharistic meals of the early communities.

It is quite possible that the story of the two disciples on the road to Emmaus (Luke 24:13-35), in suggesting a post-Easter continuation of Jesus' tradition of table fellowship, represents a narrative account of at least one of the ways the community of disciples came to recognize the risen Jesus as present among them.[32] The fellowship meal became the locus for the risen Lord's self-disclosure to his own. Certainly the centrality of the eucharistic meal in the gathering of the *ekklēsia* from the beginning as well as for the Church today that continues to recognize and encounter the risen Jesus in the breaking of the bread is supportive of this hypothesis.

Conclusion

Though the idea of God giving life to the dead enters late into the Jewish tradition, by the time of Jesus both the concept and the specific image of the resurrection of the dead were part of the Jewish religious imagination. But the resurrection of the dead was an eschatological notion; it looked forward to a general resurrection that would accompany the age of salvation.

Christian preaching begins with the Easter experience of the disciples; they are convinced that Jesus has been raised to new life and this belief is at the heart of the New Testament. But it is difficult to say just what the disciples experienced. The Easter kerygma is formulaic; the various expressions of the kerygma are binding confessions that Jesus has been raised and that there are witnesses; they give no details. The Easter stories are not historical narratives but testimonies to the Easter faith of the early communities; they are dramatic narratives, differing in details, written to bring others to that faith.

Neither a purely objective event nor a subjective experience on the part of the disciples, the resurrection is properly an eschatological event, an act of God on the other side of death and history. Thus it was a real event, an act of God on Jesus, raising him to life. If it cannot be demonstrated by the

---

[32] Haight thinks it quite possible that "the story represents broadly the historical route the disciples took to arrive at the affirmation of faith that Jesus is risen," *Jesus: Symbol of God*, 139.

canons of historiography, its mark on history is evident in the witnesses, the story of the empty tomb, and the faith of the Church. The risen Jesus was disclosed to those who followed and loved him, who had opened their hearts to him. They experienced him as present with them in a new way and themselves as sent to proclaim God's new life and hope in him to others.

The resurrection of Jesus does not reveal that all will be raised up, "but that faithful human existence such as his is called back into God's love."[33] God's love is stronger than death.

[33] Haight, *Jesus: Symbol of God*, 151.

Chapter 8

New Testament Christologies

Christology begins with the Easter experience of the disciples. They had been demoralized and scattered; the one they followed had died an ignominious and humiliating death, executed with the cruelest form of capital punishment. But their Easter experience convinced them beyond doubt that God had acted, vindicated Jesus and his message, delivered him from the bonds of death. This was astonishing news, to be shared with others. But with their proclamation came necessarily interpretation. What had happened? What did it mean? Who was this Jesus? How could they make others understand these events?

They could only express their experience in the language and symbols of their inherited tradition. They were Jews, religious men and women whose imaginations had been formed by the sacred writings of their people. Those writings were varied and diverse. They included both those texts that would latter constitute the official Jewish "canon," and others that claimed authority, those from the Septuagint used by the early Church, and still others considered "apocryphal." They would have been familiar with the traditions of Jewish hope which we considered earlier, the messianic, rooted in the preaching of the prophets, the Wisdom tradition, largely postexilic, and the apocalyptic. From these would come the earliest Christologies.

The New Testament offers a multiplicity of Christologies and witnesses to an obvious development in the Church's understanding of Jesus. The disciples did not immediately confess Jesus as the preexistent Son of God. But neither is it true that such a high Christology is only a later development, as we will see later. It would be a mistake to reduce the variety of New Testament Christologies to some kind of Hegelian unfolding, moving relentlessly from lower to higher expressions. One senses that none of the inherited symbols or figures were adequate to the disciples' experience of the one they addressed in prayer and worship as "Lord," and so their efforts to bring their faith to expression continually overflowed the limits of their language. In the process, the various titles and Christologies were stretched, overlapped, and used to explain each other as the disciples came to a deeper understanding.

The earliest Christologies, originating in early Christian preaching, are represented by fragments, titles, hymns, and formulas embedded in later Christian texts like the letters of Paul and the Acts of the Apostles. Scholars have identified them by the differences in vocabulary, imagery, style, and thought from the works in which they appear. For example, Paul quotes one of these early formulas in his letter to the Romans:

> for, if you confess with your mouth
> that Jesus is Lord
> and believe in your heart
> that God raised him from the dead,
> you will be saved.
>
> Romans 10:9

Paul is citing here a creedal formula from the early Palestinian churches, very possibly a baptismal formula. The formula demands both interior belief and outward confession of faith in Jesus as Lord, raised from the dead, and source of our salvation. Other examples include 1 Thessalonians 1:9-10 and Romans 1:3-4.

Christology can be expressed in various ways. An earlier scholarship was accustomed to focus on the origin and use of the christological titles—prophet, Messiah, Lord, Son of Man, Son of God.[1] Some scholars approach Christology by analyzing the different New Testament authors.[2] Raymond E. Brown has done a Christology on the basis of "christological moments," meaning the christological perspective taken by New Testament authors on various moments in the life of Jesus. Following the likely order of the composition of this material, from earliest to latest, Brown sees a movement backwards, from Second Coming, to Resurrection, ministry, baptism, conception, and preexistence Christologies.[3] Another approach is in terms of christological "types." Edward Schillebeeckx suggests four: Parousia, Divine-

---

[1] See F. Hahn, *The Titles of Jesus in Christology* (London: Lutterworth, 1969); Reginald H. Fuller, *The Foundations of New Testament Christology* (New York: Charles Scribner's, 1965).

[2] For example, Earl Richards, *Jesus: One and Many: The Christological Concept of the New Testament Authors* (Wilmington, Del.: Michael Glazier, 1988; also Marinus de Jonge, *Christology in Context: The Earliest Christian Response to Jesus* (Philadelphia: Westminster, 1988).

[3] Raymond E. Brown, *An Introduction to New Testament Christology* (New York: Paulist, 1994), see especially 107–08.

man, Wisdom, and Easter Christology,[4] while Roger Haight offers five: Last Adam, Son of God, Spirit, Wisdom, and Logos Christology.[5] Feminist scholars have shown a preference for Wisdom Christology, as it makes possible an approach to the mystery of the divine that is less dependent on masculine metaphors.[6] Obviously there will be considerable overlap between these various approaches, for some types may be present in a particular author who places more emphasis on a different expression. I would like to suggest four types for our consideration: Easter, Son of God, Wisdom, and Preexistence.

Easter Christologies

The earliest Christologies are centered on the post-Easter Jesus, Jesus as soon to come in judgment (*parousia*) or reigning in God's presence (exaltation). Also typical of this type is the idea that Jesus receives titles such as Messiah, Lord, and Son of God only after his death.

Parousia Christology

Sometimes called *maranatha* Christology, Parousia (Second Coming) Christology represents perhaps the oldest interpretation of Jesus, originating in the early Aramaic-speaking Palestinian communities. The apocalyptic perspective of these communities was adapted to portray Jesus as soon to come, bringing God's salvation, but also as judge. A fragment of the early kerygma in Acts 3:19-21 suggests that Jesus will be Messiah only at his future coming.

> Repent, therefore, and be converted, that your sins may be wiped away, and that the Lord may grant you times of refreshment and send you the Messiah already appointed for you, Jesus.
>
> Acts 3:19-21

Thus Parousia Christology looks to future completion of the kingdom of God at Christ's Second Coming.[7]

Schillebeeckx traces Parousia Christology to the very early Q community which lived in expectation of Christ's immanent return, just as they

---

[4] Edward Schillebeeckx, *Jesus: An Experiment in Christology* (New York: Seabury, 1979) 401–38.

[5] Roger Haight, *Jesus: Symbol of God* (Maryknoll, N.Y.: Orbis, 1999) 155–78.

[6] Elisabeth Johnson, *She Who Is: The Mystery of God in Feminist Theological Discourse* (New York: Crossroad, 1992) 94–98.

[7] Brown, *Introduction*, 110.

prayed in the Lord's Prayer "your kingdom come."[8] Variants of this tradition can be found in Mark and Paul. For example, Paul cites this tradition in 1 Thessalonians (a passage which leads for some to "rapture" theology):

> For the Lord himself, with a word of command, with the voice of an archangel and with the trumpet of God, will come down from heaven, and the dead in Christ will rise first. Then we who are alive, who are left, will be caught up together with them in the clouds to meet the Lord in the air.
>
> 1 Thessalonians 4:16-17

Two titles, both originally used in an apocalyptic context, are associated with this Christology, "Lord" (*Mari* or *Maran* in Aramaic, *Kurios* in Greek) and "Son of Man." Lord was already a divine title; according to Aramaic scholar Joseph Fitzmyer, "it seems quite likely that there was an incipient custom among both Semitic- and Greek-speaking Jews of Palestine to call Yahweh *ʾādōn, mārēʾ*, or *kyrios*."[9] In the Septuagint, *Kurios*/Lord was used to translate the Hebrew *Adonai*, which in the text took the place of the holy name Yahweh, a fact that would not have been lost on Greek-speaking Jews. Jesus was given God's name.

As a title for Jesus, Lord may have had its roots in what Schillebeeckx calls the eschatological "salvific figure" in the intertestamental literature as the bringer of salvation.[10] The New Testament letter of Jude cites the apocryphal book of Enoch 1:9:

> Behold, the Lord has come with his countless holy ones to execute judgment on all and to convict everyone for all the godless deeds that they committed.
>
> Jude 14–15

Joseph Fitzmyer argues that Paul inherited the title "Lord" for the risen Christ from the Palestinian Jewish Christian community at Jerusalem.[11] We know that some of the early communities prayed at their liturgies for Jesus to come, bringing God's salvation: in Corinth the prayer is preserved in the Aramaic formula, "*Marana tha,*" (O Lord, come) (1 Cor 16:22), while in Revelation 22:20 it appears in Greek. So from earliest moments of the tradition, Jesus was the object of prayer, with the *Sitz im Leben* for this prayer very likely being the Eucharist.[12]

---

[8] Schillebeeckx, *Jesus,* 410–11.

[9] Joseph A. Fitzmyer, "*Kyrios* and *Maranatha* and Their Aramaic Background," *To Advance the Gospel: New Testament Studies* (New York: Crossroad, 1981) 222.

[10] Schillebeeckx, *Jesus,* 409.

[11] Joseph Fitzmyer, "Pauline Theology" in the *New Jerome Biblical Commentary,* ed. Raymond E. Brown, Joseph A. Fitzmyer, and Roland Murphy (Englewood Cliffs, N.J.: Prentice Hall, 1990) 82:53.

[12] See Fuller, *Foundations,* 157.

The title "Son of Man" seems also in its earliest christological appearances to come out of this apocalyptic context. Since the phrase "Son of Man" in the New Testament occurs only in the sayings of Jesus, many scholars hold that Jesus himself may have used the title of himself (Mark 8:31; Matt 8:20), based on his reflection on the expression, "one like a son of man" in Daniel 7:13.[13] It is unlikely that Jesus referred to the Son of Man as another figure, for the Jesus-tradition is consistent in its affirmation of the eschatological finality of Jesus' mission.[14] Others think that the earliest communities identified the Easter Jesus with the Son of Man expected in the "post-Old Testament, non-Christian, Jewish apocalyptic of those days."[15] These future Son of Man sayings are found in all the Gospels. For example, "they will see the 'Son of Man coming in the clouds' with great power and glory" (Mark 13:26; cf. 14:62). Later the Son of Man takes on a creative function (Rev 1:17) and preexistence (John 3:13; 6:62).

Exaltation Christology

Another very early Christology, more common than Parousia Christology, is exaltation or resurrection Christology.[16] Exaltation Christology sees Jesus as made Messiah, Lord, and Son of God after his exaltation from the dead. It is not much of a step from seeing Jesus as coming with salvation to seeing him as reigning as Lord. Exaltation Christology is recognizable in Paul's letters and in the sermons of Peter and Paul in Acts; thus its provenance is that of Greek-speaking Jewish-Hellenistic Christianity, though some of the texts may be based on Aramaic hymns or formulas. Some examples. In Romans Paul cites an early confession:

> The gospel about his Son, descended from David according to the flesh, but established as Son of God in power, according to the spirit of holiness through resurrection from the dead, Jesus Christ our Lord.
>
> Romans 1:3-4

In this confession, Jesus is designated as God's Son by his resurrection. The idea that Jesus' exaltation or resurrection was the occasion for his messianic appointment as God's Son was widespread in early Christianity (cf. Acts 13:33).[17]

---

[13] See Brown, *An Introduction*, 109–10.

[14] See James G. D. Dunn, *Christology in the Making: A New Testament Inquiry into the Origins of the Doctrine of the Incarnation* (Philadelphia: Westminster, 1980) 35–36.

[15] Schillebeeckx, *Jesus*, 409; see also Fuller, *Foundations*, 34–43.

[16] Raymond Brown uses the term "resurrection christology" in his *Introduction*, 112–15.

[17] Dunn, *Christology in the Making*, 85.

The early christological hymn Paul incorporates into his letter to the Philippians is another example of Jesus receiving an important title, in this case "Lord," after his exaltation (Phil 2:6-11). The hymn may have been composed in Aramaic and goes back to the Palestine of the late 30s.[18] We will return later to the question of how Paul himself understands it. There are also examples of this very early christological tradition preserved in Acts. In Acts 2 Peter says

> God raised this Jesus; of this we are all witnesses . . . Therefore let the whole house of Israel know for certain that God has made him both Lord and Messiah, this Jesus whom you crucified.
>
> Acts 2:32, 36

Represented here is a two-stage Christology; the man Jesus has been exalted by God, made Lord and Messiah from the moment of his resurrection. Similarly

> The God of our ancestors raised Jesus, though you had him killed by hanging him on a tree. God exalted him at his right hand as leader and savior to grant Israel repentance and forgiveness of sins.
>
> Acts 5:30-31

There are a number of points that should be noted in these early, Easter Christologies. First, exaltation/resurrection is something that happens to Jesus; the agency is God's. Second, christological titles such as Messiah, Son of Man, Son of God, and Lord are predicated of Jesus after his exaltation; in these earliest fragments they have not yet been extended into his historical life. Third, there is yet no explicit expression of his divinity. Nevertheless, adopting for Jesus the title "Lord" was significant. Pre-Christian Palestinian Jews were already referring to God, whether in Hebrew, Aramaic, or Greek, as "the Lord" as we have seen.[19] Using *Kurios* for Jesus, initially in reference to the Second Coming, does not assert his divinity. But the fact that the term was used also for Yahweh "puts him on the same level with Yahweh and implies his transcendent status."[20] Equally important is the title "Son of God."

---

[18] See Joseph A. Fitzmyer, "The Aramaic Background of Philippians 2:6-11," *Catholic Biblical Quarterly* 50 (1988) 470–83.

[19] See Fitzmyer, *NJBC* 82:52.

[20] Ibid., 82:54.

Son of God Christologies

If the early Easter Christologies recognize Jesus as Messiah, Son of Man, and Son of God only after his death, the Gospels see these titles as applying to Jesus during his public ministry.[21] For Mark, the First Gospel, the focus is on Jesus as the Son of God. Because Mark is the major source for Matthew and Luke, the same motif can be found there, though differently developed and alongside other christological themes. In this section we will consider the Christologies of the Synoptic Gospels under the general typology, Son of God. But three preliminary observations.

First, our approach here might seem somewhat arbitrary; the argument could be made that either Matthew or Luke places primary emphasis on some other concept. In his study of Matthew, J. P. Meier remarks that "Matthew is quite capable of making important Christological statements without titles."[22] His insight is that a Christology develops out of various themes woven together in a particular work, with or without the preponderant use of a particular title. That will be our principle here. Basing the Christology of a particular author on specific titles or themes, while ignoring the whole direction of the work, can be just another form of proof-texting.

Secondly, we have already seen that the term "Son of God" in the Old Testament had a number of different meanings. It could refer to the future son of David whom God promised to adopt (2 Sam 7:14; Pss 2:7; 89:27), or to the just man in the Wisdom tradition (Sir 4:10; Wisdom 2:16-20), to angels (Job 1:6; 2:1), and sometimes, to the people of Israel collectively (Exod 4:22; Deut 14:1; Hos 11:1). Thus, when the New Testament authors use the term, "Son of God," it does not necessarily mean what it does to contemporary Christians who usually understand it in a metaphysical sense; Jesus is Son of God by nature.

Third, even if the title Son of God had various meanings in the Old Testament and underwent some development in the New, still, as Dunn observes, no other title or christological assessment "has had both the historical depth and lasting power of 'Son of God.'"[23] As a title for Jesus "Son of God" may well go back to the first Jewish-Christian community in Jerusalem,[24] most probably based on his resurrection which was seen as the moment of his appointment to divine Sonship (cf. Acts 13:3).[25] But its ultimate

---

[21] Brown, *Introduction*, 116.

[22] J. P. Meier, *The Vision of Matthew: Christ, Church, and Morality in the First Gospel* (N.Y.: Paulist, 1979) 217.

[23] Dunn, *Christology in the Making*, 12.

[24] See Martin Hengel, *The Son of God* (Philadelphia: Fortress, 1976) 60.

[25] Dunn, *Christology in the Making*, 36.

origin seems indisputably to lie in the usage of Jesus himself, who seems to have understood and expressed his own relationship to God in terms of sonship. While Jesus never describes himself as *the* Son of God in the Synoptic Gospels, there is considerable evidence that he spoke of himself as "son" in a unique way, already evident in Q (Matt 11:27/Luke 10:22), to be considered below.

Then there is the even stronger evidence of his characteristic and for the time distinctive practice of addressing God in his prayer as "Abba." Though he taught his disciples to pray in this way themselves and to regard themselves also as God's sons (and daughters), Dunn notes that "he thought of their sonship as somehow dependent on his own."[26] Kasper makes a similar point, noting that all the strata of the New Testament maintain a distinction that suggests that Jesus' relationship to the Father is different from that of the disciples (Mark 14:36; Luke 6:36; Mark 11:2; John 20:17).[27] Let us look more closely at the texts.

Mark

The Gospel of Mark opens with a twofold christological statement: "The beginning of the gospel of Jesus Christ [the Son of God]." While Jesus is both Messiah and the Son of Man who must suffer (Mark 8:31; cf. 9:31; 10:33-34) for Mark, the most significant title is Son of God, evident from its appearance at key points in his Gospel.[28] Jesus is proclaimed Son of God in the opening sentence of the Gospel, at his baptism, transfiguration, trial before the Sanhedrin, and just after his death; he also addresses God as "Abba" or "Father" (Mark 14:36) and refers to himself as the "Son" (Mark 13:32).

The baptism account is a revelation of Jesus as God's Son. Unlike accounts in Matthew and Luke, in Mark only Jesus sees the heavens torn open and the Spirit descending upon him, and hears the voice which declares, "You are my beloved Son; with you I am well pleased" (Mark 1:11). Until the end of Mark's Gospel, the real identity of Jesus is not recognized by those who encounter him, not even by the disciples, who continue to misunderstand. It is known only to the reader, and to the unclean spirits who recognize him as "the Holy One of God" (Mark 1:24), "the Son of God" (Mark 3:11), and "Son of the Most High God" (Mark 5:7).

The story of the transfiguration (Mark 9:2-8) again proclaims Jesus' divine Sonship, underlining his authority with symbols drawn from the Old

---

[26] Ibid., 32.
[27] Walter Kasper, *Jesus the Christ* (New York: Paulist, 1976) 109.
[28] Dunn, *Christology in the Making*, 46.

Testament. Peter, James, and John witness a transfiguring of Jesus' appearance; his garments become "dazzling white," a sign of otherworldly glory. Moses and Elijah, representing the Law and the Prophets, appear talking with Jesus. The cloud which overshadows them represents the divine presence, and God speaks from the cloud saying, "This is my beloved Son. Listen to him" (Mark 9:7). The expression "beloved son" appears again in the parable of the tenants (Mark 12:6); Dunn notes that this and Luke 22:29 "have a fair claim to be part of Jesus' original teaching," suggesting that Jesus sensed "an eschatological uniqueness in his relationship with God . . . as the son who had the unique role of bringing others to share in the kingdom to which he had already been appointed (Luke 22:29f.)."[29]

At the solemn moment of his trial before the Sanhedrin, the two titles of Messiah and Son of God are again joined when the high priest asks Jesus, "Are you the Messiah, the son of the Blessed One?" (Mark 14:61). Jesus replies in the affirmative, with a reference to Daniel 7:14: "I am; and 'you will see the Son of Man / seated at the right hand of the Power / and coming with the clouds of heaven'" (Mark 14:62). Again, there is no recognition of who Jesus is; the high priest accuses him of blasphemy. It is only after his death when the centurion, ironically a non-Jew, exclaims, "Truly this man was the Son of God!" (Mark 15:39) that Jesus is recognized and confessed as the Son of God. Michael Cook sees this contrastive sentence—this man/Son of God—as expressing "Mark's root metaphor."[30]

What does "Son of God" mean in Mark's Gospel? It would be difficult to conclude that Jesus in Mark's Gospel is Son of God in more than an adopted or declared sense. There is no virginal conception in Mark, no Christmas story. Jesus is the beloved of God, the Messiah and Suffering Servant who would be revealed as God's Son. He is Son of God in a functional rather than a metaphysical sense.[31]

Still, there are moments when it appears that Mark senses that Jesus' identity goes beyond what he is able to say explicitly. For example, in his story of Jesus walking on the water (Mark 6:45-52), he inserts a line in the center of the pericope that seems jarring to us. After saying that Jesus saw the disciples tossed about on the water and came toward them, Mark says, "He meant to pass by them." The line was dropped by Matthew, and Luke omits the whole story. But to a Jew, familiar with hearing the Hebrew Scriptures, it would ring some bells. There is a remarkable parallel between

---

[29] Ibid., 28.

[30] Michael L. Cook, *Christology as Narrative Quest* (Collegeville: The Liturgical Press, 1997) 95.

[31] Haight, *Jesus: Symbol of God*, 161.

this verse in context and Job 9:11, which after describing God who "treads upon the crests of the sea" (Job 9:8; cf. Ps 78:19), says two verses later: "should he pass by, I am not aware of him." Mark's story is an epiphany, drawing a careful parallel between God's self-manifestations in the Old Testament and Jesus' epiphany to his disciples.[32] The Transfiguration story may be a similar example; there are clear parallels between it and the Sinai theophany (Exod 24:15-18; 34:29-30).

Matthew

Matthew was written most probably in the mid-eighties to a largely Jewish-Christian community with an increasing number of Gentile converts. It shows a strong concern for the Gentile mission and reflects considerable tension between the Church and the synagogue; the actual break between the two may have already taken place.[33] The community has been most often identified with the church of Antioch.

Because of the church/synagogue conflict and the anxiety of the Jewish Christians, Matthew is careful to show how the coming of the Gentiles is all according to God's plan. Twelve times he introduces a pericope with "All this took place to fulfill what the Lord had said through the prophet" (Matt 1:22) or something similar. He presents Jesus as a rabbi or teacher, one who can interpret the Law with authority, and especially as a new Moses, organizing his sayings into five great discourses, paralleling the five books of the Torah or Law. Jesus is the New Israel, the fulfillment of the Law and the Prophets, the Messiah in the line of David.[34]

But Son of God may well be Matthew's most significant christological affirmation.[35] His Christology is considerably higher than that of either Mark or the Q source. The titles "Son of Man" and "Son of God" both play important roles; the former occurs more often (30 times versus between 9 and 12 times for the latter). While Matthew uses Son of Man to show Jesus as the final agent of God, the title Son of God "relates especially to Matthew's biographical interests."[36]

He brings the title "Son of God" to a new level. According to Marinus de Jonge, he "is portrayed above all as the Son who operates in union with

---

[32] Cf. John P. Meier, *A Marginal Jew*, Vol. Two: *Mentor, Message, and Miracles* (New York: Doubleday, 1994) 928.

[33] John P. Meier in Raymond E. Brown and John P. Meier, *Antioch and Rome: New Testament Cradles of Catholic Christianity* (New York: Paulist, 1983) 48–49.

[34] See Richard, *Jesus: One and Many*, 146–49.

[35] Dunn, *Christology in the Making*, 48.

[36] Richard, *Jesus: One and Many*, 155.

the Father,"[37] while for Richard, the full revelation of Jesus' identity as Son of God and Son of Man shows him as God's presence in the world (Matt 1:23; cf. 28:20b).[38] Jesus frequently refers to God as "my Father" in Matthew (16 times), and once refers to the Son of Man coming "in his Father's glory" (Matt 16:27). All but two of these references are unique to Matthew. In a tradition common to the Synoptics, Jesus three times refers to himself as "the Son." The first occurs in the so-called "bolt from the Johannine sky"[39] which comes from Q and is shared with Luke: "No one knows the Son except the Father, and no one knows the Father except the Son and anyone to whom the Son chooses to reveal him" (Matt 11:27/Luke 10:22).[40] The second is the passage where Jesus acknowledges his ignorance of the time of the coming judgment: "But of that day and hour no one knows, neither the angels of heaven, nor the Son, but the Father alone" (Matt 24:36; Mark 13:32). The third occurs in the parable of the tenants who kill the son of the owner of the vineyard (Matt 21:37; Mark 12:6/Luke 20:13).[41]

Thus for Matthew Jesus' true identity is no longer hidden. When Peter confesses his belief at Caesarea Philippi that Jesus is the Messiah, in Matthew's version he adds, "the Son of the living God" (Matt 16:16); Jesus points out that such knowledge is based on a divine revelation. When he startles the disciples by walking to them on the water, they do him homage and cry out, "Truly, you are the Son of God" (Matt 14:33). Even those who deride Jesus in his passion mock him as "the Son of God" (Matt 27:40, 43).

Most significantly, Matthew's infancy material includes the story of Jesus' virginal conception (Matt 1:18-25). Like Luke, Matthew attests that Jesus is God's Son in a unique way, from the moment of his conception by the Holy Spirit.[42]

Luke

Luke's Christology is particularly difficult to categorize. The disciples in Luke do not confess Jesus as Son of God during his public ministry, but Luke does show them referring to him as Lord for the sake of his readers.[43]

[37] De Jonge, *Christology in Context*, 95.

[38] Richard, *Jesus: One and Many*, 152–54.

[39] Kasper, *Jesus the Christ*, 109; he concludes that this phrase is a "reworking of authentic words of Jesus"; 110.

[40] Dunn says that this "expresses in summary (and rather formal) terms claims which were implicit (and occasionally explicit) elsewhere in his ministry"; *Christology in the Making*, 200.

[41] Raymond Brown sees these passages as making it likely that Jesus spoke and thought of himself as "the Son," implying a very special relationship to God; *Introduction*, 89.

[42] See Richard, *Jesus: One and Many*, 150–51.

[43] Brown, *Introduction*, 120–21.

Roger Haight sees Luke as developing a Spirit Christology, a "two-stage" narrative Christology beginning with Jesus' conception by the power of the Spirit, following him through his ministry, and ending with his exalted reign.[44]

Luke's two works should be seen as one. He presents Jesus as God's prophet (Luke 7:16, 39; 9:8, 19; 13:33; 24:19), Servant (Acts 3:14; 4:23-31), Messiah (Luke 2:11, 26; 9:20; 23:35; Acts 4:26), Savior (Luke 2:11; Acts 5:31; 13:23) and reigning at God's right hand (Acts 2:33; 5:31; 7:55-56). Perhaps his favorite title for Jesus is "Lord," used in both Gospel and Acts; in the Gospel he frequently refers to Jesus as "the Lord" (Luke 7:13, 19; 10:1, 39, 41; 2:42; 13:15). According to Richard, the key to his vision is the concept of divine visitation (Luke 7:16; 19:44) and care for humanity through Jesus in accordance with the divine plan for salvation; he describes Luke's Jesus as the "agent of God" or "the Christ of God" (Luke 9:20).[45] The notion of divine necessity is expressed repeatedly (41 times in Luke/Acts, versus 61 times in the rest of the New Testament) by the Greek *dei*, translated as "it is necessary that" or "must."[46] Perhaps this is most clearly expressed in the Emmaus story where Jesus says: "'Was it not necessary that the Messiah should suffer these things and enter into his glory?' Then beginning with Moses and all the prophets, he interpreted to them what referred to him in all the scriptures" (Luke 24:26-27).

Luke is dependent on Mark as a major source for his Gospel, and he shares with Matthew the tradition of the virginal conception of Jesus (Luke 1:35); though each evangelist develops the story independently, a number of common elements suggest their reliance on an earlier tradition. Thus, without a human father, Jesus is "Son of God" in a unique sense, from his conception. Jesus is called Son of God at his baptism (Luke 3:21-22), temptation (Luke 4:1-13), transfiguration (Luke 9:28-36), by the Gerasene demoniac (Luke 8:28), and asked if he is the Son of God at his trial (Luke 22:67-70). Luke shares with Matthew the Q logion: "No one knows who the Son is except the Father, and who the Father is except the Son and anyone to whom the Son wishes to reveal him" (Luke 10:22). So the Son of God typology is also present in his Gospel. As de Jonge says, in Luke, Jesus "is the Son of God, in his own way; then as God's representative on earth, now as the living Lord of the church."[47]

---

[44] Haight, *Jesus: Symbol of God*, 163–68.
[45] Richard, *Jesus: One and Many*, 185.
[46] Ibid., 183.
[47] De Jonge, *Christology in Context*, 105.

But behind Luke/Acts, the early exaltation typology is still recognizable. Though Luke considers Jesus as Messiah, Lord, and Son of God from the moment of his conception, in his theology "the question of Jesus' pre-existence or incarnation is never raised."[48] In the background is the early "two-stage" view which posits two modes of existence for Jesus, one earthly, the other heavenly. Similar versions of it can be found in 1 Timothy 3:16, Romans 1:3-4, and Mark 12:35-36.[49]

Wisdom Christologies

The Wisdom literature of late Judaism—Proverbs, Job, Ecclesiastes (Qoheleth), Sirach, and Wisdom of Solomon—provided another rich source for the christological reflection of the early Christian communities. But it is only in the last thirty years that the importance of the Wisdom tradition in late Judaism has been taken seriously by scholars, perhaps in part because Sirach and Wisdom are among those "deuterocanonical" books used by the early Christians in the Septuagint, the Greek version of the Hebrew Scriptures, but not included in the Jewish canon when it was drawn up by the Pharisees at the end of the first century C.E. on the grounds of their late origin and Greek language. These books, called "the Apocrypha" by Protestants, were dropped from their canon by the Protestant reformers in the sixteenth century.

In reviewing the Wisdom tradition earlier, we saw a number of themes that would recur in various interpretations of Jesus. In the tradition Sophia/Wisdom is feminine symbol, an attribute of God (Prov 1, 8, 9; Sir 34; Wis 7–9) or the personification of the transcendent God's presence in the world.[50] Sophia/Wisdom comes forth from the mouth of God (Sir 24:3), is begotten before the creation of the world (Sir 1:4; Prov 8:22-23) and plays a role in creation (Prov 8:25-31). She reflects God's glory and is an image of God's goodness (Wis 7:25-26), has a mission in the world, is sent down from heaven to make her dwelling in Israel, with God choosing the place for her tent (Sir 24:8). Sophia/Wisdom is identified with Torah (Sir 6:37; 24:22), is active in Israel's history (Wis 10–12), crying aloud in the streets (Prov 1:20). Finally, the Wisdom tradition wrestles with the plight of the

---

[48] Haight, *Jesus: Symbol of God*, 166; see also Joseph A. Fitzmyer, *The Gospel According to Luke: Introduction, Translation, and Notes* (Garden City, N.Y.: Doubleday, 1981) 197.

[49] Helmut Flender, *St. Luke: Theologian of Redemptive History* (Philadelphia: Fortress, 1967) 41.

[50] See Elizabeth A. Johnson, *She Who Is: The Mystery of God in Feminist Theological Discourse* (New York: Crossroad, 1992) 86–93.

just one, the righteous sufferer who is the victim of the wicked, who "boasts that God is his father" (Wis 2:16) and is called a "Son of God" (Wis 2:18).

Wisdom theology is woven through numerous New Testament sources.[51] Jesus himself was most probably a teacher in the Wisdom tradition. In his teaching he uses aphorisms and narrative parables (*meshalim*) and avoids the classic prophetic formula, "Thus says Yahweh." The Q source is a collection of sayings, the majority of which are Wisdom sayings, while Jesus himself is presented as the embodiment of Wisdom, protesting on his own behalf against his critics, "Wisdom is vindicated by all her children" (Luke 7:35; cf. Matt 11:19). The letter of James shows dependence on both Proverbs and Ben Sirach and Witherington calls Matthew and John "the gospels of Wisdom."[52] More to our interest here, he argues that "christological hymn fragments found in the Pauline corpus, the Fourth Gospel, and Hebrews are fundamentally expressions of a Wisdom Christology that goes back to early Jewish Christianity and reflects the fact that some of the earliest christological thinking about Jesus amounted to what today would be called a very 'high' Christology indeed. Indeed, it was a Christology which ultimately led to a full-blown doctrine of the pre-existence of the Son."[53]

There is Wisdom material throughout the Pauline corpus, for example, his stress that knowledge of God is available to all from creation and the impartiality of God's judgment towards both Jews and Gentiles in Romans 1–2:11. In this section, I would like to look briefly at some of the examples of Wisdom Christology in Paul.

Christ As the Wisdom of God

In the first four chapters of 1 Corinthians, Paul contrasts divine wisdom with the human wisdom of both Jews and Greeks: "God's wisdom, mysterious, hidden, which God predetermined before the ages for our glory" (1 Cor 2:7) and revealed in the Cross of Christ. For Paul, the wisdom of God is Christ himself; "For Jews demand signs and Greeks look for wisdom, but we proclaim Christ crucified, a stumbling block to Jews and foolishness to Gentiles, but to those who are called, Jews and Greeks alike, Christ the power of God and the wisdom of God" (1 Cor 1:22-24).

---

[51] See Ben Witherington III, *Jesus the Sage: The Pilgrimage of Wisdom* (Minneapolis: Fortress, 1994); see also Elizabeth A. Johnson, "Jesus, The Wisdom of God: A Biblical Basis for Non-Androcentric Christology," *Ephemerides Theologicae Lovanienses* 61 (1985) 335–80.

[52] Witherington, *Jesus the Sage*, 335.

[53] Ibid., 249; see 249–94; also J. T. Sanders, *The New Testament Christological Hymns* (Cambridge: Cambridge University Press, 1971).

Christ As Preexistent

The famous hymn in Philippians 2:6-11 is earlier than Paul, though he may have adapted it (perhaps adding "even death on a cross" in v. 8c) in incorporating it into his letter. The first part of the hymn describes Christ Jesus descending into human likeness to his death on a cross, the second his exaltation to glory:

> Who, though he was in the form of God
>> did not regard equality with God
>>> something to be grasped.
>> Rather he emptied himself,
>> taking the form of a slave,
>> coming in human likeness;
>> and found human in appearance,
>> he humbled himself,
>> becoming obedient to death,
>>> even death on a cross.
> Because of this, God greatly exalted him
>> and bestowed on him the name
>> that is above every name,
>> that at the name of Jesus
>> every knee should bend,
>> of those in heaven and on earth and under
>>> the earth,
>> and every tongue confess that
> Jesus Christ is Lord,
>> to the glory of God the Father.

Philippians 2:6-11

The intention of this passage has been much debated. While the language of exchange ("in the form [*morphē*] of God"/"coming in human likeness") and descent suggest a preexistence Christology, many scholars interpret the first part of the hymn against the background of Paul's second Adam Christology. Unlike Adam, Jesus the Christ does not grasp at equality with God, the temptation to which Adam succumbs in Genesis 3:5. Thus they see the hymn as representing a low Christology.[54]

But other scholars, recognizing Wisdom themes here, particularly the personification of Wisdom (Prov 8:33-31; Wis 7:22-26), see it as evidence of preexistence Christology. Witherington stresses the abasement

---

[54] Richard, *Jesus: One and Many*, 328–29; see also Dunn, *Christology in the Making*, 113–25.

and exaltation of the righteous one (Wis 3:1-4; 5:1; 5:15-16; 9:4-5) and the choice made to take on human flesh.[55] Brendan Byrne argues that Philippians should not be interpreted as representing a Christology different from Paul's. The implication of a choice to take on the human condition on Christ's part here is also present in 2 Corinthians 8:9: "For you know the gracious act of our Lord Jesus Christ, that for your sake he became poor although he was rich, so that by his poverty you might become rich." Byrne maintains that both passages rule out any interpretation of preexistence in a nonpersonal way,[56] (for example, Christ only represents God's wisdom). Though Haight considers the text still in dispute, he acknowledges that "this reading in terms of a descent christology is gaining wider acceptance."[57] If so, it means the preexistence Christology appears much earlier than has previously been thought.

Christ As the Image of God and Firstborn of All Creation

An early Christian hymn in Colossians 1:15-20 (the letter itself may be Deutero-Pauline) describes Christ as "the image of God" and "the firstborn of all creation."

> He is the image of the invisible God,
>   the firstborn of all creation.
> For in him were created all things in heaven
>   and on earth,
>   the visible and the invisible,
>   whether thrones or dominions or
>   principalities or powers;
>   all things were created through him and for him.
> He is before all things,
>   and in him all things hold together.
>
> Colossians 1:15-17

The following parallels can be drawn between the language of the hymn in Colossians and the Wisdom literature.[58]

---

[55] Witherington, *Jesus the Sage*, 260–66.

[56] Brendan Byrne, "Christ's Pre-Existence in Pauline Soteriology," *Theological Studies* 58 (1977) 321.

[57] Haight, *Jesus: Symbol of God*, 169.

[58] Witherington in *Jesus the Sage* has assembled such a list, 267, as has Haight, *Jesus: Symbol of God*, 169.

Wisdom Literature	Colossians 1:15-17
For she is the refulgence of eternal light, / the spotless mirror of the power of God, / the image of his goodness (Wis 7:26)	The image of the invisible God (15a)
The LORD begot me, the firstborn of his ways (Prov 8:22) Before all ages, in the beginning, he created me (Sir 24:9)	The firstborn of all creation (15b)
The LORD by wisdom founded the earth (Prov 3:19a) For she is instructress in the understanding of God, / the selector of his works (Wis 8:4)	For in him were created all things in heaven and on earth (16a)
Compared to light, she takes precedence (Wis 7:29b)	He is before all things (17a)
[S]he reaches from end to end mightily / and governs all things well (Wis 8:1)	And in him all things hold together (17b)

The hymn is most probably pre-Pauline. Not all scholars would agree with Witherington's suggestion that the hymn's characterization of Christ as "first born" (*prōtotokos*) asserts his uncreated status. But in indicating the priority of Christ to all things and in giving him, like Wisdom, a role in creation, it at least played a role in that development.[59] At the same time, that Paul himself thought of Christ in terms of preexistence cannot be excluded, as we saw in the previous section. We need now to consider preexistence Christology more explicitly, but first, a comment on some recent developments.

Some feminist theologians have sought to privilege Wisdom Christology over more traditional Son of God and Logos Christologies.[60] There is much to recommend a renewed emphasis on Wisdom. It seems to have provided a crucial bridge between late Jewish thinking and the development of the Church's Christology from very early in the Christian tradition.

[59] Witherington, *Jesus the Sage*, 269–71.

[60] Johnson, "Jesus, the Wisdom of God"; also Elisabeth Schüssler Fiorenza, *Jesus: Miriam's Child, Sophia's Prophet: Critical Issues in Feminist Christology* (New York: Continuum, 1994).

Even more importantly, the figure of Sophia/Wisdom represents a feminine metaphor for God's presence and saving action in the world applied by the early Christians to Jesus. Recovering this metaphor for Christology means moving towards a Christology less restricted by gender. In Elizabeth Johnson's words, "This foundational metaphor relieves the monopoly of the male metaphors of Logos and Son and destabilizes the patriarchal imagination."[61] This has important implications for anthropology as well as for Christology, for as symbol, being the Christ is not restricted to maleness, meaning that women can image and represent Jesus the Christ as well as men. "The baptismal tradition that configures both women and men to the living Christ and the martyrdom tradition that recognizes the image of Christ in the women and men who shed their blood have always born this out. Maleness does not constitute the essence of Christ, but, in the Spirit, redeemed and redeeming humanity does."[62] At the same time, without rejecting this view, Brendan Byrne's caution against neglecting the Son of God category is worth noting: "What Wisdom Christology brings out less explicitly is the sense of God's familial involvement in the work of redemption, the sense of the cost to God in the giving up of God's own Son expressed in texts such as Rom 8:4 and 8:32."[63]

Preexistence Christologies

If it cannot be said with certainty that the hymn in Colossians 1:15-20 affirms the preexistence of Jesus, that is not the case with the Gospel of John.

John

It is widely recognized that the Christology of John's Gospel is the highest in the New Testament. The familiar Prologue (John 1:1-14), another early Christian hymn, sketches in poetry the Christology of the Fourth Gospel; the Word of God, with God from the beginning, the Word that was God, the Word through whom all things were made, has become flesh and we have beheld his glory, the glory of the only begotten Son of the Father. Like Colossians 1:15-20, the Prologue is heavily informed by the Wisdom tradition (cf. Prov 3; 8:35), though *Logos* has been substituted for *Sophia*.

---

[61] Elizabeth A. Johnson, "Redeeming the Name of Christ," in *Freeing Theology: The Essentials of Theology in Feminist Perspective*, ed. Catherine Mowry LaCugna (HarperSan Francisco, 1993) 127.

[62] Ibid., 129.

[63] Byrne, "Christ's Pre-Existence," 329.

Indeed personified Wisdom themes have been woven through the whole Gospel.[64] Haight says that "the Johannine hymn both resembles the other wisdom christologies and transcends them in the direction of the incarnation of an hypostatized being."[65] However, with his preference for a Spirit Christology, he warns against reading the poetry of the hymn in a literalist manner. What seems in the Prologue to be statements about Jesus in himself become instead statements about "the realism of God's presence in Jesus" (Logos) and "the concrete visibility and availability of God's revelation in Jesus (incarnation)."[66]

But it is not clear that the Prologue of John can be reduced to poetry. It is not the Prologue that interprets the Gospel; rather, the Prologue should be interpreted in light of the gospel into which it has been incorporated. Here the portrayal of Jesus, very different from that of the Synoptics, clearly raises the question of the divinity of Jesus. In John, Jesus is recognized as Messiah (John 1:41) and Son of God (John 1:49) from the beginning. He speaks of himself as the "Son" (John 3:16, 17; 5:20, 21; 6:40; 14:13) and proclaims openly his divine origin (John 8:42) and unity with the Father (10:30, 38; 14:9). Repeatedly he uses the divine formula, "I am," the Greek *egō eimi* which is used in the Septuagint to translate the Hebrew revelatory formula "I am Yahweh" or "I am He" (Exod 6:7; Isa 43:10). While not all uses of the "I am" are equally significant, Raymond Brown calls special attention to the absolute use of the formula without the predicate, as in "For if you do not believe that I AM, you will die in your sins" (John 8:24), or "When you lift up the Son of Man, then you will realize that I AM" (John 8:28), or "Amen, amen, I say to you, before Abraham came to be, I AM" (John 8:58), and finally, "From now on I am telling you before it happens, so that when it happens you may believe that I AM" (John 13:19). Brown argues that this "absolute use . . . has the effect of portraying Jesus as divine with (pre)existence as his identity, even as the Greek OT understood the God of Israel."[67]

---

[64] Raymond Brown charts the numerous echoes of this tradition in his Appendix IV: "Features in John's Christology," *Introduction*, 205–10.

[65] Haight, *Jesus: Symbol of God*, 176.

[66] Ibid., 177.

[67] Brown, *Introduction*, 139; Richard sees these, not as revealing his being or nature, but rather his heavenly origin and role in God's dealings with humanity; *Jesus: One and Many*, 215–16.

Is Jesus Called God?

At the end of his introduction to Christology, Brown asks in an appendix, did the New Testament Christians call Jesus "God" (*theos*)? He answers in the affirmative, pointing to three texts where Jesus is clearly called God.[68] In Hebrews 1:8-9, where the context is again Wisdom theology, the author addresses Jesus in the words of Psalm 45: "Your throne, O God, stands forever and ever; and a righteous scepter is the scepter of your kingdom . . . therefore God, your God, anointed you with the oil of gladness above your companions" (cf. Ps 45:7-8). The Gospel of John, as we have already seen, begins with a hymn or Prologue, proclaiming:

> In the beginning was the Word,
>   and the Word was with God,
>   and the Word was God.

And finally, in John's Easter story of the risen Jesus' appearance to Thomas in the Upper Room, Thomas who had asked for empirical evidence comes to faith with perhaps the highest christological confession of the New Testament: "My Lord and my God" (John 20:28).

Brown also mentions nine texts that *may* refer to Jesus as God, but are dubious, either because of textual variants (Gal 2:20; Acts 20:28; and John 1:18) or because of syntax (Col 2:2-3; 2 Thess 1:12; Titus 2:13; Rom 9:5; 1 John 5:20, and 2 Pet 1:1). It is interesting that after eliminating four clearly dubious texts (Gal 2:20; Acts 20:28; Col 2:2-3; and 2 Thess 1:12) and adding the indisputable ones he ends up with eight texts which seem to confess Jesus as God, "the majority of which are clearly situated in a background of worship and liturgy."[69] His point is that addressing Jesus as God grows out of prayer and worship, and is primarily soteriological rather than ontological. We will need to consider this further in a subsequent chapter. But Brown's observation about the liturgical provenance of these texts is worth noting.

In a very significant study, Larry Hurtado has argued that the Jesus-directed "devotion" of the primitive Palestinian church effected a mutation in the Jewish monotheistic tradition which gave a "binitarian" shape to their worship by making Jesus an object of the devotion characteristically reserved for God. He illustrates this by examining six features of Christian devotion (or worship), evident from the earliest years of the Christian movement: hymns both celebrating Christ and sung to him (John 1:1-8;

---

[68] Brown, *Introduction*, 185–95.
[69] Ibid., 193.

Col 1:15-20; Phil 2:5-11); prayers addressed to him, including prayers during the liturgy (Acts 7:59-60; 2 Cor 12:2-10; 1 Cor 16:22); the use of his
name, regularly invoking Jesus (Acts 9:14, 21; 1 Cor 1:2) and baptizing in
the name of Jesus (Acts 2:38; 8:16); the Lord's Supper; confessions of faith
in Jesus; and prophecy in the words of the risen Christ (Rev 1:17–3:22).[70] It
was this cultic veneration of Jesus which explains, at least in part, why the
titles of Jesus "underwent a redefinition in early Christian circles, coming to
be used for a figure regarded as holding a heavenly and divine status."[71]

Conclusion

From the earliest days of the Church the disciples of Jesus interpreted
their experience of Jesus in symbols and images drawn from their religious
tradition, the Hebrew Scriptures and later noncanonical Jewish literature.
As they struggled to express their faith, particularly as they nourished it
through their worship,[72] they stretched the language of their tradition and
gave it new meaning.

The New Testament witnesses to a rich variety of Christologies, and
while there is a development in the ability of these early communities to
articulate their Easter faith, it is neither linear nor uniform. Christologies
can be expressed in multiple ways, there is considerable overlapping of
types in the various documents, and both low and high Christologies can
be found in the various Christian communities even before Paul.

The very early Easter Christologies (Parousia/Exaltation) show that the
risen Lord was already an object of prayer. Son of God Christologies are
first related to the Resurrection, understood as appointment to divine Sonship described in Psalm 2:7, though many scholars hold that this relationship is evident in Jesus' own words, of himself as "son" and his God as
"Abba."

The Wisdom tradition, with its feminine personification of Wisdom,
her coming forth from God, role in creation, and mission to God's people,
seems to have played an important role in attributing preexistence to Jesus,
perhaps much earlier than has generally been believed. Recovering this traditional christological symbol which is feminine rather than masculine
also has important implications for theological anthropology.

---

[70] Larry W. Hurtado, *One God, One Lord: Early Christian Devotion and Ancient Jewish
Monotheism* (Philadelphia: Fortress, 1988) 99–114.

[71] Ibid., 12–13.

[72] See Roger Haight, *Jesus: Symbol of God*, 181.

Preexistence is clearly attributed to Jesus in John, and at the end of the Gospel, Thomas confesses Jesus as both "Lord" and "God" (John 20:28). But even this language can find parallels elsewhere and earlier in the New Testament, mostly in hymns reflecting the liturgy and prayer of the early communities. Christology begins in worship.

Chapter 9

From the New Testament to Chalcedon

As Christianity began to spread beyond its original home in Judaism into the Hellenistic world of the Roman Empire, it was confronted by the challenge of finding a way to express its faith in the thought categories of the Greco-Roman world. Hellenistic philosophy was to prove helpful here, but it also represented a threat, for it was the language of a very different culture. The challenge faced by the Church was that of adopting the philosophical language of a new culture without simply "Hellenizing" its faith.

Faith and the Dialogue with Culture

That God's salvation in Christ Jesus was good news, not just for Jews, but for non-Jews as well, was evident to many by the end of the first Christian generation. Paul's letters are charged with this message; he saw his own ministry as a ministry to the Gentiles (Gal 1:16; 2:9), a "ministry of reconciliation" (2 Cor 5:18). Over half of the Acts of the Apostles is devoted to telling the story of Paul's missionary efforts. Thus the universal significance of the Christ-event was recognized very early in the life of the Church, even if the definitive and painful break with Judaism was to come considerably later.

As the Church in the post–New Testament period sought to proclaim the Gospel to the nations, it found itself in a very different culture. The citizens of the Roman Empire did not think in the messianic, Wisdom, and apocalyptic categories that had informed the religious imaginations of the early Jewish Christians. The educated of the Empire had a very different worldview, formed by Hellenistic culture and thought. Furthermore, many of the emerging apologists and theologians were converts themselves whose intellectual background was Hellenistic philosophy, not the Jewish Scriptures. It was these new Christians who brought Christianity into a dialogue with the surrounding culture, defending the faith against its critics, criticizing Greco-Roman theology where necessary, but often showing appreciation for its philosophical insights. For example, Justin Martyr (d. 165) and Clement of Alexandria (d. ca. 215) sought to illustrate how the best insights of Greco-Roman philosophy were more fully illumined by Christian revelation. Justin himself was a philosopher who after his conversion tried to present Christianity as the true philosophy, holding that "Whatever things were rightly said among all men are the property of us Christians."[1] The biblical narratives and symbols, interpreted typologically by the Church Fathers, remained primary, but they also drew on elements of Platonic, Neoplatonic, and Stoic thought to express Christian theology, concepts such as the impassability of God, the Logos, and the immortality of the soul. Today we refer to this process as "inculturation."

The process was not always an easy one. The biblical language was largely mythopoetic, while Hellenistic culture, though rich in its own myths, used the more universal language and categories of Greek or Hellenistic philosophy. We might consider this as the "scientific" language of the day. But incorporating the categories of Hellenistic philosophy presented a new challenge to Christian theology, particularly to Christology.

The New Testament church had been able to successfully balance its inherited Jewish monotheism with its faith in the risen Jesus Christ, the Lord, invoked in its worship and honored with divine names and functions. Using symbols and images drawn from the Hebrew Scriptures, the New Testament authors developed their Christologies in largely functional terms; Jesus is described from the perspective of his "mission," that is, in relation to us (*quoad nos*). Thus, we have seen Christologies formulated in virtue of his Second Coming, or his being exalted at God's right hand, or as Messiah, Lord, Son of God, Wisdom of God, and so on.

But did the New Testament authors speak of Jesus, not just functionally, but as he is in himself (*in se*)? Walter Kasper has argued that the ongoing reflection on the titles "Son" and "Son of God" within the New Testament witnesses to a transition to a more metaphysical Christology, so that Christologies of being and mission exist side by side. He sees the Fourth Gospel in particular as representing a divine Sonship that is ontologically understood, not on the basis of speculation, but in order to bring out soteriological interests.[2] Others are less ready to find ontological implications in the New Testament texts. We saw in the previous chapter that Roger Haight, noting the movement of the Johannine Prologue towards "the incarnation of a hypostatized being," warns against "misreading" the text in a "literalist" way.[3]

---

[1] Justin Martyr, *2 Apol.*12.4.

[2] Walter Kasper, *Jesus the Christ* (New York: Paulist, 1976) 165–66.

[3] Roger Haight, *Jesus: Symbol of God* (New York: Orbis, 1999) 176, 177.

It is difficult not to see some ontological implications in the Christologies of the New Testament, particularly in the Fourth Gospel. The author does far more than incorporate the Prologue. A Jewish convert with a Jew's reverence for the holy name of God, not even to be spoken aloud, would not easily use the divine formula, "I am," of Jesus, or have him proclaim so openly his divine origin (John 8:42) and unity with the Father (10:30, 38; 14:9), or have Thomas confess him as "my Lord and my God" (John 20:28), without some understanding of what he was suggesting. The argument about whether the New Testament authors intended the ontological implications suggested by their use of language perhaps cannot be resolved.

But what is without dispute is that in the post-New Testament period, as the Church continued its evangelizing mission in the different culture of the Greco-Roman world, the next generation of Christian authors understood their tradition as affirming the divinity of Jesus and began to proclaim their christological faith in ontological terms. The Apostolic Fathers, Clement of Rome (ca. 96), Ignatius of Antioch (d. 110), Hermas (ca. 150), were roughly contemporary with the later New Testament authors. Firmly monotheistic, they nevertheless presumed the preexistence of Christ as well as his role in creation and redemption, and like certain New Testament works, they did not hesitate to call Jesus God. In his *Letter to the Ephesians*, Ignatius of Antioch writes that "Jesus Christ our God was conceived of Mary" and in a *Letter to the Smyrnaeans* he proclaims "Jesus Christ, the Divine One who has gifted you with such wisdom."[4]

The Apologists who followed them, Justin Martyr, Tatian, Hippolytus, and Tertullian began to address more systematically the relation of Christ to the Father, turning to the concept of the Logos or Word, common to Hellenistic philosophy, the Septuagint, and to the Fourth Gospel, where it was used to describe Jesus as the preexistent Word of God.[5] Also significant was the Gnostic emphasis on the role of the Logos in creation as an intermediate being or emanation. From this point on, philosophy was to increasingly provide a useful intellectual framework for the Church's theology.

The Challenge of Greek Philosophy

But the philosophy of the day was not without its own dangers for Christian theology. The Greek philosophical tradition was highly dualistic,

---

[4] *Eph.* 18:2; *Smyrnaeans* 1:1.

[5] See J.N.D. Kelly, *Early Christian Doctrines* (London: Adam and Charles Black, 1958) 95–101; also Aloys Grillmeier, *Christ in Christian Tradition*, Vol. I, *From the Apostolic Age to Chalcedon (451)* (Atlanta: John Knox, 1965) 106–10.

privileging spirit over matter, the immutable over the changing, the eternal over the temporal. The highest reality was impersonal universal nature such as Plato's world of the forms, while the divine was conceived as unbegotten, immutable, ineffable, free from passion, and utterly transcendent. How different this was from the Jewish view of a God who was active in history.

At the same time, popular Greco-Roman philosophy, marked by the influence of this tradition, particularly Plato, tended toward a contempt for the body which by its very materiality was enmeshed in the world of becoming and change. Socrates went to his death with equanimity, convinced that he was about to realize the philosopher's goal of freeing the soul from the limitations of the body. His disciple Plato spoke of the soul as "imprisoned" in the body. This was very different from the Hebrew perspective, which looked on the human person as a somatic unity, a living body. Once the person died, the breath of life or spirit (*ruah*) departed and the person ceased to exist. The fact that so many Christians today still think instinctively of life after death in terms of the immortality of the soul rather than the resurrection of the body, in spite of the centrality of the Resurrection to Christian faith, is evidence of how deeply Western culture has been stamped by this Greek dualism.

The Christian apologists turned naturally to the concept of the *logos* in their efforts to explain the Church's christological faith in the new culture in which it was living. But though the term was common to the Church, given its Jewish heritage, and to Greek philosophy, it had very different connotations in each. In the Hebrew tradition, which valued the word of a person, "word" (in Hb. *dabar*) was understood as a dynamic extension of the person's personality and power. A word, once spoken, could not be withdrawn. Similarly, the divine Word was an embodiment of God's power, going forth to accomplish the divine will, in creation (Gen 1:1–2:4a; Isa 55:11), or when spoken in God's name by a prophet (Isa 9:7; Jer 7:2), usually to call the people back to God or to bring God's judgment on the nations. In the biblical tradition, God acted in history through the divine Word. In the Fourth Gospel, though the language is Greek (*Logos*), the concept is profoundly Hebraic (*Dabar*); like Wisdom, the Word was present with God in the beginning, active in creation, and took on flesh in Jesus. Thus the Hebrew Word was a *soteriological* principle. However in the Greek philosophical tradition going back as far as Heraclitus (ca. 500 B.C.E.), *logos*, which could be translated as either "word" or "reason," was a *cosmological* principle; it was understood as a principle of rationality or organization, giving form and meaning to the cosmos, just as it did to the otherwise meaningless sounds of the human voice.

In Christian theology, Logos, like its usage in the Johannine Prologue, unites the two concepts; it is active in both creation and salvation. The precise relationship between the Word and Jesus was to be debated at length in the second century. And there was always the danger, given the power of the *logos* concept in classical thought and the Gnostic emphasis on the *logos* as mediator between the ineffable God and the world of change, of reducing the divine Logos to a subordinate emanation or cosmological principle, tendencies that are evident in the theologies of Justin, Tertullian, and Origen.

The Greek philosophical distaste for the world of change was also to find expression in two heterodox movements, Gnosticism and Docetism. It is interesting that these two heresies faced by the Church in this new cultural realm very early had difficulty, not with the Church's high Christology, but rather with its belief that the Logos/Word had become flesh.

Gnosticism

Gnosticism (from the Greek *gnōsis*, "knowledge") was a syncretistic religious movement, really a philosophical religion, that may have predated Christianity; it drew on both Hellenistic and Jewish sources and was not slow in incorporating Christian symbols as well. There may have been some Christians in the church of Corinth with Gnostic leanings (the mysterious "Christ" party) and the apocryphal Gospel of Thomas was a Gnostic work. What Gnosticism offered was a doctrine of salvation through knowledge, usually a secret knowledge available only to the initiated. For example, the Gospel of Thomas begins, "These are the secret sayings which the living Jesus spoke and which Didymos Judas Thomas wrote down. And he said, 'He who finds the interpretation of these sayings will not taste death.'"[6]

Like the Hellenistic culture out of which it came, Gnosticism was highly dualistic. Its concern was redemption, not in this world, but by escaping the world's entanglements, thus, with the liberation of the person from bodily and material existence. This contempt for the bodily and the material resulted in two different expressions in practice. Some Gnostics rejected whatever had to do with the body, particularly marriage and sexuality. Others, since bodily existence belonged to the fallen realm of materiality and salvation was through a higher, spiritual knowledge, saw morality as unimportant; they practiced an antinomianism or libertinism.[7]

---

[6] *The Apocryphal New Testament*, ed. J. K. Elliott (Oxford: Clarendon Press, 1993) 135.
[7] See Kelly, *Early Christian Doctrines*, 23–28.

Those in the Christ party at Corinth, justifying sexual immorality on the basis of their misinterpretation of Paul's teaching on freedom (1 Cor 6:12-20), are probably an example of this tendency. Because Gnosticism stressed one or more mediators between the ineffable God and the material universe, they found a natural affinity with certain aspects of Christian doctrine, particularly Christology.

Docetism

Docetism was a christological expression of Gnosticism. While the Docetists easily saw Christ as a mediator, what they could not accept was that the divine Word had become flesh, with all its earthy connotations. Thus, they taught that Jesus only "seemed" or "appeared" (Greek *dokeō*, "to seem") to have a human body. Marcion taught that he had only an apparent body, Valentine that he had a spiritual or pneumatic body. And if his body was not real, then his suffering was an illusion, ruled out by the divine impassability.

Both Gnostics and Docetists denied the humanity of Jesus. Docetic tendencies must have appeared very early; arguments against them are evident in the Johannine letters (1 John 4:1-3; 2 John 7) as well as in Ignatius of Antioch (ca. 110). Ignatius protests against those who claim that Christ had suffered only in appearance[8] and "do not admit that the Eucharist is the flesh of our Savior Jesus Christ, the flesh which suffered for our sins."[9] But by the end of the second century or early third, others were denying the divinity of Jesus.

From the Third Century to Nicaea

The christological conflict known as Arianism that was to rend the Church in the fourth century expressed at least in part the struggle between two great catechetical schools, one at Alexandria in Egypt, the other at Antioch in Syria. At issue was a practical, pastoral problem, most evident in the preaching of the time, and that was how to safeguard the unity of the person of Jesus. The confession of Jesus Christ as the Son of God demanded a twofold demonstration: "first that it was compatible with Jewish monotheism, and secondly that it was different from pagan polytheism. The solution of this problem depended on the possibility of combining in God a true unity with a true distinction (between Father, Son and Spirit)."[10] Alexandria

---

[8] *Eph.* 7; *Trall.* 9; *Smyrn.* 1–3.
[9] *Smyrn.* 6.
[10] Grillmeier, *Christ in Christian Tradition*, Vol. I, 106.

stressed an incarnational *Logos–sarx* (Word–flesh) Christology, Antioch an anthropological *Logos–anthropos* (Word–man or human being) Christology.

Alexandria: Logos–Sarx

The catechetical school at Alexandria was founded in 195 by Clement of Alexandria (d. 215), but its great name was Origen (ca. 185–254). Alexandrian theology, with its reverence for the transcendence and unity of God, placed great emphasis on the Logos which somehow "enters into" or becomes "attached" to human flesh. In Roger Haight's summary phrase, its core "lies in the consistent unity or continuous self-identity of the Logos or heavenly Son through the three stages of 'its career,' so to speak."[11] The focus is always on the Logos. Thus Clement speaks of Christ as having "clothed Himself with a man," being "God in the form of a man, unsullied" and Origen, who believed that human souls preexisted in a world of spiritual beings, taught that the Logos became fused with the soul of Jesus.[12] The danger here is a tendency to slight the full humanity of Jesus, a tendency that became effective denial later in the case of Apollinaris.

Antioch: Logos–Anthropos

The other great school was at Antioch, founded perhaps by Lucian of Antioch (d. 312) in the second half of the third century. The Antiochene theologians were a fractious lot; they were responsible for several schisms and a number of their representatives were excommunicated. Antioch's emphasis was on a *Logos–anthropos* Christology which emphasized the full humanity of Jesus. Again Haight: "The core of Antiochene christology lies in a consistent vision of Jesus Christ as an historical figure or person who bore two distinct natures."[13] Antioch's focus was on Jesus of Nazareth.

The rivalry between the two schools was strong, driven in part by political interests, Alexandria against Antioch and the new capital of Constantinople. There have been competing theological schools in every age of the Church, Dominicans and Jesuits arguing over grace in the seventeenth century, Lonerganians and Rahnerians disputing over method in the twentieth. But the conflict between Alexandria and Antioch was fundamentally a struggle over theological language. How could Christians speak about the person of Jesus in a way that respected both his humanity and his divinity? How to explain the unity of Jesus with God and with us? Alexandria

---

[11] Roger Haight, *Jesus: Symbol of God* (Maryknoll, N.Y.: Orbis, 1999) 262–63.
[12] Kelly, *Early Christian Doctrines*, 154–55.
[13] Ibid., 267.

stressed the union of the divine Logos with Jesus; Antioch was concerned for his full humanity. But the struggle was not just over terminology and its use, for the effort to bring the mystery of Jesus into a philosophically conditioned language ran the risk of each affirmation being also a denial of some other aspect of the mystery. At stake was the very heart of the Church's Christology, the full meaning of God's revealing presence in Jesus.

Some Key Terms

Before we investigate the controversy between these two schools, we need to look briefly at some of the terms that they used. Part of the problem is that the terms were not always clearly distinct from each other, and might be used in several different and conflicting senses.

Term	Basic Meaning	Usage/Sense
hypostasis (Gk.) *substantia* (Lat.)	Gk. f. *hupo istēmi*, "to stand under" Lat. *sub stare*, "to stand under"	that which stands under or gives support to an object; realization; a concrete being that supports the various qualities or appearances of a thing. Thus subsistent being, a reality existing by itself, substance. (Medieval example, "transubstantiation")
ousia	Gk., substantive of vb. *einai*, "to be," "being"	being; distinct entity, nature; Cappadocian formula: one nature (*ousia*), three hypostases (*hypostasis*)
homoousios	*homo*, "same" being	one in being, consubstantial
homoiousios	*homoi*, "like" being	of like being
phusis	nature	nature, essence
prosōpon (Gk.) *persona* (Lat.)	face, countenance, mask mask, character, individual	concrete appearance; particular individual; person; "*persona*" was defined by Boethius (6th cent.) as "individual substance of a rational nature"
Theotokos	"God-bearer"	Mother of God
Christotokos	"Christ-bearer"	Mother of Christ

Theological Battles

Paul of Samosata was a bitter opponent of Origen. Concerned to safeguard the humanity of Jesus, he taught that the Word was "of one substance" (*homoousios*) with the Father, though he used the term not in the sense of the same nature or being, but as manifesting the same person of the Father. That left the question, who then was Jesus? For Paul, Jesus was a man in whom the Spirit had come to dwell. He was not God; he was "an ordinary man in nature,"[14] raised up to be God's Son at his baptism. Thus Paul's Christology was adoptionist; he had guaranteed the humanity of Jesus by a radical separation of the person of Jesus from the Word. He was condemned by the Synod of Antioch in 268.

Arius was born in Libya in 256. His background is disputed; some say his theological education was at Antioch under Lucian; Grillmeier places him within the Alexandrian tradition.[15] Ordained in 311, he became pastor of a major congregation in Alexandria about the time that Bishop Alexander of Alexandria, began preaching the Alexandrian Logos–sarx Christology. Alexander was using Origen's conception of eternal generation, suggesting the Logos or Son's divine status. In response, Arius began publishing his conclusions about the nature of the Word in 318. Affirming the absolute uniqueness of God, Arius argued that the being or essence (*ousia*) of God—who is unique, transcendent, indivisible—cannot be shared. The Logos or Word, he concluded, was created out of nothing, had a beginning in time, is dissimilar from the Father's essence and being, and must be liable to change and certainly to suffering.[16] Arius had thus reduced the Word to a demigod, a creature.[17] His theology represented a Hellenization of Christianity, turning the Logos into a mediator between the ineffable and unchanging God and the world of multiplicity and change.[18]

Nicaea (325)

Spread with the help of catchy slogans such as his famous "there was a time when he was not," Arius' theology soon had the Empire in an uproar. To address this and other issues, the Emperor Constantine called for a council which met at Nicaea in Turkey in 325. Some 318 bishops took part,

---

[14] Kelly, *Early Christian Doctrines*, 140.
[15] Grillmeier, *Christ in Christian Tradition*, Vol. One, 220–21.
[16] Kelly, *Early Christian Doctrines*, 225–30.
[17] Ibid., 230.
[18] Kasper, *Jesus the Christ*, 158.

most of them from churches of the East. Their concern was not speculation, but to affirm the teachings of Scripture and tradition. The creed of
Nicaea, claimed by Eusebius as the baptismal creed of his church, affirmed
the divinity of Jesus and his equality with the Father:

> We believe in one God the Father all powerful, maker of all things both seen
> and unseen. And in one Lord Jesus Christ, the Son of God, the only-begotten
> begotten from the Father, that is from the substance of the Father, God from
> God, light from light, true God from true God, begotten not made, consub-
> stantial with the Father, through whom all things came to be, both those in
> heaven and those in earth; for us humans and for our salvation he came
> down and became incarnate, became human, suffered and rose up on the
> third day, went up into the heavens, is coming to judge the living and the
> dead. And in the holy Spirit.[19]

The council did a number of things. First, it condemned several Arian
propositions: "And those who say 'There once was when he was not', and
'before he was begotten he was not', and that he came to be from things
that were not, or from another hypostasis or substance, affirming that the
Son of God is subject to change or alteration—these the catholic and apostolic church anathematises."[20]

Second, Nicaea affirmed in no uncertain terms the divinity of Jesus. In
opposition to Arius, the council asserted that Jesus is "God from God, light
from light, true God from true God, begotten not made, consubstantial
(*homoousion*) with the Father." But as Brian McDermott has observed, the
council did not really define what it understood by the term *homoousios*.[21]
The council's teaching was "received" by the churches, but only after considerable controversy and further clarifications in the council's aftermath.
In a real sense, the controversy reflected the struggle to find the proper
theological language to express the Church's faith.

From Nicaea to Chalcedon

In the aftermath of Nicaea controversies continued among three rival
parties, those of the Nicene party who insisted on the term *homoousios*,
the Arians who avoided it, and a moderate group in the middle, usually
referred to as the "Homoiousians" ("of like substance"), though they have

---

[19] *Decrees of the Ecumenical Councils*, Vol. One: *Nicaea I to Lateran V*, ed. Norman P. Tanner
(Washington: Georgetown University Press, 1990) 5.
[20] Ibid.
[21] Brian O. McDermott, *Word Become Flesh: Dimensions of Christology* (Collegeville: The
Liturgical Press, 1993) 166.

been unfairly labeled as "Semi-Arians." Two strong defenders of Nicaean orthodoxy, both of whom worked to include the Homoiousians, were Athanasius of Alexandria (d. 373) in the East and Hilary of Poitiers in the West (d. 367). Athanasius sought to make more concrete Nicaea's term, *homousios*, explaining it in terms of the divinity of Jesus. While the Father and the Son are distinct (other), the Son "belongs to the Father's substance and is of the same nature as He."[22] Similarly, Hilary in the West, strongly influenced by Tertullian, taught that "God the Father and God the Son are clearly one, not by a union of person, but by a unity of nature."[23] Hilary thus points to a distinction of person within a unity of nature.

Nicaea had affirmed the divinity of Jesus. But there remained the problem of safeguarding his full humanity. Athanasius and Hilary in their efforts to secure the divinity of Christ against Arius, had failed to acknowledge the implications of his humanity. Stressing the uncreated status of the Logos, Athanasius sought to remove any weakness from Jesus, suggesting that his apparent ignorance in the Gospels was a result of his restraining his omniscience.[24] Hilary, though he taught that Christ possessed a human mind and will, denied that he personally experienced real ignorance, hunger, fear, or pain, moving in the direction of a "practical docetism."[25]

Apollinaris of Laodicea (d. 390) went further, effectively denying the full humanity of Jesus. A friend of Athanasius, Apollinaris followed the Logos–sarx theology of Alexandria even though he taught in Antioch. Stressing the "one incarnate nature (*phusis*) of the divine Logos," he maintained that the Logos took the place of the human soul of Christ, or at least of the higher soul, the *nous*.[26] This means of course that Jesus was not truly a human being, as Apollinaris was apparently willing to admit: "This Christ is not a man," ran his refrain in one work.[27] As Haight says, "in the Alexandrian tradition Jesus does not seem to be conceived as an integral human being. He lacks a rational soul, or is not a human subject, or is without a principle of human individuality, freedom, and action."[28]

[22] Kelly, *Early Christian Doctrines*, 244.

[23] De Trinitate, IV, 42; cf. McDermott, *Word Become Flesh*, 169; Kelly, *Early Christian Doctrines*, 253.

[24] *The Christological Controversy*, trans. and ed., Richard A. Norris (Philadelphia: Fortress, 1980) 20–21.

[25] Thus McDermott, *Word Become Flesh*, 199.

[26] Ibid., 199.

[27] See Piet Smulders, *The Fathers on Christology* (De Pere, Wis.: St. Norbert Abbey Press, 1968) 85.

[28] Haight, *Jesus: Symbol of God*, 266.

The Cappadocian Fathers of Asia Minor, Basil of Caesarea (ca. 330–79), Gregory of Nyssa (335–94), and Gregory of Nazianzus (330–89), played a major role in securing the proper relationship between the Father and the Son; they taught that the Son was fully and equally God, not a subordinate reality (as in Arius), but eternally begotten while the Father is unbegotten. Most useful was their formula in reference to the Godhead, one divine nature (*ousia*) and three hypostases (*hypostasis*). They also affirmed the divinity of the Holy Spirit.[29]

Constantinople I (384)

The first Council of Constantinople (381) reaffirmed the faith of Nicaea and formulated its own creed, different from that of Nicaea in a number of ways. The creed eliminated the phrase, "that is, of the substance (*ousia*) of the Father" and expanded Nicaea's brief article on the Spirit by adding "the holy, the lordly and life-giving one, proceeding forth from the Father, co-worshipped and co-glorified with Father and Son, the one who spoke through the prophets." The council also added a final article confessing belief "in one, holy, catholic and apostolic church. We confess one baptism for the forgiving of sins. We look forward to a resurrection of the dead and life in the age to come. Amen."[30] The council also condemned the Apollinarans.

The period between Constantinople I and Chalcedon was dominated by the struggle between the rival theologies of Alexandria and Antioch, particularly as represented by two strong churchmen, Cyril of Alexandria and Nestorius. An Antiochene monk, Nestorius (d. 451) became patriarch of Constantinople in 428 at the time of the controversy over the title *Theotokos* ("Mother of God," literally "Godbearer"). The title had been used of Mary apparently as early as 220 in virtue of the fact that the son she bore, Jesus, had both human and divine attributes, expressed by the theological concept of the *communicatio idiomatum*, the "communication of attributes" which was implicit in Nicaea's Creed. Nestorius thought this represented an Arian and Apollinaran reduction of Christ's humanity to passive flesh animated by the Logos, thus, the Logos–sarx theology. He questioned the use of *Theotokos* for Mary in a sermon.

Cyril, bishop of Alexandria, was already irritated at Nestorius who had supported charges brought against him by some Egyptian monks. Nestorius' sermon was too much. Denouncing him to Pope Celestine in Rome, Cyril argued in a series of letters that Jesus is the "one incarnate nature of the di-

---

[29] McDermott, *Word Become Flesh*, 171–72.

[30] Tanner, *Decrees*, 24.

vine Logos," understanding it to mean that while remaining God the Logos or Son took on human life. He summed up his position as a "union in hypostasis" or "hypostatic union." To Nestorius, this sounded like Apollinaris, with his denial of the full humanity of Jesus.[31] He thus rejected the term hypostatic union, arguing that Christ was one person (*prosopōn*) in which the two natures remain distinct or separate.[32] Norris characterizes Cyril's and Nestorius' positions as christological monism and christological dualism respectively.[33] The real tragedy is that both had genuine insights, but were not able to find a common theological language to express them.

Ephesus I (431)

With conflict again growing, the Emperor Theodosius called for a council which was held at Ephesus in 431. A number of rival meetings took place. The first, presided over by Cyril, not surprisingly condemned and deposed Nestorius. Acknowledging the traditional *communicatio idiomatum*, it affirmed that Mary could be called *Theotokos*. When John, bishop of Antioch showed up, he held another meeting which excommunicated Cyril. Finally when the papal legates arrived, they endorsed Cyril's gathering which henceforth would be known as Ephesus I. Cyril's interpretation had prevailed as the authoritative interpretation of the Nicene Creed.

Though the struggle was not yet over, there were efforts underway to bring the two sides together. In August John of Antioch sent to Cyril a document known as the Symbol of Union. Confessing Jesus as "perfect God and perfect man," it acknowledged a union of two natures without confusion (Antioch's claim) as well as the unity of Christ as one person (using the Antiochian language of one *prosopōn*) and the title *Theotokos* for Mary, both Alexandrian concerns. Most interesting is the document's explicit recognition of the problem of different theological languages: "As for the evangelical and apostolic statements about the Lord, we recognize that theologians employ some indifferently in view of the unity of person but distinguish others in view of the duality of natures."[34] Cyril accepted the Symbol with a letter entitled, "The Heavens Rejoice" (*Laetentur coeli*).

Yet once again differences over how to speak about the person of Jesus threatened the communion of the churches. On the Alexandrian side, not

---

[31] See Norris, *Christological Controversy*, 26–28; McDermott, *Word Become Flesh* 253–56.

[32] Kelly, *Early Christian Doctrines*, 314–15.

[33] Norris, *Christological Controversy*, 28.

[34] Kelly, *Early Christian Doctrines*, 329.

all of Cyril's supporters were comfortable with his acceptance of the language of two natures, while at Antioch resentment over the treatment of Nestorius still smoldered. When Cyril died in 444, his successor, Dioscorus, tried to return to the one nature language which postulated that Christ's divinity and humanity came together in one divine nature, thus overcoming his humanity. From this came the heretical doctrine of Monophysitism (one nature-ism), effectively denying the humanity of Jesus. Meanwhile, in Constantinople, Eutyches, an elderly and cantankerous monk, was agitating against the Symbol of Union. The patriarch, Flavian, convened a Synod at Constantinople in 448 at which Eutyches was condemned after the patriarch read a confession of faith containing the formula, "We confess that Christ is of two natures after the incarnation, confessing one Christ, one Son, one Lord, in one *hypostasis* and one *proposōn.*"[35] His Greek read literally, "out of two natures," which caused some misunderstandings; Chalcedon would later correct it. But significantly, for the first time the words "person" (*prosopōn*) and "substance" (*hypostasis*) had been used together.

The "Robber" Council (449)

Both Flavian and Eutyches appealed to Rome, occasioning Pope Leo's famous "Tomus ad Flavian" or letter of 449, echoing Flavian's two-nature language: "So the proper character of both natures was maintained and came together in a single person. Lowliness was taken up by majesty, weakness by strength, mortality by eternity."[36] Eutyches, however, refused to accept his excommunication and with the help of Dioscorus, appealed to the Emperor Theodosius II to summon a general council. The council, which met at Ephesus in 449, was "dominated with brutal efficiency by Dioscorus."[37] Though the papal legates were present with Pope Leo's Tome, they were not allowed to read it. One of them, the deacon Hilary who was not able to speak Greek, could only shout out his disagreement in Latin.[38] Intimidating the bishops with the help of the military, Dioscorus had Eutyches declared orthodox and Flavian condemned. To make matters worse, at his signal the soldiers and monks were let into the assembly, causing such an uproar that the council has gone down in history as the "Robber Council" (*Latrocinium*) of Ephesus. It was not received by the Church.

---

[35] See Kelly, *Early Christian Doctrines*, 331.

[36] Tomus ad Flavian, in Tanner, *Decrees*, 78; Leo's tome for the first time brought Western Christology to bear in the controversy; see Kelly, *Early Christian Doctrines*, 334–38.

[37] Kelly, *Early Christian Doctrines*, 334.

[38] Grillmeier, *Christ in Christian Tradition*, Vol. One, 528.

Chalcedon (451)

When Eutyches' protector Theodosius died, the result of a fall from his horse, the new Emperor Marcian proved sympathetic to Pope Leo's request for a general council. Though Leo had wanted it to be held in Italy, Nicaea was to be the site, until Marcian transferred it to Chalcedon, near his capital on the Bosporus. The council opened on October 8, 451, with 600 bishops present (or 500, dependent on the account), as well as three papal legates. It was the largest assembly of bishops in the ancient Church.

The council accepted the Creed of Nicaea, the two letters of Cyril, the Tome of Leo, and Flavian's profession of faith. However, the text produced by the bishops remained ambiguous. After the papal legates threatened to move the council to Italy, a new commission was set up which produced a confession of faith that was acceptable to all. In summary, it read:

> we all with one voice teach the confession of one and the same Son, our Lord Jesus Christ: the same perfect in divinity and perfect in humanity; the same truly God and truly man, of a rational soul and a body; consubstantial with the Father as regards his divinity, and the same consubstantial with us as regards his humanity; like us in all respects except for sin; begotten before the ages from the Father as regards his divinity, and in the last days the same for us and for our salvation from Mary, the virgin God-bearer, as regards his humanity; one and the same Christ, Son, Lord, only-begotten, acknowledged in two natures which undergo no confusion, no change, no division, no separation; at no point was the difference between the natures taken away through union, but rather the property of both natures is preserved and comes together into a single person and a single subsistent being; he is not parted or divided into two persons, but is one and the same only-begotten Son, God, Word, Lord Jesus Christ. . . .[39]

If Nicaea had safeguarded the divinity of Jesus, Chalcedon placed equal emphasis on his full humanity, juxtaposing four carefully balanced double affirmations which echoed the earlier council: Jesus was perfect in divinity, perfect in humanity; truly God, truly man; consubstantial with the Father, consubstantial with us; begotten before the ages, in the last day the same for us . . . from Mary.

In many ways the Chalcedonian confession was a synthesis of views. Alexandrian concerns for the union of Jesus with the divine Logos were addressed by Flavian's expression, "one *prosopōn* and one *hypostasis*," as well as the repetition of the words "the same," and the emphasis that the reference to the two natures does not mean any division or separation. The

[39] Tanner, *Decrees*, 86.

reaffirmation of the Marian title *Theotokos* was also important to Alexandria. The "two-nature" language reflects Antiochian theology, as does the clear affirmation of the humanity of Jesus.

General Councils

Council	Leading Figures	Issue
Nicaea (325)	Arius (not present): "there was a time when he was not." 318 bishops present	Rejected Arius' view that the logos is created; Christ is "*homoousion*" with the Father
Constantinople I (381)	Cappadocian influence	Affirmed Nicene faith; new creed which affirmed the divinity of Spirit; our creed combination of the two
Ephesus I (431)	Nestorius: conjunction of natures, Mary is *christotokos*; John of Antioch; Cyril of Alexandria: hypostatic union; Mary is *theotokos*	Condemns Nestorius; Mary is *theotokos* but Cyril and John of Antioch excommunicate each other
Ephesus II (449) ("Robber Council")	Flavian of Constantinople: "out of two natures, in one hypostasis and in one person" (formula of union); Dioscorus of Alexandria	Dioscorus dominates; rejected Flavian's formula: out of two natures, one person. But council was itself rejected.
Chalcedon (451)	600 bishops; Tome of Leo written in support of Flavian; papal legates insist on new profession of faith	Condemns Dioscorus, accepts Tome of Leo: teaches two natures in one person and one hypostasis, truly God and truly man

Conclusion

Chalcedon did not answer all the christological questions. Subsequent councils would address Monophysite leanings in the East and questions over whether Christ had one will or two. But the council had set out the parameters for the subsequent debate. In many ways it was a great achievement.

First of all, Chalcedon represented a synthesis of the best insights of two competing theological schools. Those representing Alexandria had continued to emphasize "the union of the divine and the non-divine,"[40] making clear the presence of God in Jesus and thus in the world. The Antiocheans, with their emphasis on the humanity of Jesus, resisted any tendency to see Jesus as less than a full, integral human being. He is truly one of us. In this long struggle to reconcile the human and the divine in Jesus, the distinction made between person and nature was key.[41]

Secondly, Chalcedon exemplified the ability of the Church to express its faith in the philosophical language of the day. In the struggle to guard its faith against less adequate expressions and heterodox views, whether from the culture or from the Church, the great dogmas of Christology and Trinity were set forth in the creeds. Establishing this "rule of faith," clarifying and making explicit what in the New Testament had been at best implicit, represented a high point in a dialogue with culture that is no less important today.

Did the reformulation of the Church's christological faith in the philosophical language of the time result in a Hellenization of Christianity, as nineteenth-century liberalism and some recent Catholic theologians have maintained,[42] or was the unique meaning of the person of Jesus safeguarded even as it was newly expressed in the language of another culture?

A good case can be made that Christian theology, while adapting Greek philosophical language, actually transformed it, and in so doing, moved western culture to a new level of understanding. Walter Kasper argues convincingly that the distinction introduced by the Cappodocians between one nature (*ousia*) and the three hypostases (*hypostasis*), understood as the concrete realizations of a universal nature, was a real achievement as this distinction did not exist in the philosophy of the time. Even if hypostasis was not yet understood as person, it meant "nothing less than that the universal nature was no longer regarded as the supreme reality and that the

---

[40] McDermott, *Word Become Flesh*, 260.

[41] Dermot Lane, *The Reality of Jesus: An Essay on Christology* (New York: Paulist, 1975) 106.

[42] See Leslie Dewart, *The Future of Belief: Theism in a World Come of Age* (New York: Herder and Herder, 1966) 132–35; Hans Küng, *On Being a Christian* (Garden City, New York: Doubleday, 1976) 439–40, 450.

Greek ontological way of thinking was giving way to thinking in terms of persons."[43] In other words, rather than seeing impersonal universal nature as the supreme reality, under the influence of Christianity the most real would be seen as the existing individual *hypostasis*/substance, and ultimately, as personal.

Christianity did not completely revise Hellenistic philosophy. Its concept of God remained highly colored by Greek ideas of the divine impassability and transcendence. But in its Christology, Christianity rejected completely the Hellenistic idea of a transcendent divinity able to interact with the world only through intermediaries. Instead, it taught that in the human person of Jesus God was indeed present and active in the world. Thus God's revelation in Jesus is not just self-revelation, but self-communication; God is both transcendent and immanent.

Philosophy continued to play an important role in the development of Western theology; in the Middle Ages it was known as the "handmaid of theology." It is no less important today, guarding against fundamentalism and fideism and, when working in consort with theology, exemplifying that compatibility of faith and reason so characteristic of the Catholic tradition at its best.

---

[43] Kasper, *Jesus the Christ*, 177.

Chapter 10

Sin and Salvation

Christology also involves of necessity soteriology, the question about the work of Jesus. What did Jesus do to save us? I remember years ago when I was in divinity school sitting up half the night at a retreat house, arguing with my confreres about this question. We knew of course the "right" answers, but none of them really seemed to make sense to us. And I suspect that they don't really make that much sense to the average Christian today. A Catholic, if asked, might respond that Jesus died for our sins, offered his life as a sacrifice for us. A Protestant, better schooled in Reformation soteriology, would say that he took our place, bore the wrath of God's judgment on sin, that we might be declared righteous.

But what exactly does all this mean? How the death of Jesus could be salvific or why God would apparently require the death of his only beloved Son in order to restore us to his friendship not only escapes most people today; it also raises for them troubling questions about why God's justice would demand such a sacrifice or what kind of God such a God would be. As Roger Haight observes, when Christians today apply the dogmatic symbols in a literal way to the history of Jesus, "It begins to seem as though God wanted and even planned that Jesus die the way he did."[1]

The New Testament also wrestles with these questions. Unfortunately, the enormous power and elegant simplicity of the Reformation doctrine of substitutionary atonement, also called "penal substitution," has obscured the multiplicity of images and metaphors used by the New Testament authors as well as by the Fathers of the Church to express the mystery of our salvation. Elizabeth Johnson speaks of a "dazzling variety" of metaphors used by the early communities to tell the story of Jesus:

> They spoke in financial categories of redemption or release from slavery through payment of a price; in legal categories of advocacy, justification,

[1] Roger Haight, *Jesus: Symbol of God* (Maryknoll, N.Y.: Orbis, 1999) 85.

and satisfaction; in cultic categories of sacrifice, sin-offering, and expiation; in political categories of liberation and victory over oppressive powers; in personal categories of reconciliation after dispute; in medical categories of being healed or made whole; in existential categories of freedom and new life; and in familial categories of becoming God's children by birth (John) or adoption (Paul).[2]

In his classic study on soteriology, Gustav Aulén argues that the "classic" idea of atonement, understood as the victory of God in Christ in overpowering the forces of evil (*Christus Victor*), was gradually neglected in favor of either the "objective" Latin view, based on sacrifice and symbolized by Anselm's theory of satisfaction, or by the "subjective" view of liberal theology which, with Abelard in the background, emphasized a change in human beings rather than a changed attitude on the part of God.[3] From a slightly different perspective, Michael Slusser offers five soteriological themes which are prominent in the patristic writings and can be traced back to very early strata in the New Testament tradition: victory, atonement, revelation, eschatological judgment, and exemplar. All are rooted in the Old Testament and in the wider first-century Jewish consciousness.[4] Finally, also worthy of mention is the theme of divinization (*theosis*), so strong in the Eastern Church.

The soteriological question cannot be addressed without also addressing the question of sin, the mystery of iniquity, addressed in the story of the Fall in Genesis 3. While that account was taken historically as well as symbolically by the early Christians and the Fathers of the Church, it still has meaning for Christians today.

In this chapter we will explore the question of sin in the sense of original sin as well as the notion of salvation. We will investigate sin and salvation in the Scriptures and then consider both from the perspective of Christian history. Finally we will look at original sin and salvation from the perspective of the sixteenth century.

Sin and Salvation in Scripture

The sense that human beings are somehow enmeshed in the mystery of evil does not begin with Augustine. The Hebrew Scriptures tell the story of a people's hope for deliverance from the evil and oppression that is the

---

[2] Elizabeth A. Johnson, "Jesus and Salvation," *Catholic Theological Society of America: Proceedings* 49 (1994) 3–4.

[3] Gustaf Aulén, *Christus Victor* (New York: Macmillan, 1931) 17–31.

[4] Michael Slusser, "Primitive Christian Soteriological Themes," *Theological Studies* 44 (1983) 555–69.

result of their sinfulness; they also provide an account of the origin of humanity's sinful state in the story of the Fall.

The Fall

The account of the Fall in Genesis 3 tells the story of humankind's loss of innocence in the persons of Adam and Eve, the primordial couple from whom all men and women are descended. Placed by their Creator in a beautiful garden, they succumb to the Serpent's temptation to violate the one commandment imposed on them by God, that they should not eat the fruit of the tree in the center of the garden, under pain of death. It is easy to miss the subtlety of the Serpent's temptation: "the serpent said to the woman: 'You certainly will not die! No, God knows well that the moment you eat of it your eyes will be opened and you will be like gods who know what is good and what is bad'" (Gen 3:4-5). Seeing that the fruit was good and desiring the wisdom promised by the Serpent, first the woman and then the man eat of the fruit, only to have their eyes opened to a very different world.

The Genesis story beautifully captures the perennial temptation of human beings, not just to disobedience, but to putting themselves first, no matter the consequences. Even more, they wish to become the judge of good and evil themselves, rather than submitting to the order of creation that comes from the Creator. By refusing to acknowledge the one who alone is Creator and Lord, they are really guilty of an apotheosis or self-deification, attempting to become their own gods. The root of all sin lies here, in what Augustine calls the "*aversio a Dei*," a turning from God which is rooted in the human heart. In its postmodern form, it is the offense taken at any claim to truth that might measure human beings, denying the autonomy so dear to contemporary men and women.

The result of Adam and Eve's sin is a turning upside down of God's creation. No longer do they enjoy the intimacy with God that was their birthright. They experience an alienation, not only from God, but from creation itself, and from each other. The woman will bring forth her children in pain and labor and will be subordinate to her husband, contrary to their creation in equality and mutuality (cf. Gen 1:27). The man will henceforth find the very earth cursed, and will have to earn his daily bread by the sweat of his brow. Even their bodies are now alien to them, for they are shamed by their nakedness. Driven out of the garden, the earth becomes for them a place of exile.

The following chapters of Genesis show how all the earth is affected by their sin. The next story is about fratricide, as Cain murders his brother

Abel (Gen 4). In the story of the Great Flood (Gen 6:5–8:22), humanity barely escapes destruction as the waters of chaos, confined by God in his work of creation, rush back in, let loose by sin. Creation itself is endangered. Only through God's intervention do Noah and his family escape. In the final story of the primeval history, the willful pride of another generation results in the confusing of languages, further dividing human beings from each other (Gen 11:1-9). A myth, yes, but also a profound lesson on the destructive power of sin.

Adam does not play much of a role outside the prehistory, though he reappears in the Wisdom literature (Sir 15:14-17; Wis 2:24-25). But the story of sin and its disastrous effects is woven throughout the Hebrew Scriptures. The people are rebellious, murmuring against God (Exod 16:2, 7, 8) and falling into idolatry (Exod 32:8), even as God delivers them from bondage in Egypt. Their faithlessness and oppression of the poor are constantly denounced by the prophets, with their strong sense of collective responsibility, or what we would call today, a solidarity in evil.

Sin in Paul

Though Jesus presumes that all are sinners and calls all to repentance, Adam's sin is not mentioned in the Gospels. But he reappears in Paul's teachings on the two Adams, the first and the last (Rom 5:12-21; 1 Cor 15:22, 45). The letter to the Romans, Paul's great treatise on the universality of sin, is the New Testament's most systematic treatment on the subject. It would shape Augustine's thinking. In Romans, Paul dramatizes the history of salvation, with Adam, Sin, Death, the Law, and Christ as the cast of characters. Sin enters the world with Adam, and with Sin comes Death which affects all "inasmuch as all sinned" (Rom 5:12). Death means not just physical death, but that spiritual death that separates us from God. With the Law comes consciousness of sin (Rom 3:20); in Galatians Paul calls the Law a "tutor" or "disciplinarian" (Gal 3:24). But the Jews enjoy no advantage over the Gentiles, for both have sinned. Both are under Sin's power. In a moving passage in Romans 7, Paul describes in very personal terms the human predicament, our inability to do what is right and good even when we want to because of the law of sin at work in our members (Rom 7:23). It is only through Christ that we are set free from this law of sin and death (Rom 8:2).

While the term "original sin" does not appear until Augustine, its roots are in Paul. In Romans 5:12-21 Paul sets up a careful parallelism between Adam and Christ. Through his transgression Adam brings death (Rom

5:17), while Christ brings "acquittal and life" for all through his "righteous act" (5:18) and "obedience" (5:19). Does Paul suggest here a causal dimension to Adam's sin, doing damage to human nature? Certainly the tradition has interpreted him in this way. In its Decree on Original Sin, the Council of Trent cited this passage to argue for the baptism of infants, even infants of baptized parents.[5] At the same time, Paul's expression in Roman 5:12, "inasmuch as all sinned" (not "in whom all have sinned," as Jerome translated it in the Latin of the Vulgate) suggests that human beings have replicated Adam's sin in their own lives by sinning themselves, and so have contributed to their own alienation from God.

Thus for Paul, sin in its deepest meaning is considerably more than a question of wrong actions or "lawbreaking." It is an existential state, a condition of our being-in-the-world that affects all people. Luther recognized this. In his commentary on Psalm 51, in part a reflection on Romans 7, he wrote: "Two kinds of sin can be distinguished. There is, first, the whole nature corrupted by sin and subject to eternal death. There is, second, a kind of sin which a man who has the Law can recognize when such things as theft, murder, and adultery are committed. Even civil laws talk about this latter kind, though not very precisely."[6]

The sense of human solidarity in sin and evil is also evident in the Gospels. Luke describes humans as under the power of Satan (Luke 10:17-18); the disciples in John reflect the idea that suffering and sickness are the result of sin (John 9:2). Jesus' proclamation of the coming of God's reign or kingdom means that the reign of Satan is at an end.

New Testament Images of Salvation

The death and resurrection of Jesus transformed the disciples' understanding of Jesus and gave a whole new dimension to his preaching of the kingdom. The attentive reader notes right away that while the theme of the kingdom of God dominates the Synoptic Gospels, it appears rarely in the other New Testament writings. Paul occasionally describes it as present: "For the kingdom of God is not a matter of food and drink, but of righteousness, peace, and joy in the holy Spirit" (Rom 14:17). More often he emphasizes that the unjust or those who are ruled by "the works of the flesh" (Gal 5:19; cf. 1 Thess 2:12; 1 Cor 6:9-10) will not inherit the kingdom of God. Matthew sees the "kingdom of heaven" as initially realized in

[5] DS 1514.
[6] Martin Luther, in *Luther's Works* 12, *The Psalm Miserere*, ed. Jaroslav Pelikan (St. Louis: Concordia, 1955) 307–08.

the Church, through which the promise of Jesus to remain always with his disciples (Matt 28:20) can be realized. John refers to the kingdom in only one passage, where the context is baptism (John 3:3, 5). His usual term, "eternal life," as both a present and a future reality, shows that he has already expanded Jesus' image of the kingdom in light of the resurrection. For the kingdom has now been more deeply understood in light of the Christ-event.

From the moment of their Easter experience the disciples understood that God had acted decisively on their behalf in raising Jesus from the dead. Formed by their own Jewish tradition, they shared in the eschatological hope of God's saving intervention in the life of Israel, however differently that hope might have been expressed. Strongly influenced by apocalyptic thinking, many concluded that the resurrection of Jesus meant that the general resurrection of the dead was near; Paul's letters are written from this perspective (cf. 1 Cor 7:25-31).

But what was the precise meaning of Jesus' death? How could they put into words what the Christ-event, his life, death, and resurrection, meant to them? The New Testament witnesses to a variety of ways of expressing their sense of God's momentous work in Jesus. In chapter 6 we saw how the early Christians appealed to various Old Testament motifs, metaphors, and symbolic figures—the rejected prophet, the suffering, righteous one, redemptive or atoning sacrifice—to provide some explanation for the death of Jesus. His death was being interpreted as a sacrifice for sins even before Paul, who cites the primitive *kerygma* in 1 Corinthians 15:3: "Christ died for our sins in accordance with the scriptures." Paul shares this view (1 Cor 1:13; Rom 14:15; Gal 1:4; 3:13), but he generally links the passion and death of Jesus with his resurrection as a single salvific event (Rom 4:25).

How can we understand this mystery? What did Jesus do for us? Joseph Fitzmyer lists ten distinct images used in the Pauline writings that attempt to express different aspects of how our salvation was effected through the Christ-event: justification, salvation, reconciliation, expiation, redemption, freedom, sanctification, transformation, new creation, and glorification.[7] He sees these images, not as different answers to the question about how our salvation was accomplished, but rather as distinctive aspects of the mystery of Christ and his work.[8] Still, there is considerable variety in the way Paul characterizes the effects of the Christ event.

---

[7] Joseph A. Fitzmyer, "Pauline Theology," in the *New Jerome Biblical Commentary*, ed. Raymond E. Brown, Joseph A. Fitzmyer, and Roland Murphy (Englewood Cliffs, N.J.: Prentice Hall, 1990) 82:67.

[8] Ibid.

Mark presents the story of Jesus as a cosmic struggle against evil, personified by Satan and the unclean spirits (Mark 1:23-24; 3:11-12). Echoing Isaiah 53:10-12, he interprets the death of Jesus as a "ransom for many" (Mark 10:45), repeated in the words over the cup at the Last Supper in reference to his blood to be "shed for many" (Mark 14:24), with the idea of a vicarious death. We saw earlier that the idea that Jesus saw his death as part of his life as a "service" goes back to the Last Supper. Matthew sees the new age already breaking in with the death of Jesus (Matt 27:52), but gives no particular theological exposition of the Passion. Luke, the only Synoptic evangelist to use the words salvation and savior, describes Jesus' death and resurrection as an exodus (Luke 9:31), based on the Exodus of Israel, thus as God's definitive salvific act. But Luke's concept of salvation also includes the works of Jesus' ministry. John stresses the revelatory role of Jesus, the Word of God present in the world (Incarnation) which brings God's judgment on the world (John 3:19; 9:39). Even his death is seen from this perspective of revelation and judgment (exaltation: John 3:14; 8:28; 12:32).

Sin and Salvation in Christian History

For the Fathers of the Church, Jesus is always the mediator of God's salvation, but salvation in their understanding is much more comprehensive than the narrower notions of redemption, atonement, or justification.[9] Still less is the theme of substitutionary atonement central. Slusser's five themes—victory, atonement, revelation, eschatological judgment, and exemplar—only begin to suggest the richness of patristic thought. And though there are significant differences between the Eastern and Western Fathers in their thinking on sin and salvation, the problem of our solidarity in the sin of Adam is not absent.[10]

The Eastern Fathers in their soteriology are more incarnational and thus optimistic; with their emphasis on the divine Logos, they see creation itself as elevated and humanity transformed, even divinized, as a result of the Word becoming flesh. Most hold that the image of God remains in us fundamentally intact. They tend to interpret Romans 5:12-21 in terms of personal sin.[11] Justin blames the demons for infecting the souls and bodies

[9] Haight, *Jesus: Symbol of God*, 336; see also Robert Louis Wilken, "Salvation in Early Christian Thought," in *Catholics and Evangelicals; Do They Share a Common Future?*, ed. Thomas P. Rausch (New York: Paulist, 2000) 56–57.

[10] Henri Rondet, *Original Sin: The Patristic and Theological Background* (Staten Island, N.Y.: Alba House, 1972); see also George Vandervelde, *Original Sin: Two Major Trends in Contemporary Roman Catholic Reinterpretation* (Amsterdam: Rodopi, 1975) 2–14.

[11] See Vandervelde, *Original Sin*, 3–4.

of human beings with vice and corruption. The Word became flesh to conquer the serpent and work our salvation.[12] Still, the doctrine of recapitulation and a sense for the mystical unity of the human family in Adam leads to a view that our nature has been wounded and subject to death.[13]

The Western Fathers place greater emphasis on the redemption, the Cross, and the idea of satisfaction, introduced by Tertullian. By the third century, a "marked difference" with Eastern thought on redemption begins to emerge, including our solidarity in Adam and thus in his sin.[14] In Roger Haight's words, "western soteriology leans more on a transaction performed in Jesus."[15]

The Eastern Fathers

Irenaeus of Lyons. Born in Asia Minor but remembered for his work in the church of Lyons in the south of France, Irenaeus (d. 200) uses the metaphor of "recapitulation" to explain our salvation. In his *Against the Heresies*, the eternal Word through whom all things were created unites himself with creation by becoming man. In this way, "by becoming man, he restored anew the lengthy series of men in himself and brought them under one head (*recapitulavit*), and in short has given us salvation. Thus we regain in Christ Jesus what we had lost in Adam, namely existence according to God's image and likeness."[16] The basic idea here is that the Son of God as the Second Adam undoes Adam's fall by reenacting or recapitulating the story of his life, reversing Adam's disobedience by his own obedience. Though Adam brings death, he will not frustrate God's plan.

More controversial is Irenaeus' idea that since humankind had fallen under the power of the devil, Christ's blood was shed as a "ransom" paid to free us from his power, a theme which will find great elaboration in the later Greek Fathers.[17] Irenaeus also uses the metaphor of an exchange: "The Word of God, our Lord Jesus Christ, because of his boundless love became what we are in order to make us what he is."[18] The idea of sacrifice appears only infrequently in Irenaeus.

---

[12] J.N.D. Kelly, *Early Christian Doctrines* (London: Adam and Charles Black, 1958) 167.

[13] Ibid., 350.

[14] Ibid., 174–79, at 174.

[15] Haight, *Jesus: Symbol of God*, 223.

[16] III 18, 1; text in Piet Smulders, *The Fathers on Christology* (De Pere, Wis.: St. Norbert Abbey Press, 1968) 12.

[17] Aulén, *Christus Victor*, 42–43; Aulén stresses that what is at stake here is God acting, not with force but justly, even with the devil; 44.

[18] *Haer.* V *Praef.*; Smulders, *Fathers*, 15.

Clement of Alexandria. For Clement (d. ca. 220), the divine Logos which has entered into human flesh teaches us how to live, so that in imitating Jesus and becoming like him we become suitable for the vision of God. The theme of the Mediator suffering for us is overshadowed by that of the Logos as teacher and disciplinarian, a theme popular with the Apostolic Fathers. One of Clement's works is called *Christ the Educator* (*Paidagōgos*).

Origen. The thought of Origen of Alexandria (d. ca. 254) is extremely complex. He speaks of a defilement (*sordes peccati*) that affects all people entering the world, necessitating the baptism even of little children, but his thought here seems to reflect his theory of the original preexistence of souls and their fall into matter.[19] His thought in this case is more Platonic than Christian. He uses the language of sacrifice and propitiation to describe Christ's salvific work: "because sin has entered into the world and because sin necessarily demanded propitiation, and because propitiation came about only through a victim, it was necessary to find a victim for sin."[20] Origen was the first of the Fathers to fully develop this aspect of Christ's work, and he sees Christ's death, not merely as surrender to God's will, but as a ransom to the devil in exchange for the souls of human beings and as an offering which positively influences the Father.[21] But it is the Incarnation itself which is most truly salvific for Origen. There is a mystical dimension to his thought, for Christ the Logos unites human beings to himself, transforming them into his likeness and divinizing them.[22]

Athanasius. A presbyter of Alexandria who became bishop in 328, Athanasius has the Incarnation at the center of his soteriology. In his treatise, *On the Incarnation of the Word*, written before his twentieth birthday, he argues that the Logos has become incarnate in order to restore humanity to the state originally intended by the Creator, one of communion with God. Thus salvation is a restoration or recreation.[23] Influenced by Irenaeus, Athanasius develops his theory of exchange and the notion of divinization, already present in Irenaeus in inchoate form.

Unlike Irenaeus, however, Athanasius places some emphasis on Christ's death as a sacrifice, even a "ransom" (*lutron*), with the idea of substitution or more accurately, representation, in the sense that "the death of all was accomplished in the Lord's body."[24] He traces human misery and sin to the

---

[19] Rondet, *Original Sin*, 82–83.
[20] *Hom. Num.* 24,1; Smulders, *Fathers*, 39.
[21] Kelly, *Early Christian Doctrines*, 186.
[22] Smulders, *Fathers*, 40–41; Kelly, 184–85.
[23] Haight, *Jesus: Symbol of God*, 221; Norris, *Christological Controversy*, 18.
[24] *De Incarn.* 20; Kelly, *Early Christian Doctrines*, 380.

lapse of our first parents, yet the human will remains free and he does not suggest that we participate in Adam's guilt.[25]

The Cappadocians. The Cappadocian Fathers, Gregory of Nyssa (335–94), Basil (330–79), and Gregory of Nazianzus (ca. 329–90), see us as involved in Adam's rebellious act, with a resultant negative affect on our moral nature. Gregory of Nyssa writes, "Evil was mixed with our nature from the beginning . . . through those who by their disobedience introduced the disease." Speaking of these and the other fourth-century Greek Fathers, Kelly writes that "there was here the outline of a real theory of original sin."[26] Gregory also developed the theme of the debt owed to the devil, to whom God offered Jesus as a ransom, catching him as a fish is by the bait concealing the hook, though Gregory of Nazianzus critiqued this idea.[27]

The Western Fathers

The Western Fathers are less speculative than their Eastern counterparts. One is tempted to juxtapose the mystical and speculative tradition of Greek-speaking East with the practical, legal, and commercial interests of Rome. For example, the notion of a "transaction performed in Jesus" is exemplified by Tertullian in rather crass economic terms: "he also preserves in himself the pledge of the flesh, as earnest-money on the principle."[28]

Hippolytus of Rome (d. ca. 235), a disciple of Irenaeus, occasionally rises to dramatic heights in his prose, as in his description of the Incarnation:

> The Word leaped down from heaven into the womb of the Virgin, he leaped from his mother's womb onto the wood [of the cross], he leaped from the wood into the netherworld, he leaped upwards again to the earth . . . and leaped again from earth to heaven.[29]

But in spite of the poetry in the above passage, there is no sense in Hippolytus that the life of Jesus had salvific value, as it does in Irenaeus. For Hippolytus, deification depends on moral rather than mystical grounds, obedience to God and the commandments rather than to life with the Son. What emerges into focus is the cross on which Jesus as priest and Paschal Lamb offers the sacrifice for humankind.[30]

---

[25] Kelly, *Early Christian Doctrines*, 347.

[26] Ibid., 351.

[27] Ibid., 382–83.

[28] *De Resurr. Mort.* 51/1-3; cf. *Adv. Marc.* III 9/4; Smulders, *Fathers*, 27.

[29] *In Cant.* 2,8; Smulders, *Fathers*, 20.

[30] Smulders, *Fathers*, 21–22.

Tertullian (d. after 220) teaches that each human being bears the mark of the first sin, an inclination to sin from the fault of our origin (*ex originis vitio*). Infants share in "the contagion of the ancient death" and need baptism. Christ shared our flesh, but not Adam's sin.[31] Like Hippolytus, Tertullian focuses upon the Cross; he goes so far as to see Christ's death as the cause of his birth: "Christ, who was sent in order to die, also necessarily had to be born in order to die: for only that which has been born is accustomed to die. . . . His intended death is the cause of his birth."[32] The implication here is that Christ's life had no particular salvific value. Tertullian's legal background leads him to introduce the idea of satisfaction.[33] Yet he neither reduces the redemption to the forgiveness of sins nor separates the Cross from the Resurrection and our rebirth to eternal life.

Cyprian (d. 258) generally follows Tertullian, though he shows some independence in his theology of redemption. Yet Kelly sees a hint of the doctrine of substitution in his statement, "Christ bore us all when he bore our sins"[34] and concludes by calling attention to "the growing Western tendency to think of God as the supreme lawgiver Whose relation to mankind must be conceived in almost juridical terms."[35]

Augustine (d. 430), the bishop of Hippo in Africa, was to synthesize and pass on to the Middle Ages the Western tradition on Christ's saving work. According to Roger Haight, "No major theologian until Luther puts more stress on sin than Augustine."[36] It was he who is rightly given credit for the doctrine of original sin, as well as for its enormous influence in subsequent Western theology.

While Augustine's fascination with the power of sin is often traced to his long struggle to control his sexual nature, Rondet sees the "nub of his argument" as emerging out of the issue of infant baptism in the controversy with the followers of Pelagius. If Christ is the Savior of all, Augustine reasons, he must be the Savior of infants as well as of adults, for infants too share in Adam's sin.[37] Augustine does not hesitate to conclude that infants who died without the grace of baptism would be damned, for he rejected the Pelagian position of a middle ground between heaven and hell for unbaptized infants.[38] For him, Pelagius' view of human nature as graced and

---

[31] Kelly, *Early Christian Doctrines*, 175–76; Rondet, *Original Sin*, 60–61.

[32] *De Carne Christi* 6/6; Smulders, *Fathers*, 28.

[33] Kelly, *Early Christian Doctrines*, 177.

[34] *Ep.* 63/13; Kelly, *Early Christian Doctrines*, 178.

[35] Kelly, *Early Christian Doctrines*, 178.

[36] Haight, *Jesus: Symbol of God*, 224.

[37] Rondet, *Original Sin*, 122.

[38] Vandervelde, *Original Sin*, 19.

therefore good would mean that Christ did no more than give us a good example. His teaching was indirectly confirmed in the condemnation of Pelagius by the Councils of Carthage (418) and Orange (529).

Augustine based his interpretation on the parallelism between Adam and Christ in Romans 5, helped in part by his dependence on the Latin text of Romans 5:12 which read "in whom all have sinned." This seemed to be confirmed by Romans 5:19: "For just as through the disobedience of one person the many were made sinners, so through the obedience of one the many will be made righteous."

The darker side of Augustine's thought that was to so stamp the later Western theological tradition became evident in the conclusions he drew from this. Besides presuming the inclusion of all in Adam's sin, he argued that original sin was transmitted by concupiscence which he often identified with the human sexual drive. But he also spoke of concupiscence as embracing the whole person. As a result, human beings were in a state of rebellion against God. They had lost their true liberty (*libertas*). While they retained their freedom of choice (*liberum arbitrium*), without genuine liberty they were unable to love and serve God. He spoke of "the bondage of the free will" which meant that humans were not able *not* to sin.[39] Thus for Augustine, the human situation was desperate.

Haight summarizes Augustine's soteriological teaching in two stories. First, in his great work, *The Trinity* as well as in *The Enchiridion*, Augustine analyzes Christ's work as a sacrifice; Christ himself is an innocent victim offered to God as a "propitiation" which makes satisfaction for the sins of humankind. Since Christ takes our sin and its consequence, death, upon himself, what emerges is a theology of substitution. Second, in Book 13 of *The Trinity*, he presents Christ's death as a ransom, paid to Satan into whose power human beings had been given over because of sin. The image of Christ as "bait" for the devil appears again here, this time as a mouse in a trap. Both stories feature a transaction, done by God on our behalf.[40] Augustine's severe language, "we who were enemies," "under this wrath," "the just anger of God," "He abandoned the sinner," "made sin for us," "justified by his blood" will appear again in the Reformers.[41]

Anselm of Canterbury (d. 1109), though clearly in the Augustinian tradition, modified Augustine's theology of original sin by explaining it as a

---

[39] Vandervelde, *Original Sin*, 16–18; Kelly, *Early Christian Doctrines*, 365.

[40] Haight, *Jesus: Symbol of God*, 224–26; Kelly says that for Augustine, "the essence of the redemption lies in the expiatory sacrifice offered for us by Christ in His passion," *Early Christian Doctrines*, 392.

[41] Texts in Haight, 224–26.

privation of the justice humankind had from creation, rather than as a positive sense of hostility towards God (*amor sui, cupiditas*) as in Augustine. From Anselm's perspective, human nature was damaged rather than corrupted. Thomas Aquinas followed Anselm in this.

Anselm's presentation of Augustine's theology of Christ's satisfaction for sin was so powerfully presented that Western soteriology was henceforth stamped by it. In *Cur Deus Homo?* he asks the question, why did God become man? He answers that Adam's sin was an infinite offense as it was an offense against an infinite being which in a real sense broke the order of creation. He proposes three possible ways of dealing with this wrong: forgiveness, punishment, or satisfaction. Forgiveness would not restore the original dignity of humankind. Punishment would be necessarily eternal. Only satisfaction can fully restore the order of creation which God has established. And that, by a certain kind of logic, necessitates an infinite being, for only such a being could make the infinite satisfaction owed for such an offence. The Incarnation was God's response.

Though there is a legal aspect to Anselm's thinking, rooted in both feudal legal categories and the Church's penitential practice, his main concern is philosophical/theological; he presumes that salvation takes place within a created order of beauty, order, and goodness, which in a sense represents a self-limitation of the divine freedom. Once that order is damaged, by sin, God cannot simply restore it without involving humanity, for to do so would violate both the established order of creation and human freedom.[42] One of the strengths of his theology is that it drops the devil from the picture, so that salvation is concerned with the relationship between human beings and God.[43] The conception of satisfaction takes on the connotation of redressing an injury, albeit it an infinite one, against an infinite God.

But unfortunately, in Anselm the tendency in Western soteriological thought to understand salvation in terms of an exchange, a price paid to God for sin, reaches a high point, to the extent that the Incarnation itself is subordinated to it; God became man to make satisfaction for sins. What has been lost is that more comprehensive sense of salvation evident in the great patristic tradition of the East that places primacy on the Incarnation, with its transformation of the human. This was often expressed by the concept of divinization (*theosis, theopoiesis*), more widespread in the East

---

[42] Walter Kasper, *Jesus the Christ* (New York: Paulist, 1976) 220; cf. Haight, *Jesus: Symbol of God*, 228.

[43] Richard W. Southern, *Saint Anselm: A Portrait in a Landscape* (Cambridge: Cambridge University Press, 1990) 211.

but present in Western writers such as Hippolytus and Augustine as well.[44] But this transactional theory was not the only expression of the Western tradition.

Peter Abelard (d. 1142) provided a striking alternative, returning to Irenaeus' theory of a recapitulation and making love the motive for the Incarnation. Unlike many of Anselm's fellow monks, who did not want to abandon the idea of a payment owed to the devil, Abelard went further to reject the idea of compensation entirely, even to God. Southern expresses Abelard's thought as follows: "since Man could make no payment to God, and God need make no payment to the Devil, the purpose of the Incarnation could not be that of making any payment at all. It could only be an act of love."[45] Abelard's soteriology was both revelational and exemplary, showing us how to love both God and neighbor. Southern calls this one of the great new ideas of the twelfth century, teaching not the satisfaction of claims but rather the law of love.[46] But it was Anselm's substitutional theology which was to carry the day, particularly as read through the lenses of the Reformers.

The Sixteenth Century

While Augustine's influence on medieval theology was enormous, the Reformers in particular interpreted the doctrine of salvation in the Augustinian/Anselmian current. In their thought, the themes of substitution and vicarious punishment were to emerge with a particular clarity. Their Augustinianism is evident also in their doctrine of the radical corruption of human nature, Calvin's "total depravity."

Martin Luther

Luther (d. 1546) was deeply influenced by Augustine's pessimism; he was convinced that humankind was "under the wrath of God," even if this was an "alien work" of God, opposed to God's "proper work" of love.[47] Only Christ could save human beings from that wrath, the result of God's justified anger at sin. Taking our place, Jesus bears our sins, becoming sin itself and suffering its full effects, thus making satisfaction. Luther actually takes Anselm's thought a step forward. In the words of Paul Althaus: "For Anselm,

---

[44] Wilken, "Salvation in Early Christian Thought," 70–71.

[45] Southern, *St. Anselm*, 210.

[46] Ibid.

[47] See Paul Althaus, "Man Under the Wrath of God," in *The Theology of Martin Luther* (Philadelphia: Fortress, 1966) 169–78, at 173.

there were only two possibilities, either punishment or satisfaction. For Luther, satisfaction takes place through punishment, not of the sinner but of Christ."[48] In other words, Christ offers satisfaction to the Father through his death in our place; in this way the concepts of substitution and satisfaction come together.

As a result of Christ's sacrifice, God no longer looks on our sinfulness, but sees only the righteousness of Jesus. In this sense, our sins have been "covered over," and Christ's righteousness is attributed to us; "On his account God overlooks all sins and wants them to be covered as though they were not sins."[49] Here is the root of the Reformation concept of "forensic" or declarative justification. The believer clings to Christ through faith, receiving his righteousness, while Christ takes upon himself our guilt, sinfulness, and deserved punishment, bearing the wrath of God.[50]

John Calvin

Calvin (d. 1564) was influenced by Luther, but his theology, shaped through his own background and experience, differs in some aspects from Luther's. Trained as a lawyer, Calvin has a much more positive appreciation of law which for the justified has the positive function of ordering society and guiding the Christian. He also distinguishes sanctification from justification. For Luther, salvation means clinging to Christ's righteousness through faith. But for Calvin, the Christian, once justified, should lead a holy life in the world.

Drawing on his legal background, Calvin describes Christ as taking on for us the role of an evildoer, one condemned by a judge, just as we are guilty before God and subject to punishment. Thus Christ takes our place as a substitute, saving us from God's anger by offering himself as a sacrifice: "Christ was offered to the Father in death as an expiatory sacrifice that when he discharged all satisfaction through his sacrifice, we might cease to be afraid of God's wrath."[51] In this, Calvin's theology is similar to Luther's.

But Calvin's pessimism about the sinner's state before justification is bleak. Because of original sin, human nature, vitiated in Adam, is totally depraved:

---

[48] Ibid., 203.

[49] *Luther's Works*, 26, *Lectures on Galatians*, Jaroslav Pelikan, ed. (St. Louis: Concordia, 1963) 233.

[50] *LW*, 26, 284.

[51] Calvin, *Institutes*, II,16,6; see John Calvin, *Institutes of the Christian Religion*, Library of Christian Classics, Vol. XX, ed. John T. McNeill (Philadelphia: Westminster, 1960) 510.

Adam so corrupted himself that infection spread from him to all his descendents. Christ himself, our heavenly judge, clearly enough proclaims that
all men are born wicked and depraved when he says that "whatever is born
of flesh is flesh" [John 3:6], and therefore the door of life is closed to all until
they have been reborn [John 3:5].[52]

For Calvin, human beings cannot even cooperate with God's grace, an argument he carried through to its necessary consequence of predestination.
Children also are guilty and condemned:

> even infants themselves, while they carry their condemnation along with
> them from the mother's womb, are guilty not of another's fault but of their
> own. . . . Indeed, their whole nature is a seed of sin; hence it can be only
> hateful and abhorrent to God.[53]

The later Calvinist tradition has been summarized in five doctrines.[54]
Total depravity emphasizes that the natural or unregenerate person can do
nothing good in God's sight; for such a person, the intellect is blinded and
the will is hostile to God. Unconditional election means that God has fore-
ordained or predestined those who will be saved and those who will be
reprobated. Limited atonement is the doctrine that Christ died, not for all,
but only for believers. Irresistible grace means that being regenerated or
born again is entirely God's work. Because of sin, human beings are unable
to choose the good or cooperate with grace. Finally, perseverance of the
saints, in a word, means "once saved, always saved," and leads to the doctrine of the certainty of salvation. This extreme Calvinism, sometimes
called "hyper-Calvinism," can be seen as the fullest expression of Augustinian
pessimism.

The Council of Trent (1546–1563)

At Trent, the fathers were careful to avoid canonizing Augustinian,
Anselmian, or Thomistic views on original sin; thus they respected the diversity of theological schools within the Church. The council taught that
Adam lost righteousness and holiness, and by this sin, was changed "to a
worse state" (Canon 1), that this loss was not just for himself, but also for
his descendants (Canon 2), that original sin was one in its origin in Adam,
but communicated to each person by propagation, not imitation (Canon

---

[52] *Institutes* II,1,7; 249.

[53] *Institutes* II,1,8; 251.

[54] See Edwin H. Palmer, *The Five Points of Calvinism* (Grand Rapids, Mich.: Baker House,
1972).

3), though it did not embrace Augustine's negative view of sexual intercourse. Baptism was the necessary remedy for original sin, even for infants (Canon 4). Against Luther, the council emphasized that the guilt of original sin is taken away, not just brushed over, though concupiscence, the "tinder" of sin remains (Canon 5). The "worse state" mentioned in Canon 1 was left vague; later the preamble for Trent's Decree on Justification notes that the result of Adam's sin was not to destroy free will, but only to weaken it.[55] Indeed, the council taught that while human beings must be touched by the Holy Spirit in order to come to faith, they freely cooperate with the grace of God.[56]

Conclusion

While Christians generally say that Jesus offered his life as a sacrifice for their sins, the literalizing of the metaphors of sacrifice raises troubling questions for many Christians today. The doctrine has come to be identified with Anselm's theory of satisfaction. But this narrows considerably the rich variety of images, metaphors, and themes used in the New Testament and by the Fathers of the Church to express the mystery of our salvation.

Closely related to the soteriological question is the question of sin and the mystery of iniquity. The Genesis story of the Fall, while expressed in mythological language, sees at the origin of evil the refusal of human beings to acknowledge and reverence the Lord God. Their sin was pride, the temptation to worship themselves. Augustine called this an *aversio a Dei* or turning from God.

Adam plays scarcely any role in the remainder of the Old Testament, but he appears again in Paul, juxtaposed with Christ in Paul's two-Adam typology. In Romans Paul presents the history of salvation as a great drama, with Adam, Sin, Death, the Law, and Christ as the characters. The roots of the doctrine of original sin lie here in his interpretation of human experience, though his insights would be developed by the Fathers and ultimately be formulated by Augustine.

[55] See Rondet, *Original Sin*, 171–75; Vandervelde, *Original Sin*, 32–41; for a sophisticated treatment of original sin from an Evangelical perspective, see Henri Blocher, *Original Sin: Illuminating the Riddle* (Grand Rapids, Mich.: Eerdmans, 1997).

[56] DS 1525; cf. Canons 4–6; cf. Avery Dulles, *The Assurance of Things Hoped For* (New York: Oxford University Press, 1994) 48–50; Catholics and Lutherans today recognize a basic agreement on justification, expressed in the Lutheran World Federation/Roman Catholic *Joint Declaration on the Doctrine of Justification* (Grand Rapids, Mich.: Eerdmans, 2000).

In post-New Testament reflections on the work of Christ, the Eastern Fathers focused more on the Incarnation of the Logos and consequent transformation or divinization of humanity. The Western Fathers, less speculative, placed greater emphasis on redemption and the Cross. Augustine synthesized the Western tradition and passed it on in the Middle Ages. In reacting to the optimism of Pelagius, he taught that human beings were in a state of rebellion against God, their wills in bondage. Only the death of Christ which made satisfaction for our sins saved us from the wrath of God.

But it was Anselm of Canterbury who was to give Western soteriology its characteristic form through the sheer force and clarity of his theory of satisfaction. Christ by his death made satisfaction to God's justice, restoring the order of creation. While Abelard proposed a striking alternative, Anselm's theory won out, particularly as it was interpreted and passed on by the Protestant Reformers.

Chapter 11

A Contemporary Approach to Soteriology

While the doctrines of original sin and salvation are close to the heart of Christian faith, for many today their traditional expression becomes itself an obstacle to belief. Does one have to believe in a primeval Garden of Innocence or a set of first biological parents to make sense of original sin? Evolution rules out the first, while paleontology has yet to establish the second. Or what are we to say about the Anselmian theology of satisfaction which has dominated Western soteriology for over a thousand years? Can we believe in a God who would seem to require the crucifixion of his only beloved Son as the price of our salvation? Are we bound always to use the transactional language of the tradition—making satisfaction, taking our place, bearing God's wrath, becoming guilt and sin, offering himself as a sacrifice—to express the mystery of God's salvation offered us in Jesus? Does this language really work for our contemporaries today? Can we understand it in a new way?

Before we attempt to express the mysteries of sin and salvation in more contemporary terms, it might be helpful to make some observations about the nature of our religious language and how that language gets reflected in our theology. Our faith emerges from the reports or "narratives" of the earliest Christians who experienced God's salvation in their experience of Jesus as raised up and present among them. In their confession of him as Messiah, Lord, and Son of God, in telling his story, and in giving an account of his continued presence in their midst, they drew on the figures, metaphors, and narratives of their religious tradition, the Hebrew Scriptures. Thus our earliest theological language, the language of the New Testament, is a mostly undifferentiated mixture of narrative, metaphor, mythological imagery, and theological construction.

It is also true that Christians today frequently do not differentiate the mythological, historical, and metaphysical dimensions of their faith, as we saw at the beginning of this book in talking about the Nicene Creed, and our theologies continue to be influenced by premodern, modern, and postmodern modes of thought. Without necessarily committing ourselves to a postmodernist perspective, as we attempt to gain a more adequate understanding of both the doctrine of original sin and the mystery of salvation in Christ, it will be helpful to keep mythical, metaphysical, and properly historical explanations differentiated in our minds.

The Mystery of Iniquity

The Genesis story of the Fall represents the effort of a prescientific culture to give an account of the mystery of iniquity. The human experience of ignorance, suffering, injustice, evil, and death is all too obvious, even if the only possibility of explanation is by means of a mythological narrative. We saw in the preceding chapter how Paul developed the Genesis story into a cosmic theology with his story of the two Adams, and we traced the subsequent history of this theology of sin to its doctrinal formulation by Augustine. Theologians have argued ever since about the implications of his teaching, about the depth of its effects, the manner of its transmission, and its implications for Church and society. After the Council of Trent, Catholic theology tended to waver between two extremes, "the Pelagian thesis and the Protestant thesis of the radical corruption of fallen nature."[1] Too often, the doctrine has been interpreted in an overly individualistic way.

What might the doctrine of original sin mean from a contemporary perspective? For theology today, the doctrine speaks to the radically social nature of the human person and to the way that human freedom is limited prior even to its exercise by the network of relationships that constitutes each person as an individual.

Each of us is constituted by a multitude of social relationships, all of them touched by the competition, struggle for survival, and violence which has marked the human species since its emergence from the world of its predatory animal ancestors. Far from a primeval Garden of Innocence, evolution points to our origin in a nature "red in tooth and claw." That bloody nature has marked the human species from the beginning. Thus we are born into a world that is already scarred by the egoism, violence, injustice, and self-deception that embitters the members of the human family and pits them against each other. Our biological families are often dysfunctional; self-seeking poisons our relationships, our marriages

[1] Henri Rondet, *Original Sin: The Patristic and Theological Background* (Staten Island, N.Y.: Alba House, 1972) 175.

fail, and the weak are abused by the strong. Our cultures both shape and limit us, inculcating prejudice against those who are different from us while our social status conditions the way we perceive and relate to others. Thus our freedom is limited in all sorts of ways and our actions are never quite what we want them to be. In theological terms, death as well as life is at work in us.

In the later part of the twentieth century, the effort of theologians to reinterpret the doctrine of original sin in social terms as we have been suggesting here has been called a "situationist" approach.[2] The focus for these theologians is on the existential situation, that "being-situated" that constitutes and shapes each of us involuntarily, even prior to the exercise of our freedom. This approach accords well with the biblical emphasis on human solidarity in sin, with the post-Tridentine understanding of original sin as a privation of sanctifying grace, corresponding to limitations on human freedom and moral action that are rooted in one's concrete situation in a sinful world. The situationist approach takes the objective reality of sin in the world seriously, without reducing it to an ontological corruption of human nature. The doctrine that original sin is spread "by propagation, not imitation" is an affirmation that we sin, not because of the bad example of others or because our sexual origin is evil, but from the fact that we are shaped negatively by the sinful world into which we are born.

The formative character of one's situation, and thus the social nature of original sin, can be illustrated in the countless examples of children who grow up in dysfunctional homes where they are the victims of physical or sexual abuse, or in inner-city ghettos or barrios where peers and the threat of violence pressures them into joining gangs. In these cases, such children are not only damaged themselves, but they usually replicate the violence they have experienced in the lives of others. The complex human issues that the doctrine of original sin seeks to express are evident here. Has their situation radically limited their freedom, leading them to do evil? Yes. Do they incur guilt by reproducing the sin in the world in their own lives? Yes.

Another aspect of a contemporary interpretation concerns nature and grace. Once the Genesis story of the Fall is no longer seen as historical, nature and grace emerge in a new light. It is possible to distinguish them conceptually, but there is no such thing as "pure nature." Nature is always

---

[2] George Vandervelde analyzes this approach in the works of Piet Schoonenberg, Karl Rahner, and Karl-Heinz Wegner, as well as the "personalist" approach in his study, *Original Sin: Two Major Trends in Contemporary Roman Catholic Reinterpretation* (Amsterdam: Rodopi, 1975); see also Brian O. McDermott, "The Theology of Original Sin: Recent Developments," *Theological Studies* 38 (1977) 478–512.

"graced nature," for grace as God's free self-communication is always present in creation. Therefore, God's saving grace is available to all. The universal availability of salvation has ecclesiological implications, in that it relativizes the traditional teaching that baptism is necessary for salvation. The Second Vatican Council acknowledged for the first time that those who do not know the Gospel can attain salvation, with the help of God's grace. But this is not a doctrine of "universal salvation." The council also acknowledged the "fallen" character of the human situation, for "rather often" human beings, deceived by the Evil One, "have exchanged the truth of God for a lie, serving the creature rather than the Creator (cf. Rom. 1:21, 25)" (LG 16). This means that original sin remains a force to be reckoned with, making the proclamation of the Gospel and the community of the Church all the more important.

The doctrine of original sin is one of the great achievements of Christian theology; it is one of the few theological doctrines for which there is empirical evidence. The twentieth century's catalogue of horrors—Two World Wars, the Armenian genocide, the Holocaust, the killing fields of Cambodia, Rwanda, and Bosnia, the millions of abortions, the wars over religion and the persistence of slavery and the sexual exploitation of children, the millions who die of malnutrition or starvation—is evidence enough that there is something profoundly wrong in the human heart.

From this perspective, Brian McDermott is probably correct when he argues that the privational interpretation of original sin is not adequate to understanding its depth dimension, no matter how widespread this understanding is among Catholic theologians.[3] He finds wisdom in Augustine's view that there is in our hearts not just a lack, but an *aversio a Deo*, a positive unwillingness to love God and a complicity in evil which we experience in the confession of our powerlessness and our sins, revealing our profound need for the God who saves us in Christ, but not without our help.[4] But *how* does Jesus save us? Again, we come to the basic soteriological question at the end of our study.

Jesus Mediates God's Salvation

The rich variety of metaphors used by the New Testament authors and the Fathers of the Church to express the mystery of our salvation in Christ has been essentially lost in Western Christianity, which without any formal definition, has given quasi-magisterial authority to Anselm's theory of sat-

---

[3] McDermott, "The Theology of Original Sin," 509.
[4] Ibid., 510–12.

isfaction. Protestant theology has been largely built on this Reformation heritage, particularly Evangelical theology. In popular Catholic theology, it has often been the unarticulated subtext and it appears again in the *Catechism of the Catholic Church*.[5] Nevertheless, Anselm's theory today is increasingly seen as inadequate, for both theological and pastoral reasons.

Theologically, Anselm's theory of satisfaction is problematic for a number of reasons. First, he focuses on the death of Jesus, rather than on his entire life and ministry,[6] for it is the entire mystery of Jesus, his life, death, and resurrection, that is salvific. His approach reduces the ministry of Jesus to making an offering for sin, without any attention to his proclamation of the kingdom, his identification with the poor and the suffering, or his example of compassionate service and love.

Second, from the perspective of contemporary theology Anselm's approach is flawed methodologically. His satisfaction theory represents an attempt to do soteriology "from above," from God's point of view as it were. By literalizing one of the New Testament metaphors for salvation, Anselm has created a problematic ontological theology which "introduces the metaphysically impossible idea of a transformation of God."[7]

From a pastoral perspective, Anselm's theory has done considerable damage. Its legalism has stamped Christian preaching and spirituality with an emphasis on God's wrath and demand for reparation, to the extent that the gratuitous love and mercy of God has been obscured. Joseph Ratzinger calls it a "perfectly logical divine-cum-human legal system . . . that can make the image of God appear in a sinister light."[8] As Roger Haight asks, "How can the suffering and crucifixion of Jesus be anything but evil?"[9] In an age where the existence of so much senseless suffering and horrendous evil makes belief in a merciful and compassionate God difficult for many men and women, the idea of a God whose justice could be satisfied only by the death of an only-begotten Son makes no sense; it becomes an obstacle to faith, suggesting a narrowness in God's mercy. For feminist theologians, it seems to presume the patriarchal family structure in which the father rules over the lives of family members.[10]

---

[5] *Catechism of the Catholic Church*, Second Edition, Liberia Editrice Vaticana (Washington, D.C.: United States Catholic Conference, 1997) no. 615.

[6] See Hans Küng, *On Being a Christian* (Garden City, N.Y.: Doubleday, 1976) 421.

[7] Karl Rahner, "The Universality of Salvation," in *Theological Investigations* 16 (New York: Seabury, 1979) 208; see also Elizabeth A. Johnson, "Jesus and Salvation," Catholic *Theological Society of America: Proceedings* 49 (1994) 5.

[8] Joseph Ratzinger, *Introduction to Christianity* (New York: Herder and Herder, 1971) 174.

[9] Roger Haight, *Jesus: Symbol of God* (Maryknoll, N.Y.: Orbis, 1999) 345.

[10] Cf. Johnson, "Jesus and Salvation," 15.

Yet there are many who cling to Anselm's traditional explanation of our salvation. Much of popular Christian piety, both Catholic and Protestant, continues to be informed by it. For many Evangelicals, Anselm's satisfaction theory has been refined into the doctrine of penal substitution, which in the context of predestination holds that Christ's saving work is directed, not to all, but only to the "elect."[11] This in turn has contributed to the religious individualism which all too often has afflicted Western Christianity.

A Soteriology from Below

What would it mean to articulate a theology of salvation, not from above, but rather from below? Such a theology would take its departure from the entire story of Jesus, his life, ministry, passion, death, resurrection, and appearances to his own, particularly as it is told to us from the Gospels. It would have to take fully into account the centrality of the "reign of God" in Jesus' preaching and its importance for Christian life today. Eschewing ontological theories of salvation such as atonement, satisfaction, recapitulation, or divinization without necessarily rejecting them as metaphors would make such an approach more congenial to a contemporary culture that is often shaped by postmodern ways of thinking.

At the same time, it would not have to rule out completely any ontological statements, for there are clearly metaphysical implications to the story of Jesus which have been expressed in the dogmas of the Church. As Walter Kasper has said, "Being and meaning are indissolubly joined in the confession that 'Jesus is the Christ.'"[12] And if the Church's fundamental christological and trinitarian faith has been formally defined, the same is not true for Anselm's theology of satisfaction, despite its antecedents in the tradition. The Nicene Creed says that Jesus came down from heaven "for us and for our salvation," and though it adds "for our sake he was crucified under Pontius Pilate," it gives no particular indication as to how that should be understood.

We also need to call attention to what we saw in chapter 6. Critical scholarship does not exclude the New Testament view that Jesus saw his death, freely accepted, as part of his life and ministry. While not attributing salvific efficacy to his death itself, Jesus approached it confident in a renewed fellowship with his disciples beyond it. This view of his life and even his death as a "service" is rooted in the tradition of the Last Supper. In the

---

[11] See Gerald Bray, "Evangelicals, Salvation, and Church History" in *Catholics And Evangelicals: Do They Share a Common Future?* ed. Thomas P. Rausch (New York: Paulist, 2000) 87–89.

[12] Walter Kasper, *Jesus the Christ* (New York: Paulist, 1976) 23.

tradition, it is expressed by the concept of sacrifice in Catholic theology and as satisfaction in Protestant theology.

What then do we mean when we talk about salvation in Christ? First of all, to describe salvation as something that Jesus "does" is to risk returning to a soteriology from above, to a metaphysical account of some change worked in God or in our relationship to God, rather than something that happens existentially to us, in our experience. In the Fathers of the Church, we are saved from death, sin, and ignorance, to which Roger Haight adds guilt and suffering.[13] To say that Jesus saves us is to confess that through Jesus we come to experience God's saving presence, and so find our lives transformed.

Jesus is present to us in many ways, in the preaching of the Gospel, the contemplation of its mysteries, the celebration of the sacraments, the gathering of the community or Church in his Spirit, and in compassionate service to others in his name. Access to Jesus should not be made impossibly difficult. One does not need to have a German doctorate to understand the Gospel story; there is an immediacy in the language and imagery of the Gospel stories that can touch people separated by two millennia from the Jesus of history. At the same time, good theology can safeguard the story of Jesus from the deformations that come from partial readings or one-sided interpretations. Anselm's theory of satisfaction or the later theology of penal satisfaction are both models of clarity and economy; but neither is the whole story.

Having considered in some detail the story of Jesus in the earlier chapters of this book, we can try now to make more concrete the ways in which Jesus mediates an experience of God that is truly saving.

God's Love in Jesus Changes Lives

The Gospels make clear in the most powerful way that the ministry of Jesus was not focused on the next world. The Jesus of history, in the brief years that are available to us, spent his days teaching, healing, and reconciling real men and women.

Those whom he healed of diseases or injuries and those he set free from "unclean spirits" experienced God's transforming power in their bodies. He challenged the religious leaders of his day, some of whose lives, Nicodemus' for example (John 20:39), were changed, opened to the movements of God's Spirit. He called men and women into his company, to share his ministry and to be with him, and they "left everything" to follow him.

[13] Haight, *Jesus: Symbol of God*, 354.

The poor were clearly at the heart of his ministry. In the Old Testament prophets, justice for the poor is always a promise and sign of the messianic age. Jesus was not a social revolutionary in the conventional sense. He took no part in political movements against the occupying Roman power and cannot be construed as a prophet of radical social change, attempting to reform village life or social mores. But the centrality of the Beatitudes to his preaching, the references to "the poor and the crippled, the blind and the lame" (Luke 14:21) in his parables, the references to the vast crowd following him which he describes as "like sheep without a shepherd" (Mark 6:34) or which is described by the Pharisees as this "accursed" crowd "which does not know the law" (John 7:49)—all this points to the place that the poor, broadly understood, occupied in his ministry. This would have included the illiterate or unemployed, poor farmers and day laborers, the mentally ill, those with disfiguring diseases or bodily injuries still to be seen at city gates and church doors in the Middle East, as well as women, public sinners, and others excluded in different ways from the life of the community. Jesus made them welcome and called them blessed in the kingdom of God. Even more, he implicitly called for a transformation of their social situation, for he made it clear that our own share in God's kingdom was dependent on our efforts to succor the last and the least (Luke 16:19-31; Matt 25:31-46).

Jesus also proclaimed the forgiveness of sins. He showed a particular care for the religiously marginalized, those considered outside the law by the religious authorities. The forgiveness he proclaimed meant reconciliation with God and with the community. He was repeatedly criticized as "a glutton and drunkard, a friend of tax collectors and sinners" (Matt 11:19) for associating with them and including them in his table fellowship, showing that no one was excluded from God's reign.

The many stories of men and women whose lives were radically changed by their encounter with Jesus is testimony to the impact of his presence on others. Some of these encounters took place during his ministry. The Samaritan woman with the five husbands (John 4:42) became an evangelist, Peter, the boastful fisherman, became a leader in the primitive Church, Mary Magdalene, freed from seven demons (Luke 8:2), one of Jesus' closest followers and intimate friend, Zacchaeus (Luke 19:2) and Levi (Mark 2:14), both tax collectors, underwent conversions and one at least became a disciple. Others encountered the risen Jesus and were changed, like the two disciples on the road to Emmaus (Luke 24:13-35) or Paul, the fanatical and self-righteous Pharisee who became the Apostle of the Gentiles.

The stories are more than attractive narratives; where men and women are changed from lack of self-knowledge, unfreedom, and sin to freedom, newness of life, and care for others, grace is at work. One does not have to return to the New Testament to find evidence of lives changed by the encounter with Jesus. They are all around us; we know their names. They are stories of grace mediated by Jesus. And the presence of grace means God is there.

The Cross Is the Symbol of Our Salvation

The cross, and even more the crucifix, with its portrayal of the tortured body of Jesus, is the symbol of Christian faith and the mystery of our salvation. Christians have blessed themselves with the "sign of the cross" since the third century; Tertullian says: "We make the sign of the cross on our forehead at every turn, at our going in or coming out of the house, while dressing, while putting on our shoes, when we are taking a bath, before and after meals, when we light the lamps, when we go to bed or sit down, and in all the ordinary activities of daily life."[14]

If it is true that traditional theology and piety have stressed the death of Jesus without sufficient attention to the resurrection, too often today the reverse is true. One of the strengths of Roger Haight's book is his effort to rethink soteriology, and particularly his critique of Anselm's satisfaction theory. But like many contemporary theologians, he finds it difficult to come to terms with the Cross. He asks how torturous explanations of why the Cross has meaning and salvific value can even begin to make sense to a postmodern imagination. Following Jon Sobrino, he sees the Cross as a symbol of Jesus' entire life of choosing the kingdom of God.[15] But without a theology of the Cross Haight has little basis for discussing the mystery of suffering, evil, and death.[16]

From the time of Paul the cross has symbolized the personal price paid by Jesus for our salvation. Jewish law said that anyone "hung on a tree" was cursed (Deut 21:22-23). For the Jews, particularly for the righteous Pharisee Paul before his conversion, this was a "stumbling block" (1 Cor 1:23). But with "the logic only a rabbi could appreciate," Paul came to see the cross as that which enabled Jesus to take the Law's curse upon himself, transforming it, so that it became "the power of God and the wisdom of

---

[14] "The Chaplet, 3" in Roy J. Deferrari, gen. ed., *The Fathers of the Church: A New Translation*, vol. 40, Tertullian: Disciplinary, Moral, and Ascetical Works (New York: Fathers of the Church, Inc., 1959) 237.

[15] Cf. Haight, *Jesus: Symbol of God*, 345–47; cf. Jon Sobrino, *Jesus the Liberator: A Historical-Theological View* (Maryknoll, N.Y.: Orbis, 1993) 228–30.

[16] I am grateful to Sean Vidaurri, one of our graduate students, for this formulation.

God" (1 Cor 1:18-25).[17] Thus we are "justified" and "reconciled" through his death (Rom 5:9-10); he is our "expiation" (Rom 3:25). This is powerful, metaphorical language, as we have stressed, never to be taken literally. We can never lose sight of the mystery of the Cross, or repudiate it as a symbol.

At the same time, the death of Jesus cannot be separated from his life, ministry, and teaching; "otherwise we are turning its redemptive significance into a myth, sometimes even into a sadistic and bloody myth."[18] That Jesus is "obedient to death, even to death on a cross" (Phil 2:8) means not that he obeys some divine demand that he suffer and die as the price of our salvation, but that in faithfulness to his ministry, he refuses absolutely to respond with hostility or violence to the hostility and violence that his ministry occasioned. In theological terms, he does not respond to sin with sin.

As we have already seen, sin has a radically social dimension. The results of sin—injury, resentment, alienation, hostility—go forth like ripples from a pebble thrown into a pond, disrupting the social environment. Symbolically but truly, sin brings in its wake death. The evil that sin brings into the world is very real; it endures, beyond the death of the sinner and is not removed by forgiveness. In a real sense, we can say that the sin present in the world, the sin that is a force hostile to God's goodness and truth which touches each of us, became incarnate in the persons of the chief priests, Pilate, and all those who mocked Jesus and brought him to Calvary.

The Cross shows us a Jesus who will not turn away from God, who remains focused on the one he calls Abba, in total vulnerability, even at the cost of his life. It is the Jesus who will not sin, who clings to his Abba, refusing to break his relationship with God. He will not respond to sin with sin, for he is willing to lose his life in order to save it, as we must be (cf. Mark 8:35). This is the paradox at the heart of the Gospel. Metaphorically, Jesus' refusal to meet hostility with hostility, sin with sin is "the antidote to endless cycles of revenge and violence . . . a feeble attempt to express the radical surgery that true forgiveness and costly reconciliation entails."[19] Thus Jesus makes visible the grace that is present because of God's love for humanity; metaphorically he breaks the power of sin and death, showing us that sin does not have the last word. Jesus' entire life was to proclaim God's reign as a reign of compas-

---

[17] Joseph A. Fitzmyer, "Pauline Theology," in *The Jerome Biblical Commentary*, ed. Raymond E. Brown, Joseph A. Fitzmyer, and Roland E. Murphy (Englewood Cliffs, N.J.: Prentice-Hall, 1968) 79:13.

[18] Edward Schillebeeckx, *Church: The Human Story of God* (New York: Crossroad, 1990) 120.

[19] George Vandervelde, in a private communication to the author; see also Gil Bailie, *Violence Unveiled: Humanity at the Crossroads* (New York: Crossroad, 1995).

sion, freedom, and peace against the forces of evil, whatever dehumanizes human beings or denies them their freedom. How could he renounce those values, even to save his own life? The Cross then, rather than a curse, becomes in Christian iconography the sign of Christ's victory.

As Arthur C. McGill argues in his wonderful little book on suffering and theology, "When Jesus stands opposed to all acts of violence and to all violent powers, and when he acts to free men [and women] from those forces which oppress and torment them, he does so as the revealer of God's own essential life."[20] McGill's book is concerned with how God delivers us from evil, darkness, and death. The Augustinian/Anselmian tradition identifies the problem with the concept of sin, understood in legal terms as an offense against God's justice and will. McGill identifies it with the demonic, that "peculiar energy of destruction" so obvious in our world, the essence of which "is to twist and break apart the forms of other things, to stunt human growth, to disrupt social order, to misshape animals and trees, to obstruct the fruitfulness of the earth."[21]

McGill's argument in brief is that God's power is absolutely opposed to the dominative power of the demonic. The divinity active in Jesus is not absolute power, which is potentially tyrannical, but God's life. God's power does not bring death; it is not destructive, but life-giving. It generates the Son as God's equal, while the Son adores the Father as his origin. Though the death of Jesus shows dominative power apparently in full control, the Cross represents not the victory of the demonic, but its ultimate defeat, for "Jesus' self-offering on the cross and his whole life in Palestine is the action of the Son, and therefore an action in which a human mode of being is gathered into the inner life of God."[22]

As Christians, we too live under the Cross, knowing that dominative power can never be the lord of real life and death, nor can it separate us from our present share in God's life.[23] Even if McGill does not adequately develop the theology of the Spirit, presumed in his reference to our share in God's life, he does show how humanity in the person of Jesus enters into a life with God that makes death, not an end point, but a transition to a new life. We will consider the Spirit below.

[20] Arthur C. McGill, *Suffering: A Test of Theological Method* (Philadelphia: Westminster, 1968); republished 1982 with a Forward by Paul Ramsey and William F. May, 79.

[21] Ibid., 48.

[22] Ibid., 95; Schillebeeckx's approach is similar; he writes that "The basic choice of Jesus was to refuse power, and so his words and actions take on an unparalleled authority." *Church*, 125.

[23] McGill, *Suffering*, 98.

The Cross thus is a sign of God's love revealed in Jesus; not just his remaining united to God in the face of evil, but also because in his refusal of violence in the face of evil, he remains in solidarity with all those victims of violence throughout history. Commenting from a Jewish perspective, Harold Kushner observes that "Christianity introduced the world to the idea of a God who suffers, alongside the image of a God who creates and commands."[24] G. K. Chesterton once compared the symbol of the crucified Jesus with that of Eastern mysticism. Jesus is spread naked on an instrument of torture, the cross, vulnerable, body completely exposed, arms outstretched, open to all things, to God but also to doubt. The Buddha's figure is focused inward, content, arms and legs circling in, closing off the way to eyes and heart and genitals.[25] The point of the comparison is not to denigrate Buddhism, but rather to dramatize the vulnerability at the heart of the Gospel.

The crucified Jesus is a most apt symbol for the Christian, for we too must die to sin, to the self that turns from God, to all that is not God, and finally, in that painful final passage each of us must go through, to life itself, clinging only to God, that we might have life eternal. There is no salvation without the Cross, without pain, without a dying. Indeed, taking up one's Cross becomes the condition for following Jesus in the Synoptics (Mark 8:34 and plls), a mystery that has its own expression in Paul (Rom 6:3-5) and John (12:24). For Jesus is the way and the truth and the life (John 14:6). Like Jesus, each Christian is called and enabled to enter into the paschal mystery, to that mystery of the faithful love of God that sustains us in Christ.

God's Love Is Stronger Than Death

The resurrection of Jesus reveals that God's love is stronger than death. It show us that the deepest hope cherished in the human heart for deliverance from the finality of death, the hope for life everlasting in God's presence, is possible to those who in Christ cling to God's love. By God's love, I mean both the active and the receptive sense, God's love for us and our love for God which God's love makes possible and enables.

As we saw in chapter 7, the disciples' coming to Easter faith was a far more complex process than the Easter stories in the Gospels suggest, at least at first reading. At issue here is not the resuscitation of a corpse in history, but new life in God's future, in the eschaton, the other side of time

---

[24] Harold S. Kushner, *When Bad Things Happen to Good People* (New York: Schocken Books, 1981) 85.

[25] Paraphrasing Garry Wills' description of Chesterton's image in *Bare Ruined Choirs* (Garden City, N.Y.: Doubleday, 1972) 268.

and space which by definition is beyond our power to imagine. The disciples were able to recognize the crucified one as living and present among them because their religious tradition had already introduced the hope of a resurrection of the dead, a hope that grew out of a painful moment in Israel's history when Jews were willing to die rather than violate their covenant relationship with Yahweh.

For Paul, the resurrection of Jesus is not just the object of our hope; it is a power already transforming our lives into a new life in Christ. He speaks of desiring "to know [Christ] and the power of his resurrection and [the] sharing of his sufferings by being conformed to his death, if somehow I may attain the resurrection of the dead" (Phil 3:10-11; cf. Rom 6:4). In 2 Corinthians he speaks of our being transformed into an image of Christ (2 Cor 3:18; 4:6).

The resurrection of Jesus is a strong argument for the inspired character of the growing hope of God's people in Scripture that God will bring life to the dead, even if the resurrection itself cannot be verified by the rigorous canons of historical investigation. For the story of Jesus can only be understood against the horizon of the story of Israel, with its failures and its hope.

Jesus Gives Us a Share in God's Life

God's salvation in Christ Jesus gives us a share in the divine life, a theme developed by both Paul and John. Paul speaks of Jesus as the "last Adam" who becomes with his death and resurrection a "life-giving spirit" (1 Cor 15:45) and says that God has sent the spirit of Jesus into our hearts, that we also might cry out, "Abba, Father" (Gal 4:6). In Romans 8, a chapter which brings to a close his great drama of salvation history, he speaks of our own share in the divine life through the indwelling Spirit. Three times he reminds the Roman Christians that "the Spirit of God" or the "Spirit of the one who raised Jesus from the dead" or simply that it is "his Spirit that dwells in you" (Rom 8:9-11). He does not always distinguish clearly between Jesus and the Spirit, even saying at one point "the Lord is the Spirit" (2 Cor 3:17, 18). It is this indwelling Spirit that is the source of the Christian confession of Jesus as Lord (1 Cor 12:3), the Spirit which manifests itself in the rich diversity of spiritual gifts and ministries given for the building up of the Church (1 Cor 12:4-11).

The author of the Fourth Gospel develops a rich theology of the divine indwelling in Jesus' farewell discourse (John 14–17). The Father who dwells in Jesus (John 14:10) will send the Spirit to the disciples to be with them always (John 14:16); the Spirit is sent in the name of Jesus (John 14:26) or by Jesus himself (John 15:26). In his great final prayer Jesus says that he has given his disciples the glory he received from the Father, "so that they may be one, as we are one, I in them and you in me" (John 17:22-23). Thus in the Johannine theology of the divine indwelling there is already present in rudimentary form what would become the doctrine of the trinitarian life of God.

God's Love in Jesus Creates a New People

If we share in God's life, then we have a new communion or fellowship (*koinonia*) with one another. Using this word *koinonia*, Paul tells us that God has called us into fellowship with his Son Jesus (1 Cor 1:9), that we have a communion in his Body and Blood, that in sharing in the one bread of the Eucharist we become ourselves one body (1 Cor 10:16–17). Thus our salvation in Christ makes us a new people, an assembly or Church (*ekklēsia*). Just as God's salvation in Jesus is mediated by the story of Israel, so that salvation, that hope, that life remain visible and accessible in history in the community committed to his way of life and living in his Spirit. In this way salvation itself becomes historical, not a transhistorical, metaphysical event. Christianity is a radically incarnational faith, which means that grace becomes visible, enfleshed, present in history. It is also a radically social faith, binding us in the Spirit to Christ and to one another.

Historically, the Church is the continuation in history of the new family Jesus establishes, dedicated to hearing the Word of God (Mark 3:33-35). It is this eschatological Israel, gathered by Jesus in the persons of his disciples, with the Twelve at the center, that becomes the new People of God (though God does not repent of the gifts given or the calls issued to the Jewish people; cf. LG 16). The Church mediates God's salvation in Christ through its preaching (*kerygma*), teaching (*didachē*), worship (*leitourgia*), ministry (*diakonia*), and shared life (*koinonia*). For all the sin *in* the Church and even *of* the Church (though official Catholicism is reluctant to speak this way), grace is always mediated grace. Those who are touched by the Word proclaimed, by communion in the Spirit of Jesus, by bread broken and shared, by ministry in his name, find salvation and life through his community.

Theologically, salvation in Christ unites us in Christ to one another and demands a new relationship with all men and women. The Church is always at the service of God's reign. The individualistic understanding of salvation so typical of much of American Christianity is very much at odds with the

New Testament and contributes to the privatization of religion so typical of secular American culture.[26] While salvation involves a personal relationship with Jesus, it can never be reduced to that. As Gerhard Lohfink says, analyzing the Last Supper at Corinth as an example, "One can have communion with Christ only and always in communion with one another."[27] To be "in Christ," a phrase which appears some 164 times in the Pauline letters, should not be understood in an individual sense. "It means belonging to the realm within which Christ rules, and that realm is his body, the community."[28] Christ's reign makes a real claim on us; it breaks down all divisions based on race, class, or social status. The Eucharist creates this communion by inserting us into the Body of Christ.[29] In Latin America, the privatization of faith results in the anomalous situation of Christians in government or the military worshipping in the same faith and often the same local community with those they have tortured.[30] And there are analogous offenses of commission and omission that divide our own ecclesial communities. When Paul rebuked the Corinthian Christians for not "discerning the body" (1 Cor 11:29), he had such offenses against communion in mind. The "Body of Christ" is both the Christian community and the eucharistic bread; both are truly his Body.[31]

Is Jesus the Source of Our Salvation?

In the preceding section I have tried to articulate a soteriology from below. We have explored how Jesus mediates salvation. We saw that God's love made present in Jesus changes lives, is symbolized by the cross, proves stronger than death, creates a new people, and gives us a share in the divine life through the Spirit of Jesus. Such a soteriology is relational and revelatory rather than transactional. It specifically seeks to avoid literalizing one of the New Testament metaphors, and it does not offer a mythological or metaphysical metanarrative, explaining salvation in terms of some kind of transaction or exchange, a transformation in God effected by Jesus.

[26] Cf. Robert N. Bellah, "Religion and the Shape of National Culture," *America* 181/3 (1999) 9–14.

[27] Gerhard Lohfink, *Does God Need the Church?* (Collegeville: The Liturgical Press, 1999) 255.

[28] Ibid., 260.

[29] See J.-M. R. Tillard, *Flesh of the Church, Flesh of Christ: At the Source of the Ecclesiology of Communion* (Collegeville: The Liturgical Press, 2001) 38–39.

[30] See William T. Cavanaugh, *Torture and Eucharist: Theology, Politics, and the Body of Christ* (Oxford: Blackwell, 1998).

[31] This view is particularly strong in Augustine; see Tillard, *Flesh of the Church*, 39–62.

This approach to soteriology comes close to that of Roger Haight, whose proposal is to retrieve the forgotten tradition of Abelard that he sees as "more appropriate to the New Testament witness that Jesus reveals a God whose justice unfolds within the larger context of gratuitous and forgiving love."[32] Haight's soteriology presents Jesus as one who reveals and symbolizes the encounter with God and becomes an exemplar of human existence (357–58).

But our approach here differs from Haight's at a number of points. First, it seeks to deal more explicitly with the Cross as a paradoxical symbol of our salvation, indeed, as a symbol of God's love in Christ that stands resolutely opposed to all violence and worldly power. God's power is life-giving, not dominative. Failing to come to terms with the paradox of the Cross risks missing God's mysterious self-revelation in suffering and marginality, a theme quite congenial to the postmodern mentality. Haight does not really deal adequately with the Cross. He seems to find no positive value in the Cross itself, except as a symbol of Jesus' life.

Second, unlike Haight, our approach is willing to affirm that Jesus is the universal source of salvation, though in a qualified way. Toward the end of his book, Haight observes that "modern christology is split between those who retain the idea that Jesus caused or causes the salvation of all and those who do not." He argues that only through some metaphysical construct can one argue that Jesus had a causal influence on the salvation of those who have never come into contact with him historically, or lived before him (349). The most that Haight seems able to admit is that Jesus causes the salvation of Christians by symbolically or sacramentally revealing God's loving presence, or that he does not constitute but reveals God's love as something that has always been operative (359–60). Haight acknowledges that he "leans on the side of pluralism" (398). Jesus is "a normative revelation of God" for Christians, but there are other normative revelations for those in other religions (403).

I think it entirely possible that there are other mediators of salvation, personal or transcendent. The mainstream of Catholic theology recognizes that both non-Christian religions and secular realities such as devoting oneself to transcendent values, for example justice, peace, or humanity, can serve as mediations of salvation for non-Christians.[33] Whenever men and women search for the truth, are touched by goodness, or contemplate the beautiful, the Spirit of God is present. As Michael Amaladoss argues in an

---

[32] Haight, *Jesus: Symbol of God*, 360.

[33] Francis A. Sullivan, *Salvation Outside the Church? Tracing the History of the Catholic Response* (New York: Paulist, 1992) 181.

address on proclaiming Christ in the context of the pluralism of religions, salvific encounters take place in and through other religions, not in spite of them.[34]

The magisterium of the Church has been more cautious. Pope John Paul II has gone further than any pontiff in history in his appreciation of other religions. In his encyclical, *Redemptoris missio*, he acknowledges that the Holy Spirit is active in the heart of every person, and that the Spirit's activity can also affect "society and history, peoples, cultures and religions" (no. 28).[35] Twice he has called the leaders of the world's religions to come together at Assisi to pray for peace, in 1986 and again in 2002. Yet in reaffirming the universality of salvation in Christ, he speaks only of "participated forms of mediation" which acquire meaning and value from Christ (no. 5; cf. LG 16). Thus he does not move the magisterium forward on this point.

But is Jesus the *source* of the salvation for all human beings, as Christians have traditionally asserted? Here I would answer with a qualified affirmative. Jesus is the source of human salvation, not by some work accomplished or transaction enacted, but as a constituent embodiment of the saving work of God who speaks the divine Word into space and time and sends the Spirit into history, enabling us to participate in the divine life. We share in this life because of the trinitarian nature of our salvation, which is always communion in the mystery we identify symbolically as Father, Son, and Spirit.

With his preference for a Spirit Christology as an alternative to traditional Logos Christology, Haight makes Jesus a unique mediator of the Spirit for Christians, but not the incarnation of the Word, as in Logos Christology. Thus, his Christology does not acknowledge the ontological union of the divine with the human in Jesus. This in turn effects his doctrine of the Trinity. He recognizes that the doctrine of the Trinity is dependent on Christology (479) for, given the self-revelation of God through Jesus, "the historical genesis and intrinsic structure of Christian faith, revelation, and salvation are functionally trinitarian" (484). The word "functionally" here is key, for he grants the trinitarian structure of historical revelation, the "economic" Trinity, but not what is generally referred to as the "immanent" Trinity, which holds that the inner reality of God is differentiated.

But other theologians are reluctant to move towards a "unitarian" understanding of God *in se*. Joseph Bracken argues against the tendency of theologians like Haight to reject the notion of an immanent Trinity. He finds it "too radical" in that "it seems to set aside almost two thousand

---

[34] Michael Amaladoss, "Pluralism of Religions and the Proclamation of Jesus Christ in the Context of Asia," Catholic Theological Society of America, *Proceedings* 56 (2001) 1.

[35] John Paul II, *Redemptoris missio*, no. 28; see *Origins* 20/34 (1991) 541–68.

years of careful theological reflection on the reality of God as derived from Scripture and Tradition." But it is also "not radical enough," as it fails to come to terms with the deeper issue, the need to move from a metaphysics of being to a metaphysics of becoming as the appropriate way for understanding both the doctrine of the Trinity and the God-world relationship.[36] Bracken's process approach provides a powerful alternative to those who would maintain that trinitarian language applies to God only in relation to us. Instead, he affirms a God who is not just personal, but intersubjective. In other words, relationality is at the heart of the Christian understanding of God.

Though her methodology makes her less insistent on arguing for intradivine distinctions considered apart from the economy, Catherine Mowry LaCugna also argues for person as the primary ontological category for understanding the Trinity. She returns to the Cappadocian insistence that God's *ousia* (nature) exists only as relation or *hypostasis* (person): "The whole point of the original doctrine of the Trinity was that God (God's *ousia*) simply does not exist except as three persons. Vice versa, the divine persons are not other than the divine *ousia*, they are the *ousia*."[37]

On what grounds does Haight with his "functionally trinitarian" understanding of Christian faith substantively reinterpret what has been intrinsic to that faith since the fourth century? His real concern is to enter into dialogue with postmodern intellectual culture (490). He offers a number of specific arguments. The first is from the relation of the trinitarian symbols to religious knowing. Haight tends to deal with both Trinity and Christology primarily in terms of symbols. Yahweh, Spirit, Word, Wisdom, and Logos are metaphors; the first names the utterly transcendent, the others are used for God's presence and action in the world (472). But these "symbols, metaphors, or models" come from the world of religious experience; such language is "not objectively representational, or immediately referential, or propositionally descriptive" (471). The language of religious symbolism does not give so much factual knowledge as it symbolizes encounters with God in history.

The christological models Haight offers earlier in his book, Last Adam, Son of God, Spirit, Wisdom, and Logos Christologies, are also based on symbols, including three of those that reappear in his argument about the doctrine of the Trinity. He is correct about the nature of such symbols. But

---

[36] Joseph A. Bracken, "Trinity: Economic *And* Immanent," *Horizons* 25/1 (1998) 8.

[37] Catherine Mowry LaCugna, *God for Us: The Trinity and Christian Life* (HarperSan-Francisco, 1991) 389.

I would caution about reducing New Testament christological evidence to symbols and models which are already a step or more removed from the immediacy of the texts. This is not unlike an older approach that did Christology almost exclusively in terms of titles such as prophet, Messiah, Lord, Son of Man, Son of God, and so forth. The New Testament offers a good deal more. There is considerable narrative and figurative testimony to Jesus' divine Sonship and even preexistence, including his use of Abba, the virginal conception in Matthew and Luke, various efforts to link him to Old Testament theophanies (Mark 6:45-52; 9:2-8), the accusation of blasphemy reported in the Gospels (Mark 14:64; Matt 26:65; John 10:33, 36; cf. 19:7), the very adoption of the divine title Lord (*kurios*), the fact that he was an object of worship from the earliest period, even that he was addressed as "God" in John and Hebrews, as we saw in chapter 8.

By the same token, Haight's claim that Spirit Christology dominates the New Testament (474) is at least debatable. While focusing on Luke's Gospel as an example of Spirit Christology, elements of which he finds also in Paul and John, not all would agree that this is the foundational aspect of Luke's Christology (163).[38] He also argues that the doctrine of the immanent Trinity is not in the New Testament (474). But Wisdom and Logos Christologies as well as passages that use preexistence language of Jesus (John, Hebrews, and most probably Paul) clearly indicate at least the beginning of questions about the nature of God, as Haight himself acknowledges (481), as do the theologies of the divine indwelling in Paul and especially John. Haight sees the hypostatization of the Logos in the second century as a literalizing or reification of a metaphor (475); others see it as a clarifying of what is already implicit in the New Testament.

Finally, in his analysis of the doctrine of the Trinity, Haight argues that the unicity and unity of God are always a given. Trinitarian theology is primarily soteriological in emphasis, concerned to affirm that God is truly encountered as God in Jesus and the Spirit. This was the Fathers' concern at Nicaea in the controversy with the Arians. Haight says "This presence of true God in Jesus is the supposition behind Logos language: this is not the 'ordinary' presence of God as creator, but the intimate presence of God for human salvation" (485). But how is this presence of God in Jesus different from God's presence in other Spirit-filled persons or in other forms of mediation? Is his Jesus like Marcus Borg's, who places Jesus among the "many

[38] For example, John H. Wright argues that "The prevailing New Testament Christology seems, strictly speaking, to be neither Logos Christology nor Spirit Christology, but a Christology of divine sonship." See "Roger Haight's Spirit Christology," *Theological Studies* 53 (1992) 730–31.

mediators of the sacred"?[39] Is it a question of degrees? "Ordinary" versus "intimate"? Haight is not really able to answer this. Earlier he rejects the metaphors of "inspiration" and "possession," choosing instead "empowerment," which enhances human freedom without overpowering it (454–55). But it is not clear that this really resolves the issue the Fathers were wrestling with at Nicaea. In rejecting the subordinationist teaching of Arius, Nicaea affirmed the consubstantiality of Jesus with God: "God from God, light from light, true God from true God, begotten not made, consubstantial with the Father." In this way the fathers affirmed that it was the living God who acted in Jesus, God *in se*.

Haight wants to affirm that God is truly, intimately present in Jesus, but it is not clear how that presence is truly different from God's presence through the Spirit in others. His preference for a Spirit Christology leads him to interpret the trinitarian teaching of the Church in purely economic terms. But this raises a serious question. If the God revealed in the economy, *Deus pro nobis*, is not God *in se*, then is the God who is active in the economy really God? Has God really saved us? This was the issue that the Fathers of the Church were wrestling with as they reflected on the biblical tradition and the faith of their Churches, and from it came the doctrine of the Trinity. In Catherine LaCugna's contemporary formulation, the doctrine affirms "that God as such is communicated in Jesus Christ."[40]

Conclusion

In the effort to give a contemporary account of the mystery of salvation it is important to keep in mind the nature of our religious language, both the undifferentiated mixture of narrative and metaphor, mythological imagery and theological construction of the Bible, as well as the various kinds of narrative we use to express our faith.

A contemporary, "situationist," approach to the mystery of iniquity interprets the doctrine of original sin in light of the radically social nature of the human person. Not just ourselves but our freedom to a considerable degree bears the imprint of our social situations, each of which is touched by sin. This approach takes the reality of sin seriously, without reducing it to an ontological theory of a corrupted nature. It also recognizes that nature and grace can be separated conceptually, but not in reality, for from

---

[39] Cf. Marcus J. Borg, *Meeting Jesus Again for the First Time: The Historical Jesus and the Heart of Contemporary Faith* (HarperSanFrancisco, 1994) 37.

[40] LaCugna, *God for Us*, 42.

the perspective of the theology of creation, nature is always "graced nature." Still, there is wisdom in Augustine's view that there is in the human heart something profoundly wrong, as is obvious from the violence and injustice so evident in our world, showing our need for God's grace.

While the mystery of our salvation in Christ has been understood in Augustinian/Anselmian terms for over a millennium, Anselm's theory of satisfaction is problematic for both theological and pastoral reasons. Ultimately it is a soteriology from above.

In attempting to develop a soteriology from below, we followed Roger Haight's approach, which sees Jesus as revealer and exemplar of our salvation. However we moved in a different direction from Haight at several significant points. First, we tried to show how the Cross of Christ remains a preeminent symbol of Christian faith and the mystery of our salvation. Only in the Cross, indeed in the whole mystery of his Passion, do we see Jesus' radical refusal of the way of evil, the demonic, giving himself instead into the hands of Abba. In refusing to meet evil with evil, he reveals the non-dominative, life-giving power of God, the God whose love is stronger than death, the God whose power is revealed in weakness. Therefore any contemporary soteriology must give more attention to the place of the Cross in Christian spirituality and life.

Second, unlike Haight, we affirmed with the Christian tradition that Jesus is the source of our salvation, though in a qualified way. Implicated in this expression of the tradition is the doctrine of the Trinity, for through Christ and in his Spirit we share in the inner life of God. To live "in Christ" is to be related consciously to the mystery of the divine life as Father, Son, and Spirit. The doctrine of the Trinity shows us that "it is the very being of God to be in relation. God is not a self-contained self, but One whose very being is constituted by the relations of interpersonal love."[41] Therefore Jesus is not just revealer and exemplar; Jesus is the embodiment of the mystery of God who in his Spirit gathers us into the divine life.

Finally, we departed from Haight in regard to the doctrine of the Trinity. While the doctrine did not appear in articulated form until the fourth century, there is already evidence in the New Testament that the way Jesus was confessed, proclaimed, and addressed liturgically by the early Christians had implications for their understanding of God. Wisdom and Logos Christologies, narrative and figurative testimonies to Jesus' divine Sonship, as well as the theologies of preexistence and the divine indwelling all witness

---

[41] Michael Downey, *Altogether Gift: A Trinitarian Spirituality* (Maryknoll, N.Y.: Orbis, 2000) 55.

to the conviction that God was present and active in Jesus. The doctrine of the Trinity, which develops out of a concern for the work of Christ and the Spirit and ultimately depends on it, articulates the Christian experience of the self-revelation of God through Jesus and in his Spirit. Jesus is the symbol of God's presence—understanding symbol in its full and deepest sense. In Jesus the mystery of God is embodied and made efficaciously present. Jesus is Emmanuel, God with us (cf. Matt 1:23).

Glossary

ALLEGORY: from the Greek *allēgorein*, "to speak figuratively," a symbolic representation. Allegorical language is symbolic language.

ANTHROPOLOGY, THEOLOGICAL: a cultural, social, and philosophical understanding of the human person, rooted in a theological vision.

APOCALYPTIC: from the Greek *apocalypsis*, "uncovering," "revelation." Used of a type of literature which claims to be a revelation of the future, usually granted to a visionary, and often concerned with the end of the world or the present world order.

APOCRYPHAL: from the Greek *apocryphos*, "hidden," apocryphal books are Jewish or Christian writings for which divine authority is claimed but which were not recognized as having such authority by the religious community, and thus were not included in its "canon" or official collection. The expression "the Apocrypha" is used by Protestants to refer to those six books in the Catholic Old Testament canon that were included in the Greek translation of the Old Testament, known as the Septuagint. Catholics refer to them as the Deuterocanonical books (see below).

CATECHESIS: from the Greek *katēkhizein*, "to instruct," "to teach by word of mouth," particularly in preparation for baptism. The word is rooted in the Greek *katēchein*, "to resound," "to echo." Catechesis was generally oral instruction, though catechetical material appears in New Testament books.

CANON: from the Greek word for "reed," hence a standard for measuring. The word is used of authoritative statements or lists, thus of the decrees of Church councils, for Church laws (canon law), and for the collection of books accepted as having divine authority.

DEUTEROCANONICAL BOOKS: the seven Jewish books (1, 2 Maccabees, Tobit, Judith, Sirach, Wisdom, and Baruch, plus some additional parts of Daniel and Esther) that have been included in the Catholic Old

Testament canon since the earliest days of the Church. Because they were not included in the Jewish canon established after the fall of Jerusalem (70 C.E.), they were removed from what became the Protestant canon by the Reformers in the sixteenth century.

DOXOLOGY: a formula of praise to God, usually liturgical and trinitarian in form.

ECCLESIOLOGY: area of theology and doctrine concerned with the Church.

ESCHATOLOGY: from the Greek *eschatos*, "last" or "furthest," refers to teachings about the endtimes or "last things."

EXEGESIS: the critical interpretation and exposition of a text.

FIDEISM: originally described the position denying that the human mind could attain to knowledge of God's existence or nature apart from revelation; generally describes an uncritical approach to faith and theology which leaves no room for critical reason.

FORM CRITICISM: a literary science that seeks to identify the different literary forms in the Bible and identify the original literary form of a particular text.

HELLENIZATION: influencing or transforming a culture through the adaptation of Greek ways of thinking and speaking.

HERMENEUTICS: from the Greek *hermēneuein*, "to interpret." The science of interpretation.

HETERODOX: deviating from accepted standards of belief and doctrine; non-orthodox.

HISTORICAL CRITICISM: investigation of the historical background or *Sitz im Leben* of a text.

HOMOOUSIOS: one in being, consubstantial.

HOMOIOUSIOS: of like being.

HYPOSTASIS (Gk.)/SUBSTANTIA (Lat.): that which stands under or gives support to an object; realization; a concrete being that supports the various qualities or appearances of a thing. Thus subsistent being, a reality existing by itself, substance. (Medieval example, "transubstantiation").

INTERTESTAMENTAL: referring to literature originating in the period between the last canonical Old Testament book and the first Christian books. For example, some of the late Jewish apocryphal writings or the Qumran literature.

KERYGMA: from the Greek *kērux*, "herald," kerygma means proclamation or message.

LITERARY FORM: type or species of literature (e.g., legend, law code, prophetic oracle, apocalyptic vision, miracle story).

MESSIANISM: that complex of ideas concerned with Israel's future salvation, particularly as mediated by the prophetic preaching.

MILLENNIALISM: the belief, variously expressed, in a "thousand year" reign of Christ in the endtime.

MONOPHYSITISM: from the Greek *mono*, "one" and *phusis*, "nature," the belief that Jesus had only one, divine nature.

ONTOLOGICAL: a philosophical term referring to the underlying metaphysical principles or structure of reality.

ORTHODOX: literally "right praise," the adjective orthodox is used of teaching which is in agreement with the faith of the Church, as opposed to heterodox or heretical teaching. Also used of the Eastern or Orthodox Churches after the split between East and West in 1054.

OUSIA: being; distinct entity, nature; Cappadocian formula: one nature (*ousia*), three hypostases (*hypostasis*).

PAROUSIA: from the Greek *parousia*, "presence" or "arrival," refers to the Second Coming of Christ in the endtimes.

PERICOPE: a section of a narrative complete in itself, for liturgical reading or analysis; for example, a miracle story.

PHUSIS: nature, essence.

PROSŌPON (Gk.)/PERSONA (Lat.): concrete appearance; particular individual; person; "*persona*" was defined by Boethius (sixth century C.E.) as an "individual substance of a rational nature."

RAPTURE THEOLOGY: the belief of some Evangelical Christians that in the endtime those Christians still living on earth will be "caught up" with the just to be united with the Lord (1 Thess 4:17). There is disagreement as to whether this will take place before, during, or after the "great tribulation" of the last days.

REDACTION CRITICISM: literary discipline that seeks to discover the particular theology, emphases, and point of view of an author.

SEPTUAGINT (LXX): Greek translation of the Hebrew Scriptures done at Alexandria in Egypt, probably in the first half of the second century B.C.E. According to an ancient legend, it was the work of 72 scholars who accomplished the work in 70 days, hence the name.

SOTERIOLOGY: from the Greek *sōtēr,* "savior," the doctrine of salvation.

SOURCE CRITICISM: investigation of the literary source(s) of a particular text.

TEXTUAL CRITICISM: the discipline that seeks to establish the original ("critical") text or version of a biblical book.

THEOTOKOS: "God-bearer," Mother of God.

Index of Names

Index of Subjects